Springer Series

FOCUS ON WOMEN

Violet Franks, Ph.D., Series Editor

Confronting the major psychological, medical, and social issues
of today and tomorrow, *Focus on Women* provides a wide range
of books on the changing concerns of women.

Albert R. Roberts received his D.S.W. from the School of Social Work and Community Planning at the University of Maryland. He is an Associate Professor of Sociology and Social Welfare and Coordinator of the Social Welfare Program at the University of New Haven. Dr. Roberts was formerly Assistant Professor of Sociology and Coordinator of Social Work Field Placements at Brooklyn College of the City University of New York. He is the author of numerous articles and the author/editor of five previous books, two of which are *Correctional Treatment of the Offender* and *Childhood Deprivation*. The latter is a book of original essays on physical and emotional abuse of children.

Dr. Roberts has been a project director, principal researcher, and consultant for several juvenile justice and correctional rehabilitation programs. His current research and teaching areas include family violence, juvenile justice and delinquency prevention, program evaluation, research methods, social work education, stress and illness, and services to children and families.

Sheltering Battered Women
A National Study and Service Guide

Albert R. Roberts, D.S.W.

with the assistance of
Beverly J. Roberts, M. Ed.

Foreword by
Nancy A. Humphreys, D.S.W.

SPRINGER PUBLISHING COMPANY ■ New York

Springer Publishing Company, Inc.
200 Park Avenue South
New York, New York 10003

81 82 83 84 85 / 10 9 8 7 6 5 4 3 2 1

Library of Congress Cataloging in Publication Data

Roberts, Albert R.
    Sheltering battered women.

    (Springer series, focus on women; 3)
    Bibliography: p.
    Includes index.
    1.   Abused wives—Services for—United States.
I. Roberts, Beverly J.   II. Title.   III. Series.
HV699.R63   362.8'3   80-19827
ISBN 0-8261-2690-1
ISBN 0-8261-2691-X (pbk.)

Printed in the United States of America

Contents

■ TWO

Guide to Program Planning and Resources

■ THREE

Prevention Strategies

Foreword

The battered woman is not a new problem. Rather, it is society's awareness of this problem that is new. Society's recent interest in, and sensitivity to, the issue of violence, particularly in relation to such problems as child abuse and wife battering, has made it possible for the many victims to come forward and seek help. The blame-the-victim syndrome has long been in effect, often leading victims to believe that their condition was somehow their own fault and that there was nowhere to turn. Today, however, thousands of victims of spousal abuse are coming forward to seek assistance without shame. Such an overwhelming expression of need has been followed by a rather haphazard evolution of new service programs to meet these needs; these programs are often in the form of emergency services.

The increased attention to the issue of wife battering is evident in the recent action by President Carter to establish an Office of Domestic Violence within the Department of Health and Human Services to coordinate federal efforts in providing services to victimized family members. At this writing, federal legislation is pending before Congress which would provide special funding, albeit limited, for a variety of social services for battered women. These new efforts speak to an emerging awareness of, and concern about, this special population group. They are also testimony to the attempts on the part of this society, through government, to respond to the needs of this now-better-understood victim group.

This book reports data on the first national survey conducted on emergency shelter programs for battered women. What is obvious from the data reported is that the need for help far exceeds our current capacity to provide it. The experiences of the existing emergency shelter programs for battered women argue eloquently for the need for comprehensive services for this population. The material poses practical questions and offers realistic answers which can be used by professionals and paraprofessionals alike, board member, citizen, and policy maker. The experiences of the various shelter programs are reported here in terms of the struggle of those who seek to help battered women by establishing and operating emergency service programs. Such programs are intended to offer victims an alternative to their problematic life situation.

Written in a clear, direct, and highly informative style, this book can serve many and varied uses. The style of reporting is sufficiently specific that the book can serve as a guide, as suggested by the author, to enable those interested in working with battered women to understand this special population group, to learn interventions to meet their needs, and to assist them in making critical life choices and decisions. The wide scope of materials ranges from a practical guide for appropriate action that would serve as a useful training tool for those who work directly with battered women, to a police training document. Thus the material offers information about usual police and court procedures, the law, and the kinds of psychological and social reactions experienced by the battered woman. This report should be read by social workers and other helping professionals, in all settings, who seek to serve the family as a unit or individual members of the family.

Survey data of the kind made available in this book offer important insights into the critical task of knowledge building for practice intervention with battered women. Because our attention and interest in the battered woman is so recent, it goes without saying that there are many helping professionals who have little practical firsthand knowledge about this population. The dearth of experiences of those who currently serve the battered woman inevitably has caused many helping professionals to rely on their own assumptions, or current social views, which may be colored by society's insensitivity or by an outright sexist definition of the problems of battered women. Like any initial survey effort, the data from this study is more suggestive of further research directions than it is definitive of the subject at hand. Knowledge building through more research is the key to effective social service programs for battered women. The need for knowledge building is particularly strong given the paucity of previous research efforts in relation to this client population as well as the fact that our view of the battered woman may be steeped in a variety of social attitudes which may not be an accurate representation.

In addition to documenting the experiences of the shelters themselves, the overarching conclusion from the survey data is that battered women shelters operate and survive in spite of a fairly hostile and insensitive external environment and without adequate or secure funding. A considerable amount of the resources of shelter staff must be channeled into securing funds for the maintenance of programs. This book includes an excellent chapter on how to explore and secure funding, including a sample grant application proposal which could be readily used by anyone interested in beginning an emergency shelter program to serve this population. Although the book was primarily written for professionals and paraprofessionals who work with battered women, several sections could be applied to work with high-risk populations of suspected or potential battered women. The chapter by Fields and Lehman was originally written as a practical guide for battered women to assist them in exploring their options and planning constructive action.

It is interesting to note the findings of the study in relation to the role played by social workers in emergency shelter programs. Because of the critical lack of funding, only a few shelters can afford to employ the services of a full- or part-time professionally trained social worker. However, social workers have elected to become heavily involved in the delivery of services to battered women, often in the capacity of volunteers and in a dominant representative role on boards of directors and advisory groups of individual shelters. With adequate funding, social workers could be a major professional helping group serving this population. The social work professional perspective offers a unique qualification to working effectively with battered women.

To be successful, intervention with battered women must move beyond accepting the status quo of their life situation. Attempts to change the individual must also include a change-oriented posture with the social system itself. The goal of intervention with battered women should be both to enable the individual to change and be equipped to participate in society, and to change society and its attitude toward the battered woman. Such an approach to social services offers rich opportunities for the social work profession since, unlike other helping professions, social work has traditionally incorporated a person-in-situation orientation. Historically, social work has utilized both a social change–social reform orientation and an individual helping orientation, seeking to work with individuals in combination with broader efforts aimed at improving the larger social conditions. Sometimes these efforts have been less than successful, but they have nonetheless been a major tenet of the social work mission.

Given social work's history, principles, and dual thrust for change, it is in a unique position to recognize, conceptualize, and implement effective social service programs for the battered woman. The needs of the battered woman are not unique in that they parallel the needs of all human beings to see self and situation within the context of the broader social environment and to have options for changing and growing. Social work principles, its commitment to multiple modes of intervention, the diverse skills of practitioners, and the varied practice settings all complement what needs to be done to service battered women adequately along with other disadvantaged groups. However, a review of current practice indicates that social work has only recently begun to explore its role and commitment in relation to the social service needs of women and of battered women as a special target population. This book, authored by a social worker, is an important step in the process of helping social work understand the special needs of women, and in particular, battered women, and providng a data base from which effective social service programs can be developed.

It is important to recognize that emergency shelters represent only one of the critically important services needed by this client population. By definition, emergency shelters are temporary and provide help only to the battered woman in crisis. What is needed, and sorely lacking, is a comprehensive range of services particularly suited to the needs of the battered woman and the members of her family, including the abusing spouse. The recent policy statement on battered women adopted by the National Association of Social Workers Delegate Assembly, reprinted in Chapter 6, speaks to the range of legislative initiatives that would yield a comprehensive approach to social services for the battered woman. As the data reported in this study suggest, to a considerable extent the emergency shelter is the only major service system currently available for battered women. It operates as an island of safety in an otherwise sparse, if not altogether missing, set of needed social services.

Shelters are an important link in what must become a comprehensive network of social services to meet the needs of battered women. Shelters today, because of the lack of funding and insensitivity on the part of the established social service community, tend to operate in isolation and often experience considerable hostility from the established social service agencies. Such stopgap emergency services have the potential, if not complemented by a network of services, of proving ineffective. Without adequate outreach and critically necessary follow-up services, shelters can become revolving doors offering little more than a temporary way station for the battered woman who uses this service only during times if intense crisis and who, because of the lack of adequate follow-up services, returns to the violent home with no additional options for the long-term than existed previously. The compelling conclusion of the data from this study is the stark reality of the tremendous need for the social work profession and the social service industry to recognize and address in a more forthright manner the needs of battered women. Social workers should take leadership in attempting to move the established social service community to build a supportive network of services around the vital services now provided by battered women shelters. We can only hope that, as the attention to the problems of battered women increases, so will the realization of our collective responsibilities to provide a comprehensive network of social services for this needy and vulnerable client population.

Nancy A. Humphreys, D.S.W.
President of the National Association of Social Workers
Washington, D.C.
February 1980

Preface

The late 1970s have ushered in the long-overdue emergence of shelters and other crisis intervention services to aid battered women throughout the United States. With the growing recognition of the fact that wife battering is a recurring agony for millions of American women has come efforts by human service professionals and paraprofessionals to develop 24-hour hotlines, secure emergency shelters and networks of volunteer homes, crisis counseling services, and welfare and court advocacy programs. This book focuses on the shelters and services available to battered women in this country.

The primary goals of this handbook are twofold: (1) to report on the findings of the first national study of the organizational structure and functions of 89 intervention services for battered women and their children, and (2) to offer the reader practical assistance in the form of procedural guides and recommended techniques for fostering program planning and development. Thus this volume attempts to provide a stimulus, a factual knowledge base, and a resource guide for those individuals concerned with and actively involved in providing services for battered women.

The book is divided into four principle parts. Part I focuses on the nature and extent of newly emerging intervention services and shelters for abused victims and their children. It provides a readily accessible national perspective on the hotlines, counseling services, and emergency shelters geared to helping beaten women. The aim of Part II is to offer practitioners and concerned citizens specific methods and procedures for aiding battered women. Part III addresses the current and projected trends in the delivery of services. Recommendations for program planning are categorized on three levels: primary, secondary, and tertiary prevention. The fourth part, the Appendix, includes a directory of the respondents to this study along with descriptive information on each and a list of community foundations which may serve as funding sources for shelters and related services.

Acknowledgments

In recent years many individuals have dedicated themselves to resolving the plight of battered women. I would like to pay special tribute to Erin Pizzey, founder of Chiswick Women's Aid in London, England, and author of *Scream Quietly or the Neighbors Will Hear*. Her crusading efforts in providing shelter and support services to abused women and their children have inspired others throughout the Western world to do the same. I am indebted to the 89 respondents to this study, who are actively involved in giving refuge to beaten women. Without their candid and thorough responses to my research questions, the book would not have been possible.

I gratefully acknowledge the important contributions made by the following individuals: Imogene Baldwin, Bella Celnick, Sharon E. Cook, Rosemarie E. Dalton, Marjory Fields, Janet A. Geller, Charles E. Higginbotham, Judith Kaufholz, Carolyn A. Krill, Anne McGlinchey, Ginger McMahon, Fran Tomczyk and Edward G. Thomson. I am especially appreciative of the care and attention given by Ursula Springer and Barbara Watkins in the production of this book.

Finally, I want to express my deepest gratitude to Beverly, my wife, who was primarily responsible for writing Chapter 4 on sources of funding. I am indebted to Beverly for her unfailing good humor as she spent countless hours editing and typing the manuscript and preparing Appendix B. Her critical reading of the manuscript, probing questions, and insightful suggestions have done much to enhance this work.

■ one
FINDINGS OF THE NATIONAL STUDY

■1
Introduction

Millions of women throughout the United States live in terror and agony because they have been beaten repeatedly by their husband or boyfriend. Each year thousands of these battered women make the decision to escape to a safe place. There is a rough road ahead for the abused woman who decides to leave the assaultive male and seek the services of an emergency shelter. Although it is she who has been victimized again and again, it is she who—for her own protection—must flee from her own home. In so doing, every precaution must be taken so that her husband will not find out where she is.

Can she confide in anyone about her whereabouts? If she passes the information on to her closest neighbor, will the neighbor mistakenly let it slip to her husband or children, who could then accidentally tell the abusive husband? Or, worse, would the husband, knowing of the friendship his wife and neighbor share, threaten to harm the neighbor's family in a frantic attempt to learn where his wife and children have gone? It is best if no one knows where the woman has gone.

What about the children's activities, their schooling and friendships? Those, too, face disruption. The risk is all too great that the abusive husband would contact school to get to the children and cajole, coax, or threaten them or their friends in an effort to find out where his wife is staying. Thus, all previous activities and associations—enjoyable ones which helped make the abusive home situation tolerable for months or even years—all must be temporarily halted in the woman's valiant effort to come to grips with her future.

3

While the emergency shelter provides a "safe" existence, it is far from an easy or comfortable one. Many shelters are filled to capacity or overcrowded with a diversity of women and children of varying ages and backgrounds. Many shelters are so hard-pressed financially that the amenities of "home" are sorely lacking. Furniture is generally worn and second-hand, and the shelter itself is usually in need of repair. The sudden change in life style is confusing for children, who want to know why they have been uprooted so suddenly and ask how soon they will be able to return "home."

Some of the woman's most difficult decisions lie ahead: coming to grips with the realities of her situation through individual and/or group counseling sessions; learning her legal rights and options; determining what the future course of action will be—return home with the hope that it won't happen again, or initiate legal action; getting oriented vocationally, be it brushing up on work skills now 10 or 15 years old, or learning for the first time about the labor market. Money will be a major problem. Is it preferable to get an unskilled job immediately, anything that happens to be available, or to invest the time (and money) in vocational training or a college education with the goal of finding a more financially and personally rewarding job? Should she move in with relatives until she can earn her own living, thus placing an extra burden on loved ones who may well be facing problems of their own?

And what about the welfare system, that "awful mess of a system" which is constantly described in the media as much abused and a drain on the honest taxpayer? Now, that system, with all of its red tape, forms, waiting lines, questions, and impersonality may become an essential way for the woman and her children to stay afloat financially.

The road ahead is a difficult one, fraught with personal and financial problems. But for many women who know the unspeakable despair of physical brutality at the hands of their husbands, this is the road they must take. A woman *does* have a choice. She has the opportunity to regain her dignity and self-respect; in many localities she can also enlist the assistance of crisis intervention programs which will help her day or night.

The large number of calls for help reaching women's crisis centers each year and the growing number of these centers suggest that there is an urgent need for crisis intervention services for battered women. Yet few research studies have been conducted on centers which provide services for these women. To obtain information on the objectives, goals, and activities of these centers nationally, an exploratory study was undertaken in the summer of 1978. The purpose of this study was to gather information on the following:

1. The specific activities of the programs that are directed at crisis intervention with battered women

2. The length of time the centers have been in operation
3. The operation of an emergency telephone hotline
4. The initial procedures which are used in crisis intervention
5. The funding sources
6. The organizational structure as it relates to a board of directors, an advisory board, and staffing patterns
7. The types of problems which have been encountered
8. The total number of callers annually
9. The strongest features of the crisis intervention service
10. The centers' present needs
11. The positive and negative aspects of encounters with the police and courts

Statement of the Problem

Wife abuse is the latest in a series of family-related adversities to gain recognition as a severe and much underreported occurrence. As with child abuse before it, wife battering is not a "new" problem. What is relatively new is the awareness of its magnitude and the availability of crisis intervention services where none existed previously. Once the butt of thoughtless jokes (like "When did you stop beating your wife?"), wife abuse has finally been recognized for the very real and serious problem it is.

Statistics which have been collected by the police, courts, and researchers make clear the fact that wife battering is a social problem of major proportions. Moreover, it has been taking place—unreported and untreated—for generations. Recent articles point to the growing awareness of its prevalence. According to the *U.S. News and World Report* (Sept. 20, 1976) there are police and/or family court complaints from almost one million battered women annually in this country. This figure is only the tip of the iceberg, since many cases never appear in official police department and court statistics.

National data on the prevalence of wife battering have recently become available. Professors Straus, Gelles, and Steinmetz have conducted an extensive nationwide study on the extent of family violence. These prominent sociologists studied "a nationally representative sample of 2,143 families" and found a high level of spouse abuse. Their study shows that 16 out of every 100 American families "experience at least one incident in which either the husband or the wife uses physical force on the other" (Straus, 1979). Many of the violent acts which were reported "were minor assaults such as slapping, pushing, shoving, and throwing things." But more than 6 percent of the couples were found to have engaged in more severe forms of violence such as punching, biting, kicking, beating, hitting with an object, or using a gun or knife. From their study sample, Straus and associates were able to make an approximation of the national prevalence rate of spouse abuse for the 47 million couples in the United States. This finding showed a prevalence rate of serious violent acts taking place "in almost three million American homes" each year.

- Wife abuse has grave consequences. The FBI has reported that domestic violence is one of the most common, yet least reported, of crimes. In 1971, FBI statistics indicated that almost one-third of all female homicide victims had been murdered by their husbands. In 1975, the FBI Uniform Crime Reports indicated that murder within the family constituted one-fourth of all murders, and one-half of the family-related homicides involved spouse killing. The dilemma of family violence results in danger not only for the women but potentially for the police as well. As stated in the FBI Uniform Crime Reports (1979), between 1969 and 1973, the number of police officers killed responding to disturbance calls such as family quarrels and fights was reported as 77; that number had increased to 101 between 1974 and 1978. Police are therefore somewhat hesitant about answering domestic relations calls for fear of becoming a substitute target in a husband-and-wife argument. In addition, police know that, if they do intervene, the quarrel is likely to continue after they have left the scene; if the woman does press charges against her husband, she may well change her mind before the trial and drop the charges from fear of physical reprisals by her spouse.

 Wife battering can be life threatening for the abusive male as well; he may be killed accidentally in a woman's attempt to defend herself. A woman brought to trial for killing her husband in self-defense may not receive recognition from the court for the trauma she had undergone. Years of violence at home could be followed by years of institutional violence and degradation in a women's prison.

The New York Coalition for Battered Women compiled statistics documenting the prevalence of the wife beating problem in one large metropolitan area—New York City.

- In New York City Family Courts 6,680 new family offense petitions were filed by wives in 1977, 4,804 for alleged assault; 1,695 for threats and harassment; 181 for other complaints.
- During 1978, the 3 shelter facilities for women and their children in New York City served 1,300 families.
- The Borough Crisis Centers in 4 municipal hospitals served 2,800 battered women.
- AWAIC (Abused Women's Aid in Crisis) served 4,000 women in 1978 with their hotline, referral and counseling services (Swan, 1979).

The above statistics are based on the number of battered women who requested assistance. Since many abused women did not inform any community agencies of their plight, the actual number of victims may be 2 to 3 times greater than these statistics indicate.

Steinmetz (1977) conducted a study of violent behavior among a random sample of 57 families living in Delaware. The findings are shocking: In 6 out of 10 families, Steinmetz found some form of violent physical behavior, with 10 percent of the families indicating that they had a history of extreme spouse assault. Similarly, Gelles's (1972) study of 80 New Hampshire families revealed that conjugal violence occurred in 55 percent of the families. More revealing is his finding that, in 26 percent of the sample, spouse abuse happened regularly, occurring from an average of once a month to, in extreme cases, every day.

In a study conducted by Flynn (1977) and seven of his graduate students, Flynn estimated that wife battering was prevalent in 10 percent (4,700) of the 47,000 families residing in Kalamazoo, Michigan. One of his findings is particularly revealing: Whereas women were most often the victims of nonfatal assaults, both women and men were found to be victims of homicide fatalities. Abusive men often rely on their physical strength when they beat women, but when a battered woman attempts to retaliate or defend herself, she generally uses a weapon. The use of such weapons has led to fatalities.

Battered women have traditionally been reluctant to seek help. If "seeking help" would not protect her from further physical abuse and if there was no place to go to escape from the assaults, then what was the use of seeking help? For many years this was the plight a battered woman faced. All too often these women have been ashamed of being victims of spouse abuse. They have endured repeated assaults because of an overriding desire to keep the family together, uncertainty over where to get legal aid and social work services, fear of poverty, guilt that they are in some way to blame for the abuse, and fear of intensified physical reprisals if they left home or filed a complaint against the husband.

A woman who does consider divorce is faced with stark realities: How would I live? Where could I take the children that is safe? Where would I get money for food and other necessities? Most battered women, upon leaving their husbands, have immediate financial needs; they require assistance from relatives or friends, and many will have to rely on public assistance to make ends meet.

Obtaining a job becomes vitally important. But women who have suffered severe bodily blows have suffered blows to their self-esteem as well. The average abused woman has been a housewife for 15 years. Her lack of confidence coupled with a lack of job skills, and the resulting fear of poverty, is a major factor in convincing the woman to remain with her husband and his assaultive ways. It is, therefore, necessary for these women to receive vocational counseling, evaluation, and training before the job hunt begins. The keen competition of the labor market can be depressing even for a self-confident, skilled, and experienced person; so one can readily imagine the detrimental effect it can have on a person who lacks self-esteem, is unsure of her vocational potential, and has not worked for many years (if at all).

What resources exist for the rapidly growing number of women who are seeking relief and a safe place to stay? In years past their pleas for assistance to court personnel, the police, local social service agencies, and/or telephone operators would likely have been met with indifference or ignorance of available resources. There is growing awareness of the shattering problems of abused women among women's groups, social workers, the news media, philanthropic organizations, and the federal government. This awareness has led to the establishment and recent proliferation of hotlines, counseling services, and 24-hour emergency shelters geared to helping abused women. To date, the nature and extent of these newly emerging crisis intervention services and shelters for abused victims and their children has not been documented. This study provides the first national perspective on crisis intervention services for battered women.

As of the summer of 1978, emergency services for battered women had been developed in 111 locations throughout the United States. The findings contained here are based on the 89 programs participating in this study. There are three objectives which are common to most of the programs studied: (1) to provide a safe and secure environment for abused women and their children; (2) to provide emotional support and counseling for battered women; and (3) to provide information on women's legal rights, assist with court appearances, discuss permanent housing options, and explore future life goals and directions.

Methodology

A listing of 128 battered women's programs (see Appendix A) was developed by the following means:

1. Making inquiries through wife abuse programs in the New York metropolitan area and local chapters of women's organizations. These inquiries revealed that Warrior's (1978) listing was the best available source for names and addresses of programs for battered women.[1]
2. Asking the telephone information operator in each of the 212

---

[1] Grateful acknowledgement goes to Betsy Warrior for her important work in the movement to develop direct services for battered women.

Standard Metropolitan Statistical Areas (SMSA) of the United
States to check their local directories under the headings,
"abused women," "battered women," "wife abuse," or "wife
battering service."[2]
3. Cross-indexing the list compiled from the telephone information
   operators with Warrior's list to produce one comprehensive
   directory.

A detailed 23-item questionnaire was developed, pretested with
three administrators of programs for battered women, revised, and mailed
along with a cover letter to battered women's programs throughout the
country. Within one month after mailing questionnaires to the 128 centers,
the post office had returned 17 of them because the addresses of the centers
were unknown. The result was a sample of 111 battered women's programs; 4 months after mailing the questionnaires, replies had been received
from 89 (80.2 percent) of the 111 centers. All 89 respondents indicated that
they provide crisis intervention services to abused women. The respondents represent a cross-section of shelters in urban, suburban, and rural
areas in almost every one of the 50 states.

Providing shelter to battered women is a relatively new area of
intervention within the human service field. Although this book raises
critical issues and questions, and provides a thorough review of approaches
for helping abused women, only tentative conclusions can be drawn for the
following reason: In the past two years, there has been an incredibly rapid
proliferation of programs to help abused women; recent estimates indicate
that as of the summer of 1980, there were over 300 shelters in existence.

---

[2]In many instances, several calls had to be made to each metropolitan area because
some localities allow their information operators to check only two listings for each caller.

■2
Background and Functions of Programs

Overview of Intervention Services

It was 8:43 A.M. when Mrs. Phyllis Reed picked up the receiver. The caller at the other end sounded desperate and terrified; but now, at least, there was a chance that she would get to a safe place.

"I think I have a concussion. He beat me again last night. I'm not staying another night with him. I need a safe place to go to."

Mrs. Reed works for a local battered women's shelter. In a calm and concerned manner, she asked the caller if she would like to go to the hospital. The caller said that she would but had no way of getting there and no one to take care of her two children. Mrs. Reed told the caller that she would send the police to provide safe transport for her and the children to the hospital. A staff member from the shelter would meet her at the hospital.

During 1977, over 110,000 calls were made to 89 intervention programs for battered women throughout the United States. Most victims who turn to a battered women's program for assistance make their first contact through a crisis telephone line. Generally, these hotlines are operational on a 24-hour, 7-day-a-week basis and are staffed by trained volunteers or CETA workers. During the initial contact, it is the hotline worker's responsibility to encourage the caller to ventilate, determine whether the woman is in immediate danger, and make arrangements for shelter or other emergency services if needed. The hotline worker may also inform the caller of additional services which are available within the community.

Rosemarie is 21 years old and has been married for almost 3 years. She is frightened, depressed, and very unhappy with her life. Her husband has beaten her many times during the past 3 years and, in fact, the first beating occurred when they were engaged. He always apologizes the next day and promises not to drink so much. Rosemarie has never had a job, and she has no bank account of her own. The "last straw" occurred when the husband threw an ash tray at her; it missed and instead hit her 2-year-old daughter on the forehead, just missing her eye. Rosemarie has decided that she and her daughter must leave.

What should a woman take with her when she and her children leave home for a temporary shelter? The answer depends upon how much time she has between making the decision to leave and the departure. For some women there is no time for planning. Either during or immediately following a brutal assault, a woman may decide that she must get out *immediately*, that leaving the home is literally a life-or-death decision. In such cases, a woman may be able to escape with only the clothing she and her children were wearing at the time. However, in other cases, the woman has given thought to leaving the abusive situation. For instance, there may have been a history of beatings which became progressively more severe. After each assault, the husband may have apologized and said that it would not happen again. This may have been followed by periods of peace and quiet where all seemed well. But a woman finally reaches a point where—while she fervently hopes that there will never again be a beating—she recognizes that there probably will be. So she may plan ahead, gathering information about a local emergency shelter "just in case" it should happen again.

For women in this type of situation where some advance planning is possible, it is recommended that they take with them important documents such as the marriage certificate, children's birth certificates, school records, medical insurance cards, and any other legal papers. These records may be needed to obtain welfare funds, to change the children's schools, or for divorce or other legal proceedings. In addition to legal documents, the woman should take whatever cash is accessible at home and also credit cards and bank books (as long as the accounts are in her own name or jointly in the name of the woman and her husband). Finally, she and her children will need clothing and toiletries, and the youngsters should take a few of their favorite playthings. Some shelters request that women bring their own linens. However, as stated previously, the most important thing when faced with a life-threatening situation is *getting out*.

All shelters are able to provide emergency items for women who escaped with nothing but the clothes they were wearing at the time. For women who do not have time to pack essential personal items, some temporary assistance is available through food banks and clothing donations administered through churches and Salvation Army offices. In a number of areas, police transport and protect the women on a quick return home to pick up clothes and other belongings.

Following an assault, there are two reasons for going to a nearby hospital emergency room: The first and obvious one is to get appropriate medical treatment, and the second reason is to have the hospital records reflect that the injuries resulted from an assault by the spouse. These records may become important evidence in subsequent legal proceedings. However, there may be a problem in obtaining prompt emergency medical services. The abusive male may prevent the woman from leaving the home to seek medical attention. Or a woman may arrive at the emergency room with no money to pay for treatment and no medical insurance coverage; depending upon the rigidity of the hospital's policies, she could be turned away. Hospital emergency room personnel are starting to become aware of the seriousness of wife abuse and the vital opportunity they have for identifying and treating assault victims. Emergency room staff need to be trained to recognize the signs of wife abuse so that they can arrange for immediate assistance and, if needed, referral to a safe home. Tragically, many hospitals have yet to institute any procedures for the identification, treatment, and referral of battered women, resulting in the loss of a valuable opportunity to break the cycle of violence.

One example of a successful training effort for hospital staff is a program pioneered by O'Dea Culhane, the Nursing Coordinator of the Peter Bent Brigham Division of Boston's Affiliated Hospitals Center. Culhane has designed domestic violence curricula to train hospital staff including emergency room physicians, nurses, social workers, and admissions secretaries. The training objectives are:

> to identify the underlying problems of domestic violence; to discuss the short and long-term needs of victims; to identify hospital and community services available to victims; and to learn how to document information about patients and gather evidence that may later be used in a court of law. (Center for Women Policy Studies, July, 1979)

If the woman is unable to get to the shelter on her own, a shelter staff member will generally offer to meet her at a neutral place, such as a police station or hospital, and transport her to the shelter. Another alternative is to request that the police provide safe transport to the shelter. It should be noted that some of the respondents who indicated that they had a good working relationship with the police further indicated that, when they contacted the police department on behalf of the victim, police were more responsive than when the victim approached the police on her own.

With nonemergency callers, when there does not appear to be immediate danger and shelter is not necessary, arrangements are made for the woman to come to the office for an intake interview and counseling. If the hotline does not have the capability to provide counseling services, or if specialized services are needed, a referral is made to the appropriate community resource, such as a marriage counseling agency, family service agency, vocational rehabilitation center, community mental health center, or Legal Aid.

How long do women spend at a temporary shelter? The length of stay varies, but one determinant is whether the center has its own building for housing women and children (and the capacity of that residence) or whether volunteer homes are used. In the former circumstance, shelter is generally provided for a maximum of between 3 and 6 weeks, although women are sometimes able to remain longer if their situation warrants it. On the other hand, the stay in volunteer homes is usually quite short, with a maximum duration of 3–4 nights being the general rule.

To help offset the considerable expenses of maintaining a shelter and staff, many programs charge a nominal fee for room and board. Examples of these charges are as follows: A shelter in Boston requests $1.25 per person per day for food and $1.50 per family per day to defray the cost of utility bills; an Athens, Ohio, center charges $5.00 per day for women and $2.00 per day for children; and a Lancaster, Pennsylvania, program has a fee of $1.00 per night for the woman and her children. It is inferred that no woman is turned away because of inability to pay.

Battered women often need legal advice; they may want to initiate divorce proceedings or obtain a restraining order. Since the financial status of an unemployed married woman is computed on the basis of her husband's income, many abused women do not qualify for Legal Aid. The legal procedures vary from state to state. It is therefore imperative that women be referred to qualified legal counsel in their own state to learn about their legal rights. For instance, in some states, the abused woman must file for separation from her husband before she can obtain a restraining order. In other states, judges are reluctant to issue an order of protection since some women change their minds several hours later. Even with a restraining order, enforcement is difficult since the violent husband may return at any time and the police cannot provide 24-hour surveillance of each abused woman.

In most of the 50 states a man who rapes his wife cannot be charged with rape. But in a few states (Delaware, Oregon, and Nebraska, with a similar law set to go into effect in New Jersey in 1979), legislation has been passed to the effect that marriage can no longer be used as a defense against rape. It is probable that other states will adopt such legislation in the coming years. The first case to be tried under the new law took place in Salem, Oregon, in December 1978. Greta Rideout charged that on October 10, 1978, her husband, John, raped her. Mrs. Rideout received supportive services from the Women's Crisis Service in Salem. The jury returned a verdict of not guilty (*Time*, January 1, 1979, p. 86). (See Chapter 5 for a more detailed analysis of battered women's encounters with the criminal justice system.)

Length of Time Programs Have Been in Operation

Services for battered women have been developed only recently. Recognition that there is such a problem as battered women was a long time coming, and as usual, there is a time lag between recognizing the need for a service and obtaining the funds necessary to establish urgently needed programs. The survey questionnaire was mailed during the last week of June 1978. Just over 50 percent (45 centers) responded that they had been in operation for 1 year or less (Table 2–1). In other words, as recently as the summer of 1977, one-half of the responding programs did not exist. Of the 14 programs that recently became operational, 9 waited until September 1978 to respond (3 months after receiving the questionnaire). The majority of these indicated that, having begun their service during the preceding few months, they had been gaining experience and had waited until September to respond because they wanted to be more knowledgeable about the center's operations.

A total of 13 agencies reported being operational 4 years or more, but of these, only 4 programs are serving battered women exclusively. The

TABLE 2–1. Length of time center has been operational

Time	Frequency	Percentage
1 year or less	45	50.6
2 years	20	22.4
3 years	11	12.4
4 years	4	4.5
5 years	3	3.4
Over 5 years	6	6.7

remaining 9 are multiservice agencies serving abused women in addition to rape victims, female alcoholics, or women experiencing a crisis—whatever its origin.

Physical Setting

The transitional nature and growth phase of these women's centers was made evident by some responses which mentioned present physical facilities (for example, a YWCA residence) and then stated that in a specified amount of time they would be moving to a private house. Several others indicated that, if they could secure additional funds, they were hoping to rent a building with more adequate space. As indicated by the 17 questionnaires returned from the post office marked "addressee moved, no forwarding address," 17 programs either moved or closed their center completely.

The respondents indicated that 48 (53.9 percent) of the crisis intervention services were located in a separate facility, 18 (20 percent) used private homes for emergency housing of battered women, and an additional 19 (21 percent) used areas of the local YWCA. In addition, several programs mentioned that they use churches, motels, hospital clinics, and mental health centers. In most cases, these other types of facilities were used to house the overflow of those women and children which could not be accommodated in the shelter or private homes.

Several respondents reported that they have both a separate facility for their shelter and the use of private volunteer homes when the shelter is overcrowded. For example, the Women's Support Shelter in Washington State uses 37 private rooms and the cooking facilities of a YWCA. With 2 to a room, they can house a maximum of 75 people; and when the YWCA shelter is full, they utilize private homes. Other combinations of facility use also became evident. Several centers had offices in a YWCA, county office building, or private office building, but they provided emergency shelter through an underground network of "safe homes." The North Country Women's Center in upstate New York is presently located in an apartment and is looking for a house to rent. The Abused Women's Alternative Resource Exchange (AWARE) in south Florida has a private house which serves as its central shelter; when the need arises it relies on private homes. Sunflower House in Oregon reported that it is possible for women to be sheltered at their community center, but the staff usually place them in private homes or shelters because it is "safer" that way.

Programs for battered women face two major concerns, which quickly became apparent from a review of the responses: (1) There is an urgent need for more space for the women and children who are seeking emergency shelter, and (2) the actual location of the shelter is divulged only to those who absolutely need to be involved because security is of paramount importance. Publicity about services for battered women will always give a telephone number (and maybe the address of a social service agency with which it is affiliated, or their administrative offices if separate from the shelter site) but never the shelter's address. In many cases those who answered the questionnaire gave their address as a post office box rather than a street address. Typically, shelters have no signs or other identifying information posted outside the residence to distinguish it from the other houses or buildings in the area.

Criteria for Admission

In order to provide services which will be beneficial to the largest number of women, some shelters have established a written policy of eligibility criteria. An example of a center with specific criteria for admission is the Battered Women's Shelter of Winston-Salem, North Carolina. To be eligible for services the woman must:

1. Be a victim of a violent act
2. Be a recipient of life threats
3. Have a spouse who is abusive to the children
4. Have been forced to leave home due to a family disturbance
5. Have no friends or relatives who can help
6. Be a resident of Forsyth County
7. Be willing to take part in the shelter program

Women are excluded from the program if they:

1. Have a drug or alcohol abuse problem
2. Are coming directly out of prison
3. Are minors unaccompanied by a female parent or guardian (unless the minor is the battered woman)
4. Have a family member with an active communicable disease
5. Have a child who is severely emotionally or physically handicapped (unless the mother can make other arrangements for the child)
6. Are unwilling to participate in the shelter program

A second example is Brandon House in San Jose, California, which provides emergency shelter for a maximum of 30 days to women and their children who are in a crisis situation. Individuals have to be ambulatory, free of severe medical or mental health difficulties, and free of chronic alcohol/drug problems. Also excluded are boys over the age of 12.

My Sister's Place, in Athens, Ohio, admits women who are over 18 years of age, have been physically and/or emotionally abused, and have no place to go. Shelter is provided for a maximum of 3 weeks. The woman must be a resident of Athens or one of the three other neighboring counties. Children over the age of 12 cannot be housed at the shelter except in rare instances (and only with the approval of the board of trustees). Released state hospital patients are usually referred elsewhere. No woman is allowed shelter privileges more than twice due to the large number of women seeking refuge there. After being housed at the center, women may return for individual and/or group counseling.

A final example is Oasis Women's Center of Alton, Illinois. This program serves women in crisis due to battering, rape, separation, divorce, depression, and/or anxiety. Up to 7 days of temporary lodging are provided for women and their children, however, male adolescents over 14 years of age are referred elsewhere. The admissions policy at Oasis also excludes: persons in acute medical or psychiatric distress; minors (unless accompanied by mother or they are emancipated); and repeaters who have demonstrated no progress toward stabilization.

Security

For the safety and protection of battered women, the address of the shelter must be kept anonymous. A variety of cautious measures were reported by shelter personnel so that a victim's whereabouts are not accessible to an enraged and violent husband or boyfriend. The three primary security measures utilized by the shelters in this study are:

1. Holding meetings with police, welfare, and building department personnel to emphasize the urgency of keeping the address of the shelter confidential.
2. Informing all staff and residents of the dangers of divulging the shelter's address, and reserving the right to ask a resident to leave if such information is given out.
3. Cautioning the victim, upon leaving the shelter (to return to her former home or to set up a new home elsewhere) not to divulge the shelter's address.

One shelter in New York City, lacking funds and in need of many repairs and furnishings, had wisely determined that the top priority was expenditure of funds for installation of a high-quality burglar and fire alarm system. Another center requires women coming to the shelter to swear an oath that they will never reveal the shelter's location. Finally, a program in the Northeast rents the entire floor of a motel and, from time to time, switches from one motel to another to make it more difficult for an outsider to uncover their location.

House Rules of Shelters

The women who seek an emergency shelter come from a variety of backgrounds, with varying personal habits and beliefs. Because of the trauma they have experienced at the hands of their husbands, they and their children suddenly find themselves uprooted. Although the home was the site of the assaults, it was also a place of comfort and solace. The women who enter a temporary shelter are in varying states of physical and emotional health. For there to be a sense of order at the shelter, to maintain security, and so as not to impinge upon the rights of the other residents, shelters generally establish house rules. In some cases the rules are communicated verbally; in others, they are typed and presented to the woman at the outset so that she is fully aware of what is expected. Herewith (in no particular order) is a compilation of the types of regulations which are commonly set forth:

- No alcoholic beverages or non-prescription drugs (e.g. sleeping pills) will be allowed in the shelter. Prescription drugs will be kept in a centralized location and dispensed by a staff member.
- Except in extreme situations, women will be expected to provide clothing and personal items for themselves and their children.
- Smoking is prohibited in sleeping areas because it is a fire hazard, but smoking is permitted in certain designated areas (e.g. living room and dining room).
- Violence toward any other person will not be tolerated. No lethal weapons will be allowed in the shelter.
- All residents are expected to maintain their own and their children's sleeping quarters.
- All residents are expected to share in the following household activities: cleaning, cooking, shopping, washing, and babysitting for those children not in school.
- Any resident who reveals the location of the shelter will be asked to leave. Residents may not have any visitors at the shelter. When planning to meet with friends, it is required that the meeting take place outside the shelter.
- Women with children will be responsible for supervising their youngsters. Women with children of school age are expected to see that their children are up and ready for school on time.
- House meetings and group sessions are each held once a week at designated times, usually in the evening. All residents must attend.
- A locked area is available for all valuables.
- Everyone is to be in by 11:00 P.M. After that time, the doors are bolted for security reasons.

- On a resident's last day at the shelter, the woman's room and that of her children should be thoroughly cleaned so that the next woman to use that area—a woman who is in crisis just as the woman being discharged had been—will have a clean room.
- The center reserves the right to ask a resident to leave if the house rules are not respected.

Emergency Telephone Service

The operation of a 24-hour telephone crisis intervention service serves to facilitate timely and immediate assistance to distressed victims of spouse abuse. The telephone crisis line, when operated by trained and experienced hotline operators, can provide an immediate and accessible channel to crisis intervention services. Providing a telephone crisis line maximizes the availability of assistance to victims when the victim has the greatest need for assistance.

Volume of Calls

In 1977 alone, it is estimated that over 110,000 women sought the aid of crisis centers for battered women. The high volume of calls reaching services for battered women suggests that there is a growing demand and crucial need for these crisis centers. Only 26 of the 89 responding programs had records of the total number of calls they had received during 1977. These 26 programs reported receiving a total of 32,137 calls (or an average of 1,236 calls per respondent). Many of the other programs either said that they do not maintain a log of callers or were not operational for the full year of 1977. Therefore, an extrapoliation of the annual number of callers to the 89 programs in this survey can be made by multiplying the average total volume per program (1,236 callers) by 89. The result is my estimate of over 110,000 calls received annually for hotlines for abused women, contingent upon 89 hotlines being operational for 1 full year or more. In view of the growth phase these hotlines and shelters are experiencing, this figure is a low estimate.

The respondents were asked to provide frequencies on those who called seeking information as well as those who were seeking emergency shelter. Of the 32,137 calls logged in by 26 programs, a total of 25,513 women requested information, and 6,624 women requested emergency shelter. Although the high number of callers in search of emergency shelter indicates a critical need, it would be useful if future research obtained additional information on the nature of calls. For instance: How many callers are seeking information about legal services or admission to the shelter with the hope of being prepared to obtain help if another beating occurs? How many callers are seeking referral to another agency, such as public assistance or Alcoholics Anonymous? How many callers are seeking information for a relative? How many are repeat callers? And how many are prank calls or hang-ups? Record-keeping and case management systems should be planned and implemented at battered women's programs nationwide. These record-keeping systems would generate more rigorous data on the volume and types of callers.

Telephone Methods

Table 2–2 reveals that 65.1 percent of the 89 services use the "direct" telephone method, meaning that there is 24-hour staffing of the telephone line. It is expected that all calls will be answered by someone who is knowledgeable about crisis intervention techniques and the services provided by that particular center. The direct-line telephone system is the method whereby a call comes directly into an office and is answered by the hotline worker without any interference. This method of telephone service is the quickest and most efficient way of connecting a victim caller with a hotline operator or counselor.

Another 20 percent (18) of the programs reported using a combination of a direct line plus an answering service. For the most part, the direct line is in operation during typical business hours and the answering service takes over at all other times to provide 24-hour coverage. An additional 2 programs said that they use an answering service only. The answering service may be one of the most ineffective telephone methods because the operator, who is not trained in handling crisis calls, merely relays the message to a regular staff member. The primary drawback to this system is that it necessitates requesting the caller's name and phone number, which is often perceived as threatening and cold by a victim in crisis. In addition,

TABLE 2–2. Telephone methods

Method	Frequency	Percentage
Direct line only	58	65.1
Direct line and answering service	18	20.2
Direct line, patch, and answering service	3	3.4
Direct line and patch	2	2.2
Patch and answering service	2	2.2
Answering service only	2	2.2
Other:		
Through YWCA switchboard	3	3.4
Direct line, then after 5 P.M., switch		
to mental health crisis line	1	1.1

Note. Based on a total of 88 responses.

if the woman is calling from her home phone at a "safe" time of day for her, she would not want to risk that the call would be returned when her husband might be at home. Or the victim may be calling from a telephone booth or from her home at a time when she may be fearful of her husband returning at any moment. Services without the funds to employ staff around the clock have utilized answering services with the hope that some response by a phone operator—and the hope that a staff member will be able to return the call—is better than no response.

The "patch" system in combination with a central switchboard or answering service was used by 7 programs during the evening hours. This method allows the telephone to ring directly into a specified switchboard where an operator, by turning a manual switch, can connect the victim with the crisis worker at a given phone number. This type of phone service allows victim callers to be patched into a trained counselor who can take the call on her telephone at home. The advantages of the patch line are obvious. The main disadvantage is that it results in opening the line, thus interfering with the clarity of tone and ability to hear clearly.

A telephone message machine usually informs the caller of the hours that the center is open and may give callers another phone number to call during the late-night hours. Fortunately, only one program has found it necessary to resort to the impersonality of a telephone answering machine to record callers' messages on evenings and weekends.

Method of Publicizing the Center's Telephone Number and Service

Over three-fourths (70 out of 89, or 78.7 percent) of the centers have their telephone number listed in a local telephone directory, generally with a post office box number or the address of a separate administrative office rather than the actual street address of the shelter.

Due to the high volume of domestic relations cases encountered by the police, it was significant to learn that 73 (82 percent) of the respondents had their telephone number listed with police dispatchers and desk sergeants. (The respondents reported wide variation in their contacts with police, from highly negative encounters to very positive ones. The role of police intervention is discussed in Chapter 5).

In five additional cases the shelter was so new that the listing had not yet appeared in the telephone directory, but the respondent stated that the number would be listed in the upcoming directory. Because of the rapidity with which some shelters are established, it is recommended that the directory assistance operator have up-to-date information and specialized training in assisting crisis callers.

It is vitally important that battered women's intervention programs make every effort to establish linkages with community leaders and local agencies. It seems that many entry-level facilitators to services for abused women have been overlooked. Although large numbers of battered women receive emergency medical treatment, only 21 of the 89 centers reported that they had listed their telephone number and the nature of their service with the emergency room of nearby hospitals. Members of the clergy, physicians, and school personnel sometimes learn about particular women in their community who have been abused. Yet only 6 centers stated that they listed their service with local churches; only 4, with private physicians; and only 2 with nearby schools.

While many of the centers did not seem to have an ongoing referral network with the health and welfare agencies in their communities, several centers reported that they had established good relationships with concerned professionals and community resources. Examples of the kinds of agencies that have aided battered women's programs are: family court, Legal Aid bureaus, the National Organization for Women (NOW), welfare departments, suicide prevention centers, Salvation Army officers, community mental health centers, family service agencies, statewide adult and child abuse registries, Traveler's Aid, probation departments, rape crisis centers, and district attorney's offices.

Busiest Day for Callers

Monday was reported as the busiest day of the week for hotline calls by 38 (or 52 percent) of the 73 programs responding to this question (Table 2–3). Friday was cited by 20 programs as their busiest day for callers. One explanation for the high volume of Monday calls is that during the weekend the husband is usually at home; there is more time for activities which can lead to conflict and which result in beatings. Furthermore, because of the husband's presence on the weekend, it is more difficult for the abused

TABLE 2–3. Busiest day for callers

Day of the Week	Number of Respondents
Monday	38
Tuesday	6
Wednesday	1
Thursday	3
Friday	20
Saturday	4
Sunday	1

Note. Based on a total of 73 responses.

woman to find a safe and private place from which to call for help. Thus the Monday calls may be a build-up of victims who were beaten at any time during the weekend and felt unable to call for help without risking further abuse. By the same token, perhaps the reason for Friday as the second-busiest day is the wife's recollection of previous weekends and the dreaded anticipation of the upcoming weekend.

Busiest Time of Day for Callers

Although most programs for battered women provide 24-hour telephone service, it is not surprising that the largest number of calls comes during the morning hours—8:00 A.M. to 12:00 noon—when the husband has most likely gone to work (Table 2–4). Although night calls are not as frequent as morning calls, interviews with staff members at three of the New York–area programs revealed that the night calls are usually of a more serious and crisis nature than the morning calls.

Improved record keeping and further research should be planned to determine the types of callers likely to call at specific times. It is important to ascertain the extent to which the high volume of morning calls is for informational purposes or for emergency medical care and shelter. Are the morning callers likely to be making inquiries so that in the event of another beating the woman knows whom to call and where to go for safety? In contrast, are the late-night calls made by women who have just been seriously injured and manged to escape? If so, the implication for staffing is that 24-hour hotlines and shelters should be certain to have counselors who have been trained in crisis intervention working on the evening shifts. Especially since evenings are the time when traditional social service agencies are closed, it is vital that a woman in crisis who contacts a hotline at midnight be able to receive the proper assistance.

TABLE 2–4. Time of day with highest frequency of calls

Time of Day	Number of Respondents
Midnight–4 A.M.	4
4 A.M.–8 A.M.	1
8 A.M.–12 Noon	26
12 Noon–4 P.M.	17
4 P.M.–8 P.M.	15
8 P.M.–Midnight	7
No particularly high volume time— all times equally busy	2

Note. Based on a total of 72 responses; 17 respondents gave no response to this question.

Initial Crisis Intervention Procedures

When asked to provide information on their initial procedures, the majority of the centers ranked their responses into three procedures in order of actual use: (1) assessing the caller's immediate situation and needs, (2) making arrangements for emergency shelter, and (3) exploring options and making a referral to an appropriate community resource. It became apparent that most of the programs have established initial procedures which utilize crisis intervention techniques. The individual respondent's descriptions varied somewhat because of differences in vocabulary, training, and experience. This analysis describes the major steps used by battered women's programs in intervening with a crisis.

The procedures used by each center vary somewhat depending upon the caller's particular circumstances. The flexibility to meet the individual needs of each victim is an important characteristic of a client-centered service. Keeping that in mind, there emerged general procedures common to many of the centers. Of the 89 respondents to the questionnaire, only 63 (70.8 percent) answered this question, the others—almost one-third—leaving it blank.[1] Of those who answered this question, a total of 43 indicated that their primary concern is to determine the woman's immediate condition. In assessing the battered woman's situation, a determination is usually made of the danger or immediate threat of further physical abuse and also of the need for immediate medical attention, police intervention, emergency shelter, emotional support, or information.

Of the 43 respondents whose initial procedure is to assess the seriousness of the situation, 25 reported that they first determine whether the woman is in imminent physical danger. The remaining 18 placed their emphasis on assessing the overall situation and determining the woman's immediate needs. Supportive listening, by allowing the woman to ventilate about her situation, was reported as the primary initial procedure by 12 centers. An additional 18 programs mentioned supportive listening as their second procedure, making a total of 30 who recognize the importance of encouraging the women to talk about their problems.

Many of the callers express an urgent need to find a safe place to stay. Thus the second step in crisis intervention for 19 respondents is suggesting or making arrangements for emergency housing. In delineating their second procedure, 9 other respondents reported they assess the

---

[1]A combination of factors probably contributed to the high no-response rate to this particular question, including the inexperience of many centers and nonprofessional staffing patterns. Also, over three-fourths of the questions in the study were of the structured, check-off type. In contrast, the initial procedures question was open-ended, and some respondents may not have taken the time to do a thorough job.

situation by trying to understand what problems and needs the callers have. An additional 9 programs indicated that their focus is on supportive listening and allowing the caller to ventilate her feelings about herself and the problem.

The victim, who may have feelings of fear, helplessness, anger, guilt, and anxiety, needs to express her feelings to a supportive listener. In addition to enabling the caller to ventilate, it is important for the crisis counselor to determine what feelings and problems the caller is experiencing. At the same time, the caller should not be pressured to open up if she is not ready to do so.

The most frequently cited third procedure is exploration of options and alternative community resources (26 respondents). It is important for the abused woman to become of the resources which are available. However, depending upon the circumstances of the call, the woman may be receptive to this exploration immediately, or she may need to have basic needs—shelter, medical attention, sleep—tended to first before she is able to concentrate on weighing available options and making important decisions.

The Women's Crisis Service in Salem, Oregon, provided the researcher with printed information on its initial procedures, written in clear and concise terms. The following procedures pertain to the basic issue of whether the woman is in immediate danger or not. These procedures were developed as a training guide for counselors to assist the woman who wants to remain at her home:

1. Offer support and information for the future.
2. Remind her we have a 24-hour line.
   Remind her of legal resources.
   Remind her of other resources.
   Remind her of other options.
3. Tell her not to, in anger, tell him (the abusive male) the avenues open to her.

If the woman feels the need to leave, the following procedures are undertaken:

1. Find out if she has transportation.
2. Does she have friends or relatives she can stay with?
3. Arrange for a safe place to meet and how you can recognize each other.
4. Tell her she can take half the money from the relationship.
5. Have her take the children with her. [Find out] how many children she has and what ages. Having the children with her is 9/10's in her favor if she goes to court.

6. Have her take legal papers, i.e., birth certificates, marraige certificate, social security, insurance, etc.
7. Does she need/want to leave the area?
   a. Does she have the money to do so?
   b. Friends/relatives she can stay with out of the area?
8. If she leaves, how much effort will he put forth to find her?
9. When meeting with her, take information on referrals with you.

To further illustrate the crisis intervention methods of programs for battered women, the initial procedures utilized by seven of the respondents are presented below.

Aid to Women Victims of Violence, Cortland, New York

Determination is made of whether the client is in immediate danger or is calling to explore alternatives. Gather information as to what precipitated the call and the important needs. The advocate uses listening techniques, provides information on available services, and makes arrangements for further action or follow-up (personal) contact. The advocate will meet the victim at the hospital, police station, or [other] neutral ground [and bring her to the shelter].

Stop Abuse, Inc., Everett, Washington

First, always ask if client is in immediate danger. If so, tell her to get her and the children out of the house and go to police station or phone booth. Then, give client an opportunity to vent her situation. Next, outline possible options. Describe the help that is available and ask client what she wants to do.

Sojourner Truth House, Milwaukee

Assess present situation; assess immediate need for protection. What does the woman want/neeed? Make appropriate referrals. Admit her and children into shelter.

Thurston-Mason YWCA Women's Shelter Program, Olympia, Washington

First comes immediate safety: Is everyone safe with no injuries? (Refer to hospital if not.) Second, assess situation and her needs: Does she have any resources to call upon? Third, listen and give support for what *she* wants to do. Come to shelter (if appropriate) or go to a friend or relative's, or stay in present situation and know the options available for the future.

North Country Women's Center, Inc., Canton, New York

Try to ascertain the basic problem. Try to calm the person if she is upset. Offer shelter or a "breathing space." Try to offer help with specifics such as lawyers, physicians, counselors, social services, police, etc.

Aid to Battered Women in Black Hawk County, Cedar Falls, Iowa

Counselor assesses situation. If immediate threat, woman is encouraged to call police. If emergency shelter is needed, counselor explores possibilities—friend, relative, neighbors, or volunteer home. If volunteer home is needed, counselor meets woman at police station and accompanies her to volunteer home. The next morning, follow-up is provided. If there is no immediate danger and emergency shelter is not necessary, information is exchanged over the telephone and a meeting is arranged.

Marital Abuse Project of Delaware County, Inc., Media, Pennsylvania

1. Assess the immediate danger (i.e., finding out where she is, where attacker is, whether she has been injured, whether her husband has a psychiatric history). If in danger, tell caller to contact police, to get out of the house to safest place available, that you will also call police.
2. If she doesn't want to call police and is injured, encourage her to go to the hospital (she may have internal injuries).
3. Meet caller at police station or hospital.
4. Make sure caller and her children have a safe place for the night.
5. Arrange for victim to meet with you or other staff member the next day to continue counseling and explore her options.

Important Service Features

The responses to the question: What do you consider to be the strongest or best feature of your emergency service as it is now constituted? indicate that their strengths fall mainly into three categories: (1) the availability of comprehensive or specialized services, (2) availability and security of the emergency shelter, and (3) commitment or special skills of staff. Data presented in Table 2–5 show that the majority of respondents (47) pointed to either the 24-hour round-the-clock nature of their hotline (25 respondents) or the availability of emergency shelter (22 respondents) as the strongest feature of their service.

TABLE 2–5. The strongest or best feature of the services

Strongest or Best Feature	Number of Responses
Specialized or comprehensive service features	53
24-hour, 7-day-a-week service	25
Individual counseling service	8
Welfare, legal, and court advocacy	7
Support and caring service	5
Ability to provide comprehensive program	3
Transportation to bring victim to shelter	2
Vocational training	1
Mediation program for abusers	1
Alumnae group of former residents	1
Shelter	32
Availability of emergency shelter	22
Provision of safe and secure shelter	7
Comfortable environment	1
Underground network of homes	1
Location of shelter (near hospital)	1
Staffing	24
Dedication and high quality of volunteers	7
Commitment and dedication of staff	6
Staff's skills	5
Child advocate on staff	1
Good communication among staff	1
Large size of staff	1
Social worker with good access to both legal and social service resources	1
Thoroughness of staff training program	1
Training for volunteers	1
Interagency and community support	19
Referral service and cooperation with other agencies	13
Acceptance in the community/good community support	6
Philosophy	7
Flexibility in meeting individual needs	3
Emphasis on self-help	2
Empowerment of women	1
Being nonjudgmental	1

Note. The total strong points is 135 since many of the 89 respondents listed more than one "strongest or best feature."

Comprehensive or Specialized Services

The strongest feature reported by the Women's Association of Self-Help (WASH) of Bellevue, Washington, reflects the emphasis many of these programs place on 24-hour availability of crisis intervention services. This program reported that it provides immediate crisis counseling on the telephone or in person, any time of the day or night, without fees or an appointment. In addition to the provision of 24-hour emergency services, respondents singled out other features, including counseling services; welfare, legal, and court advocacy; an overall "caring program"; and transportation to bring victims to the shelter. The following examples are particularly noteworthy:

- A program of child advocacy in recognition of the fact that an environment in which a husband has battered his wife is an environment in which the children have suffered as well, emotionally and possibly physically too (Women's Advocates, St. Paul, Minnesota).
- An alumni group (Catherine Booth House, Seattle).
- A mobile unit which is available to pick-up clients (Abused Persons Program of Montgomery County, Maryland).
- A short-term (10-session) group treatment program for abusive husbands (Victims Information Bureau of Suffolk, Inc.—VIBS—Hauppauge, New York).
- Advocacy and continued involvement with women who have sought help (YWCA Battered Women's Program of Bellingham, Washington).
- Provision for a legal consultation for clients who cannot afford to pay for the service and who are not eligible for Legal Aid services. The purpose of the consultation is to clarify the woman's legal rights and the legal action she may choose to take (Women's Crisis Center, Kalamazoo).

Emergency Shelter

About one-third of the respondents (32) singled out the availability, nature, location and/or security of their shelter or volunteer home network as their strongest feature. Typical in this regard were the following responses:

- A safe shelter immediately available without red tape and bureaucratic delays (Shelter for Abused Spouses and Children, Honolulu).
- We are open 24 hours a day and will shelter any woman who needs a place to stay (The Women's Center, Providence).
- Immediate availability for a client to come in to a safe place and speak with a professional counselor (Abused Person's Program, Montgomery County, Maryland).

Staffing

With regard to staffing, 24 respondents viewed the dedication, commitment, special skills, and/or training of their staff as the program's strongest feature. Several of the respondents emphasized the commitment of their staff by pointing out that many worked 50 to 60 hours a week, evenings and weekends, for low salaries.

The Battered Women's Crisis Center of Austin, Minnesota, was particularly enthusiastic about its "highly motivated and dedicated volunteer advocates. They are ready and willing to go at all times. They are well-trained and have had most positive feedback from the community." Similarly, Women's Advocates in Pocatello, Idaho, reported that it has a dedicated corps of 45–50 women who volunteer their time and services. Finally, Services for Abused Females in Fresno reported that it is staffed by well-trained professionals.

Program Philosophy

Finally, some programs responded that their strongest service features were the result of their overall program philosophy or their ability to garner interagency and community support. For instance, Phoenix House, Inc., of Columbus, Ohio, was most proud of its concept of "total services, not just physical or psychological or legal." The Women's Support Shelter, in Tacoma mentioned its comprehensive counseling program (available to residents of the shelter and to the community) which is based on self-help and empowerment of women. Finally, the Wichita Women's Crisis Center stressed its successful coordination with other agencies: "Although problems arise," stated the Kansas program, "the overall cooperation, response and sensitivity to the problem [from other agencies] has been excellent."

Major Problems

The respondents were asked to list the major problems confronting their program. Difficulty in securing funding stands out as the most frequently cited problem facing the majority of battered women's programs (58). A second major problem encountered by these programs relates to staffing (40 programs); of this number, attrition of volunteers was cited by 26 programs, and staff turnover was mentioned by 14. The third-most frequently cited problem is the lack of cooperation on the part of local police (26 respondents). Other problems common to several programs are: poor interagency relations and inadequate referral links (16 respondents), threats of angry husbands (15), a lack of cooperation from the courts (8), inability to house all who need shelter (7), chronic hotline callers (4), and a lack of community awareness about the problems faced by battered women and the services available (3).

Needs: Staffing, Facilities, and Services

The centers were asked what changes they would make if they had the money, and 83 of the 89 programs responding to this study answered this question. The responses fell into three general categories: those involving improvements of staffing, of facilities and equipment, and of services (see Table 2–6). Responses cited most frequently for each category were: Hire additional paid staff (60 respondents, or 72.3 percent); obtain a separate shelter facility for a larger building (43, or 51.8 percent); and increase the number of outreach groups (9, or 10.8 percent).

As would be expected, programs first want to provide the most basic services: some type of emergency shelter, a crisis telephone line, and at leastminimal staffing coverage. Once the bare minimum has been accomplished, programs can look toward providing services which will enhance their level and scope of service. For instance, Women in Transition in Philadelphia wants to establish a 24-hour hot line (rather than a line operating only during the day) and have the funds to pay their telephone counselors. A program counselor at the Women's Resource Center, Traverse City, Michigan, expressed her frustration about the limitations on what the center is able to provide when she commented, "Our 'emergency service' is only our weekday counseling at the center and placement in private homes. It is very warm, personal, and caring but totally inadequate."

The types of proposed facility changes ranged from upgrading the present site to establishing a network of shelter programs. For instance, the Stop Abuse Center in Everett, Washington, is using volunteer homes for shelter because it does not have the funds to acquire a large house. Sometimes when a victim has many children, there is not enough bedding to go around. The center relies upon donations of old sleeping bags, toiletry kits, and children's toys and games to make the brief stay at a volunteer home more comfortable.

Staffing

The general need for additional full-time paid staff was the need indicated by 30 respondents rather than specific type of staff, but other respondents mentioned the need for professionals with particular specializations: 7 programs would hire child care workers; 7 others specified

TABLE 2–6.   The changes services would make if they had the money

Agency Needs	Number of Responses
Staffing	69
Hire or expand full-time paid staff	30
Hire child care worker(s)	7
Hire social worker(s) and counselors	7
Hire a lawyer	6
Hire staff training specialists	6
Increase staff salaries	4
Stipend for volunteers	3
Increase fringe benefits for staff	2
Hire a bookkeeper	2
Hire a professional fund raiser	2
Facilities and equipment	50
Shelter:	
Larger facility	21
Separate shelter building	14
Open a shelter	8
Satellite system of shelters and offices throughout the county	2
Equipment:	
Buy a van to transport women	11
Office furniture	3
More beds and linen	2
More phone lines	1
A library	1
Recreational facilities	1
More equipment for children's programs	1
Additional services	50
Increase number of outreach groups	9
Activities for children	6
Make services more comprehensive	5
Emergency funds to help women pay security when moving to new housing	5
Expand to 24-hour staffing	4
Research and follow-up studies	3
Family counseling	2
Emergency funds for clients' court costs	2
Assertiveness training workshops in community	2
More counseling services	2
Extend length of time women can stay in shelter	2
Vocational training for those lacking employment skills	2
Legal counsel (free of charge)	2
Provision for medical services at the shelter	1
More nutritional food	1
Scholarships for women to take college courses	1
Extend hotline to 24-hour service	1

the hiring of social workers or counselors; 6 would hire an attorney; and an additional 6 expressed interest in employing training specialists or consultants to provide training for volunteers and other staff.

Within these staffing categories, some programs provided further detail on their staffing needs. For instance, of the 7 respondents indicating the need to hire a social worker or counselor, some simply said they wanted to hire a social worker; others stated their need for counselors or caseworkers experienced with crisis situations; 1 center specified that it would hire a social worker for the purpose of providing outreach. Hiring a bookkeeper and a fund raiser were each mentioned by 2 centers. The remaining few responses involved increasing salaries or fringe benefits for existing staff or providing a stipend for volunteers.

The following are specific illustrations of the respondents' staffing needs:

- The North Country Women's Center, Inc., of Canton, New York, expressed the desire to hire feminist counselors and lawyers.
- The Women's Crisis Shelter of Las Vegas wants to hire additional staff, particularly from among the ranks of formerly battered women.
- The Women's Crisis Center of Brattleboro, Vermont, and the Aiding Women from Abuse and Rape (AWARE) program in Juneau, expressed the need for staff specifically for the children.
- The YWCA Battered Women's Crisis Center in Marietta, Georgia, stated a need for staff training.
- Sojourner Truth House of Milwaukee wants the services of a medical person, either in-house or on retainer.

Facilities and Equipment

The need for more space to house abused women in crisis was described by over one-half (43) of those who responded to this question. Approximately one-quarter (21) of the centers indicated that living conditions at their shelter are overcrowded. Some of these respondents said that they would like a shelter large enough to accomplish the following goals: serve a larger number of women and children; expand the service area to include battered women in surrounding counties; provide more office space to allow for greater privacy when counseling clients; and provide play areas for the children.

Since some programs rely on hotels, motels, and private homes for emergency shelter, it is to be expected that they would state the need for their own shelter (14 programs). Similarly, these programs which have no shelter would like to develop one (8 programs). There were 2 centers who wanted to have a network of small shelters in different parts of the county, while 2 others expressed the need to renovate the existing shelter to provide additional bedrooms and a more pleasant atmosphere.

Acquisition of equipment for the shelter was also mentioned, although to a far lesser extent than requests for improved shelter space. The most frequently stated equipment need was a van for transporting women and children (11 programs). Other items, mentioned by 1 or 2 centers, were office furniture, more beds and linen, additional telephone lines, a library, recreational facilities, a washer and dryer, and toys and equipment for the children's program.

Typical responses regarding facilities needs are:

- The Battered Women's Shelter of Winston-Salem expressed the need for a washer and dryer, as well as wanting to have a play area for the children.
- The Spring, Inc., of Tampa has hopes for a larger shelter and a separate walk-in counseling facility.
- The Women's Center of Providence stated simply that it needs a facility which can accommodate more than 20 persons at one time.
- Sunflower House, a multiservice agency located in Corvallis, Oregon, would "like to see a shelter care facility that is specifically for domestic violence." The center feels that it does more than any other program in the area to aid battered women "but it still is not enough."
- The Women's Transitional Living Center, Inc., of Orange, California, proposed having two facilities: "one for 72-hour emergency transitional care, and a second facility for those clients who desire long-term transitional care.
- The Women's Crisis Service of Salem, Oregon, made the following request for comprehensive service delivery: "More emergency shelters placed within and without the city limits, and a satellite system consisting of longer term living units where interested women could group together after leaving the emergency shelter to continue their support for each other."

Services

The most frequently cited service needs are: outreach groups (9 programs), activities for the children (6), emergency funds to provide women with loans for security deposits and rent when moving to new housing (5), expansion to 24-hour staffing (4), and research and follow-up work on clients (3). Additionally, mention was made of providing the following types of services: free legal services, more counseling services (general), family counseling, vocational training, extending hotline to 24-hour service, greater length of stay for women who need it, assertiveness training workshops (two responses each); more nutritional food, scholarships, and free medical services at the center (one response each).

Specific illustrations are:

- The Women's Support Shelter in Tacoma would like to make greater use of the media for education and outreach.
- The Abused Persons Program in Montgomery County, Maryland and the YWCA Spouse Abuse Program in St. Joseph, Michigan, expressed the need for vocational training for those lacking employment skills.
- The Catherine Booth House of Seattle wants to provide family counseling and to increase the number of outreach groups.
- Hubbard House of Jacksonville, Florida, hopes to develop a comprehensive child care service.
- Sojourner Truth House of Milwaukee needs more effective security and money for legal retainers.
- Women's Association of Self-Help (WASH) in Bellevue, Washington, would like scholarships for women to take classes when they cannot afford the fees.

In addition to the specific service needs which are delineated by the respondents, those respondents who expressed a need for more staff and equipment were also concerned with the provision of additional services. For example, the 11 respondents who need a van anticipate using the vehicle to provide transportation services to battered women and their children. Similarly, the respondents who stated a need for an attorney, child care workers, and/or counselors would then be able to provide additional child care services, legal services, and counseling services to their clients. The way in which the respondents phrased their answers formed the basis for the categories in this section. More specifically, if a respondent expressed a need to hire an attorney, her phrasing indicated a staff need rather than the function of the new staff member, which would be to provide legal services.

■3
Organizational Structure of Programs

Generally, the organizational structure of centers and programs for battered women consists of a board of directors; a director/coordinator; and a staff of volunteers, CETA workers, or—in some cases—a small core of paid staff. The directorate body of each program usually discusses issues related to battered women and establishes policies for the program. Most boards meet once a month. For the most part, boards direct their attention to developing broad policies and assisting in fund raising, while leaving operational decisions to the director. In some cases, however, boards do take responsibility for establishing all policies and procedures, become involved in the actual running of the center, and make decisions on employee hiring and firing.

The director/coordinator is usually responsible for a combination of staff supervision, fiscal administration, grant proposal writing, speaking engagements (community outreach and publicity), and establishing liaisons with community leaders and agencies. The most frequently cited staffing pattern consisted of nonprofessional volunteers and CETA workers. Almost half of the 89 respondents also employed formerly battered women and/or professional counselors.

Board of Directors

Table 3–1 shows that almost all of the respondents have a board of directors. In response to the question, Do you have a board of directors? 81 centers (91 percent) answered "yes," while only eight answered "no."

TABLE 3–1. Number of centers having a board of directors

	Frequency	Percentage
Yes	81	91.0
No	8	9.0

TABLE 3–2. Size of board of directors

Number of Board Members	Frequency	Percentage
1– 5	4	6.2
6–10	16	24.6
11–15	23	35.4
16–20	8	12.3
21 or more	14	21.5

Note. Of the 81 programs which reported having a board of directors, 65 provided information on the total number of board members, while 16 (20 percent) did not reveal the size of their board.

There was variance in the size and membership of the boards (Tables 3–2 and 3–3). Almost half of those responding to this question (39 out of 65, or 60 percent) reported that their board consisted of between 6 and 15 members. But one-quarter of the programs had relatively large boards consisting of either 16–20 or more than 21 members.

The most frequently cited profession of a board of directors member was attorney, followed closely by social worker. Also well represented were formerly battered women, nurses, teachers, counselors, and other mental health professionals (for example, vocational rehabilitation counselors or alcoholism counselors). Also included on some boards, although to a lesser extent than the aforementioned, were clergy, physicians, police officers, nonbattered women from the community, judges, and students.

The purposes and functions of the boards of private agencies may vary, but in general there are three major purposes of a board of directors (Sorenson, 1950):

1. To secure effective administration of the agency. The board is, ultimately, responsible for the agency's overall performance, even though it usually delegates day-to-day administrative responsibility to the director/coordinator.
2. To create public acceptance of the work of the agency through citizen participation.

TABLE 3–3.   Types of professionals and community leaders on board of directors

	Frequency	Percentage
Lawyers	36	69.2
Social workers	34	65.4
Formerly battered women	31	59.6
Mental health professionals	27	51.9
(primarily counselors)		
Teachers	23	44.2
Nurses	23	44.2
Community women	17	32.7
Clergy	16	30.7
Police	16	30.7
Judges	6	11.5
City officials/legislators	5	9.6
Legislative aides	5	9.6
Physicians	5	9.6
Students	5	9.6
Probation officers	3	5.7
Psychologists	3	5.7
Volunteers	3	5.7
Activists	2	3.8
Bankers	2	3.8
Other	7	13.5
Accountant	1	
Assistant district attorney	1	
Director of council on status of women	1	
Director of head start program	1	
Engineer	1	
Librarian	1	
Newspaper editor	1	
YWCA as governing board	11	21.2

Note. Based on a total of 52 responses. Respondents were asked to list the types of professionals and/or community leaders involved in their board of directors. A limitation to this question was revealed when respondents indicated that their board consisted of lawyers, social workers, and so on without specifying the number of such professionals on their board. The responses provided information on whether one or more persons in a certain profession were on the board. Thus, this table underrepresents the total number of professionals involved.

3. To provide continuity to the agency. From time-to-time, the director and other staff members may leave for another position, but the board remains (Johns, 1960).

According to Ehlers et al. (1976), the functions of the board of directors at private, voluntary agencies include establishing policies, helping to raise funds, overseeing the operation of the agency, validating the agency's services, and improving public relations.

Although the structure of almost all of the battered women's centers includes a board of directors, many of the respondents seem to have a loosely knit board which does not contribute significantly to raising funds or improving public relations. The above is inferred from the fact that most battered women's programs are functioning on shoestring budgets, and they often encounter resistance from community leaders and public agencies when seeking their assistance.

Advisory Board

No one program can operate successfully in a vacuum and provide the comprehensive services its clientele need. A new program is especially pressed when trying to gain acceptance and cooperation from established mental health, social service, and criminal justice agencies. Developing an advisory board can serve to lay the groundwork for interagency cooperation and shared agency responsibility in delivering optimal services to abused women. An advisory board can help to identify the battered woman's critical need for legal, medical, and social services. Board members in administrative positions at state, local, and private agencies can sensitize their associates and employees to the vital work of centers for battered women. Developing positive interagency relationships is important. It can result in local agencies' knowing where and how to refer a traumatized victim of spouse abuse so that she can receive immediate assistance. It can also provide a coordinated approach to referring these women for a full range of supportive services.

When advisory committees and councils are organized by human service agencies, it is to solve specific problems. However, when a battered women's center plans to develop an advisory board it is usually to solve one major problem: public and interagency relations. Through the right personal contacts—with administrators of health, welfare, and criminal justice agencies—advisory board members can hope to assure interagency cooperation; and by having community leaders on the board, abused women and abusive males may more readily recognize the important work of these programs. For example, one center in the New York metropolitan area is planning an advisory board with members such as a professional football player, the commissioner of the Sanitation Department, attorney William Kunstler, a police captain, bank vice-presidents, and legislators. One of the primary goals of this type of advisory board would be to improve the image of the battered women's center and to influence people who are ignorant of the issues to realize that wife battering is a genuine problem and that crisis intervention programs are desperately needed. This study found that the type of member most frequently represented on an advisory board is a social worker, attorney (many of

TABLE 3–4. Number of centers having an advisory board

	Frequency	Percentage
Yes	44	52.3
No	40	47.6
No response	5	

TABLE 3–5. Size of advisory board

Number of Board Members	Frequency	Percentage
1– 5	4	11.1
6–10	15	41.7
11–15	3	8.3
16–20	9	25.0
21 or more	5	13.9

Note. Of the 44 programs which reported having an advisory board, 36 provided information on the total number of board members, while 8 did not reveal the size of their advisory board.

whom are working for Legal Aid), registered nurse, or representative of the police department or the criminal court.

Slightly more than half (44, or 52.3 percent) of the 84 respondents to this question reported having an advisory board (Table 3–4). Just over half (24 of 44) of these programs which reported having such a board stated that it consists of either 6–10 members (15 respondents) or 16–20 members (9 respondents) (Table 3–5). Some of the programs which do not have an advisory board offered the following explanations: (1) The board of directors doubles as an advisory board; (2) they have no need for an additional board (beyond the board of directors); (3) they are in the process of trying to organize an advisory board.

The types of professionals included on the advisory board were similar to those of the board of directors (Table 3–6). The two most frequently represented professionals here (as with the board of directors) were social workers (including administrative directors of social service organizations) and attorneys. However, in the make-up of advisory boards, social workers had a slight edge (28 to 23), whereas attorneys had been the most represented group on the board of directors. The involvement of nurses remained high, with nurses on 12 advisory boards compared to 23 nurses on boards of directors. A significant difference in the composition of

TABLE 3–6. Types of professionals and community leaders on advisory boards

	Frequency	Percentage
Social workers	28	63.6
Legal aid attorneys	23	52.3
Nurses	12	27.3
Judges	9	20.4
Mental health professionals (primarily counselors)	9	20.4
Police officers	9	20.4
Battered wives	7	15.9
Clergy	6	13.6
Legislators	6	13.6
Teachers	4	9.0
Business people	3	6.8
City or county prosecutors	3	6.8
Community women	3	6.8
Representatives of private nonprofit organizations	3	6.8
Volunteers	2	4.5
Professors of criminology	2	4.5
Real estate salespersons	2	4.5
Public relations director	1	2.3

Note. Based on a total of 44 responses. Respondents were asked to list the types of professionals and/or community leaders on their advisory board. A limitation to this question was revealed when respondents indicated that their advisory board consisted of social workers and legal aid attorneys, etc., without specifying the number of such professionals on their board. The responses provided information on whether one or more persons in a certain profession were on the board. Thus, this table underrepresents the total number of professionals involved.

the two groups is the representation of formerly battered women. Although they were the third-ranking category (mentioned 31 times) for membership on the board of directors, they were seventh-ranked on advisory boards, being included on only 7 such boards (15.9 percent). The percentage of judges and representatives of criminal justice agencies increased such that they were represented on 20.4 percent of advisory boards while sitting on only 11.5 percent of boards of directors. There was also a considerably lower percentage of teachers and a slightly lower percentage of clergy serving on the advisory boards, 9.0 percent and 13.6 percent respectively.

A major problem facing these newly emerging crisis intervention programs is securing adequate funds. Executives from business, industry, and financial institutions have the background and personal contacts which could be highly beneficial to programs in need of operating funds. Yet this study found that such representatives have generally not been included on the boards of centers for abused women.

When a board is comprised solely of social workers and counselors, formerly battered women, and leaders of local women's groups, the outcome is often a program which strives to meet the many needs of the target population but without adequte funding to turn the projected goals into reality. Without sufficient funding even the most carefully planned emergency shelter and treatment program cannot survive. Therefore programs should give serious thought to the most effective methods of fund raising, one of which is to include locally prominent business leaders and legislators on the advisory board. (Further information on funding sources is given in the next chapter.) Another approach is for a newly developing battered women's program to join forces with an established social welfare agency such as a local family service agency, the YWCA, or the Salvation Army, if an arrangement can be made so that the parent organization will provide all or most of the program's funding. In this way, the new program could benefit from the established agency's program development and administrative expertise. Fiscal operations would be more likely to follow generally accepted accounting procedures.

Staffing Patterns

The predominant staffing pattern is nonprofessional and volunteer workers. Information reported in Table 3–7 indicates that the majority of centers are staffed by six or more volunteers and three or more CETA workers. Undergraduate and graduate students were mentioned frequently, providing the opportunity for the center to acquire free labor while the student has an on-the-job learning experience (for which college credit is usually given). In addition, almost half of the programs had counselors and a formerly battered woman on staff. Only 29 (approximately one-third) of the centers had a full-time social worker on staff; 32 programs reported having a clerical worker. One center reported that it employs consultant lawyers and psychologists on an hourly basis when needed. The small number of consultants that seem to be employed by battered women's programs may be a consequence of the fact that survey respondents sometimes neglect to fill in the "other" category on a questionnaire when it is appropriate to do so.

The following types of personnel were mentioned by three or more centers: attorney (11 centers), psychologist (7), nurse (6), vocational coun-

TABLE 3–7. Total number of staff by positions

	Most Frequent Types of Staffing			
	1 Staff Member	2 Staff	3–5 Staff	6 or More
Volunteers	2	3	6	50
CETA workers	10	6	23	18
Social workers	21	2	6	
Counselors	17	10	10	4
Vocational counselors	4	1		
Lawyers	9	2		
Former battered women	6	11	17	9
Psychologists	5		2	
Undergraduate students	11	4	5	4
Graduate students	8	5	4	3
Clerical staffs	27	5		
Nurses	7			

Other Types of Staff	
Community organizers	Art therapists
VISTA workers	Training Directors
Child care workers	Paralegal aides
Housekeepers	Cooks
Assistant directors	Housemothers
Youth outreach workers	Advocates
Volunteer coordinators	Group leaders
Fund raiser/researchers	Sociologists
Maintenance workers	Recreation aides
Teachers	Part-time consultant lawyers
House managers	Part-time consultant psychologists
Dance therapists	

selor (5), house manager (5), advocate (5), VISTA volunteer (4), and volunteer coordinator (3). The following staff positions were listed by 2 centers: teacher, children's coordinator, administrative assistant, assistant director, and maintenance worker. Finally, several types of staff positions were mentioned by just 1 program: cook, art therapist, dance therapist, training director, group leader, paralegal aide, sociologist, recreation aide, and fund raiser/researcher. The more extensive and elaborate staff lines are reflective of centers which are secure financially, which already have sufficient personnel in essential capacities, and which serve large numbers of clients.

It should be noted that at least some of the responsibilities entailed in positions such as children's coordinator, group worker, or recreation aide are being handled by counselors and social workers of many centers.

Although most of the programs did not have a full-time coordinator of children's activities, a play therapist, or a teacher, several respondents are aware of the need for such a staff person. As reported in Chapter 2, 7 respondents indicated their need to hire child care workers if they had the funds to do so. Attending to the children's psychological, physical, and educational well-being remains an area of profound need for the vast majority of programs.

■4
Funding Sources

Obtaining operating funds is one of the most significant problems facing these centers, many of which are survivng on a shoestring budget. Their staff usually consists of volunteers and CETA workers and; when funding levels permit, professional social workers and counselors are hired. Most of these centers are relatively new. They are the outgrowth of concerted efforts on the part of local community groups, women's groups, YWCA staff, and rape centers. Some progress is being made. The consolidated picture of the wide range of sponsors which have funded battered women's services reveals the potential for others who seek funds from the public or private sector.

Of all the funding mechanisms—public and private—the single most frequently mentioned source of funds was CETA, the federal grant program which provides funds for economically disadvantaged, unemployed, and underemployed citizens. Of the 89 respondents to this survey, 88 provided information on their source(s) of funding. A total of 57 programs (64.8 percent) reported having CETA workers on staff. The acronym CETA is so widely used that several respondents did not seem to know what it stands for or how the money is made available. CETA stands for the Comprehensive Employment and Training Act, which is handled by the Employment and Training Administration of the federal Department of Labor. Federal funds go directly to "prime sponsors" in local areas (under a formula based on population). The funds are then made available by the prime sponsor to persons and organizations who can provide jobs in a variety of semiskilled, skilled, and professional occupations. Since the funds are channeled through the local areas, some respondents had the misconception that the program had originated at the city or county, rather than the federal, level.

Utilizing CETA workers appears to be a blessing to some programs and a bone of contention to others. Because these programs for battered women operate on such tight budgets, it is advantageous to hire workers who are paid by an outside source. Some programs conceded that without CETA-funded positions their programs would not be able to operate. By the same token, however, some project directors complained that their CETA workers lacked the motivation, work attitude, and skills necessary to do the job properly. For example, a center in Massachusetts reported: "In retrospect, using Title VI CETA monies to pioneer an endeavor of this sort presented overwhelming obstacles. Finding committed, self-motivated paraprofessionals from the CETA work pool has been very difficult and often discouraging." Professionally trained social workers and counselors, so desperately needed, are not usually able to be hired through CETA because of the way in which the legislation is written and the low ceiling on salaries. Even in cases where a counselor could meet the criteria, the maximum salary that a CETA worker may earn (approximately $12,000 annually) is too low to attract most experienced and capable professionals. Programs which are barely scraping by cannot afford to hire a professional and experienced staff, especially when CETA workers are available to take on the job.

Several programs reported that they had encouraged selected formerly battered women to register for the CETA program. Because of their lack of job skills, lack of recent work experience, and need for an income (particularly among women who were separated from their husbands), such women fit the requirements set forth in the CETA guidelines. These women, when they become eligible for a CETA position, can be selected to work at a battered women's shelter, or they can be placed in another type of job setting.

Following CETA funding, the most frequently mentioned funding sources reported were grants from private foundations (34, or 38.6 percent), individual donations (19, or 21.6 percent), the United Way (17, or 19.3 percent), and donations from community groups (14, or 15.9 percent) and churches (10, or 11.4 percent). An additional 5 organizations said that they hold fund-raising events to bring in additional moneys.

Local church and civic organizatons represent an excellent (and often overlooked) source of partial support, providing not only direct financial assistance but also valuable services such as transportation and needed items for the shelter such as food and used furniture. Local chapters of national organizations are generally interested in providing assistance to residents of their community who have the greatest need. As distinct from grants at the federal level—which require that a center demonstrate that it has developed a unique or innovative type of program—church and civic organizations are concerned only that there be an identifiable need in the community and that a viable program be developed and maintained to meet that need. The following are a few of the organizations which have been approached by the programs responding to this survey: Zonta International, Junior League, B'Nai B'Rith, Rotary and Templeton groups, and local women's centers. Local businesses and individual merchants are another source of partial support which is often overlooked. In addition to outright donations, they can also be approached for needed furniture, appliances, and food.

Grants from Private Foundations

As mentioned previously, grants from private foundations represented a source of funding for over one-third of the centers in this study. The well-known big-name foundations, such as the Rockefeller Foundation, Ford Foundation, and Mellon Foundation, are interested in supporting innovative research and development programs; they are not likely to provide funds for a locally based emergency shelter. The types of foundations most likely to fund a program for battered women are *community foundations*. Many times these foundations are named for the city, county, or state in which their interests lie, for example, the Rhode Island Foundation, the Philadelphia Foundation, the Milwaukee Foundation, or the San Francisco Foundation. Furthermore, the community foundations typically restrict their giving to a specific region, and their policy of giving is stated quite clearly. For instance, the Pittsburgh Foundation's funds go for projects within Pittsburgh and Allegheny County; the Kalamazoo (Michigan) Foundation serves to benefit residents of Kalamazoo County; and the California Community Foundation makes grants principally to California organizations. These types of foundations usually place emphasis on charitable, educational, and civic activities such as education, social welfare, hospitals and health agencies, youth agencies, and the visual and performing arts. A list of 219 community foundations, presented in alphabetical order by state, appears in Appendix B.

A reference book which represents the most comprehensive source of information on private foundations throughout the United States is the seventh edition of *The Foundation Directory* (Lewis, 1979), published by the Foundation Center in New York and revised approximately every 2 years. The current edition provides information on over 2,800 foundations. It does not include all of the community foundations listed in Appendix B because the criteria for including a foundation in the directory are such that many community foundations are excluded on the basis of their small grant volume and/or insufficient assets. However, the directory does list many foundations which, while not considered "community foundations," should be approached because of their expressed interest in local giving.

Cleveland Foundation, The
700 National City Bank Building
Cleveland 44114   (216) 861-3810

Community foundation established in 1914 in Ohio by bank resolution and declaration of trust.

Purpose and Activities: The pioneer community trust which has served as the model for most community foundations in the United States; purposes are to assist public charitable or educational institutions in Ohio; promote education and scientific research; care for the sick, aged, and helpless; improve living and working conditions; provide facilities for public recreation; promote social and domestic hygiene, sanitation, and the prevention of disease; research into the causes of ignorance, poverty, crime, and vice. Unless specified otherwise by the donor, grants are limited to the Greater Cleveland Area and are not made for capital, sectarian, or religious activities. Grants for specific programs, with emphasis on higher education, hospitals, health and medical research, social services, the aged, child welfare, community and economic development, and criminal justice. No grants to individuals, for endowment funds, or operating budgets. Report published annually.

Financial Data: (yr. ended 12/31/75):   Assets, $179,815,000 (M); gifts received, $4,200,000; expenditures, $9,533,000, including $9,184,000 for 445 grants (high: $225,000; low: $1,000).

Officer: Homer C. Wadsworth, Director.

Distribution Committee: H. Stuart Harrison, Chairman; Mrs. Scott R. York, Vice-Chairman; George B. Chapman, Jr., Robert D. Gries, Frank E. Joseph, George F. Karch, Mrs. Drue King, Jr., William J. O'Neill, Jr., Thomas F. Patton, Walter O. Spenser, Thomas V. H. Vail.

Trustees: Central National Bank of Cleveland, The Cleveland Trust Company, National City Bank, Society National Bank of Cleveland, Union Commerce Bank.

Write: Homer C. Wadsworth, Director.

Grant Application Information: Grant application guidelines available; initial approach by telephone; submit 11 copies of proposal; no application deadline; board meets 5 times a year.

IRS Employer Identification No.:   340714588

Reprinted with the permission of Marianna O. Lewis, editor of *The Foundation Directory,* published by The Foundation Center, New York, N.Y., 6th ed., 1977.

FIGURE 4–1.   Sample *Foundation Directory* listing.

Each *Foundation Directory* listing provides basic information on the foundation's purpose and activities, financial data, grant application information, and the name of a contact person. Figure 4–1 shows the entry on the Cleveland Foundation, which in the 1-year period ending December 31, 1975, made 445 grants totaling $9,184,000. The Cleveland

Foundation is reported to be the largest community foundation (based on assets) in the country; other community foundations make considerably fewer awards, and their grant expenditures are far less. It is important to emphasize the fact that there is heavy competition for foundation support, and often extremely worthy projects are not able to be funded.

The Foundation Center, chartered in 1956 in New York, is "the only independent, not-for-profit organization in the United States dedicated entirely to the gathering, analysis and dissemination of factual information on philanthropic foundations" (Lewis, 1977). The center operates one library in New York City [888 Seventh Avenue, New York, N.Y. 10019; (212)975–1120] and one in Washington [1001 Connecticut Avenue, N.W., Washington, D.C. 20036; (202)331–1400], which are open to the public without charge. In addition, "cooperating collections" are available to the public in 45 states, Mexico, and Puerto Rico.

Women's programs interested in more detailed information than that which the *Foundation Directory* provides may check other reference volumes (an example is the Foundation Center's *Foundation Grants Index*), or they may contact certain foundations directly to request a free copy of their annual report. A complete collection of annual reports is available for perusal by the public at the Foundation Center libraries.

By reviewing a copy of a foundation's annual report, one can readily determine its giving pattern. One should examine the total number of grant awards and the total expenditure, as well as the number and amount of awards in the particular category of interest, that is, social services. Although a foundation may express an interest in funding social service programs as one of several areas of support, a review of its grant awards may reveal that few grants have been made for that purpose. In particular, one may discover that a foundation has not yet provided funding for any programs which provide services to battered women. Such knowledge can be helpful in approaching the foundation. As an example, one might preface a letter in the following manner:

> I have reviewed the X Foundation's *Annual Reports* from the past 2 years and notice that only 6 awards (out of a total of 45 grants) were made in the social services area. Furthermore, none of the awards have gone for programs to serve battered women and their children. Yet I am aware of the X Foundation's expressed interest in strengthening the social service resources of our county. I believe that the program I am about to propose will provide the abused women of our county with the sort of comprehensive service delivery network they so desperately need.

Variations on the above approach would be made as appropriate. For instance:

The X Foundation has clearly demonstrated its support for social service programs by having awarded 20 grants in this area during the past 2 years. Based on the foundation's strong commitment to social services, I am hoping that you will be interested in funding the Battered Women's Hotline and Shelter Program of Y County.

And for those cases in which a community foundation's annual report does not indicate a particular interest in social services programs, one might write:

I recognize that the predominant funding interests of the X Foundation are health care and education and that the overwhelming majority of your grants are in those areas. Nevertheless I ask you to consider funding for Y County's Battered Women's Shelter. In many cases, our shelter has offered a life-saving opportunity to women who have been severely beaten by a husband or boyfriend. Without the 24-hour availability of an emergency shelter such as ours, the physical and mental health of these women would be further endangered.

By beginning the letter in a way such as this, the grants writer has immediately established that she has done her homework by researching the foundation's grant-making history. Following the opening statement, the writer would describe the nature and background of the organization she represents. The writer would then document the need for the services, including supportive data such as:

- The number of women already being served monthly and the total served to date (if the program is already in existence)
- Local police statistics on numbers of domestic violence calls annually
- Statistics from local hospital emergency rooms (if such are available) on women victims of assault and battery where a husband or boyfriend was the perpetrator
- Quotes from respected people, such as physicians, police administrators, and legislators, on the local, state, or national level, who are sensitive to the critical need for establishing programs for abused women

This would be followed by a concise description of the proposed program and the specific services to be provided. The educational and experiential background of the center's director, and the names and positions of the members of the board of directors and advisory board (if they have been selected) should also be included. Finally, an estimated budget figure should be given along with information on any financial support which has already been made available.

In most cases foundations request that applicants submit their initial inquiry in the form of a brief letter (two pages is sufficient), but some foundations do have their own forms which need to be completed. It is best to inquire about the foundation's policy before submitting a request for funding. The letter should contain a statement to the effect that more detailed information on the program is available if the foundation is interested. In general, private foundations do not want to be inundated with massive 30-page proposals; an informative letter is sufficient to elicit a response—either the foundation is interested and will seek further information (including in some cases, a personal meeting) or it is not. This is distinct from grant proposals to government agencies, which are usually lengthy, quite detailed and all-inclusive, and are submitted on official forms.

The following are some examples of grants that have been awarded by foundations to programs serving battered women:

- San Francisco Foundation (California): $29,048 to Casa de las Madres, San Francisco, for administrative support.

- Boettcher Foundation (Colorado): $25,000 to Volunteers of America, Denver, to establish a pilot safe house for battered women.

- Piton Foundation (Colorado): $12,000 to the Human Development and Research Center of Colorado (located in Evergreen) to plan and operate counseling and emergency housing center for battered women and their children.

- Dayton Hudson Foundation (Minnesota): $15,000 to Bradley Angle House (Portland, Oregon) for general support of shelter for battered women and their children. (*Foundation News*, 1979)[1]

- Hartford Foundation for Public Giving (Connecticut): $75,000 to Hartford Interval House to help establish services and temporary shelter for battered and abused women.

- Winston-Salem Foundation (North Carolina): $35,000 to YWCA of Winston-Salem, Battered Women's Services for the following purposes: to provide shelter and counseling for battered women and their children, & to work with courts, probation and mental health departments for court-imposed counseling for the abusive male.

- Cleveland Foundation (Ohio): $55,000 to Women Together of Cleveland

---

[1]The amount of these grants as originally reported in the *Foundation News*, January–February, 1979, pp. g-3, g-5, g-6, and g-15; they are reprinted with the permission of Marianna O. Lewis, editor of *The Foundation Directory*.

for shelter and supportive services for battered women and their children. (*Foundation News*, 1978)[2]

• McKnight Foundation (Minnesota): $10,000 to Harriet Tubman Women's Shelter of Minneapolis, for new crisis shelter for abused women.

• Chicago Community Trust (Illinois): $46,200 to Legal Assistance Foundation of Chicago for a Legal Center for battered women.

• Wallace Alexander Gerbode Foundation (California): $7,560 to Casa de las Madres of San Francisco, to help underwrite developmental efforts for this agency for abused women. (Noe, 1978)

Funds from Government Sources

A total of 54 respondents (61.3 percent) obtained some or all of their funding from a government source, either city (15 respondents), county (9), state (16), or federal (14). (This tabulation does not include CETA funds, which were reported by 57 programs, as discussed earlier in this chapter.)

Federal Funding

At the federal level, the most frequently mentioned program was the Law Enforcement Assistance Administration (LEAA); 8 respondents reported receiving LEAA support. Fiscal year 1979 marked the second year of funding under LEAA's Family Violence Program. During the 1979 funding cycle, LEAA targeted six to eight grants (ranging in size from $75,000 to $150,000) for rural communities and networks of small communities having a maximum population of 75,000. An additional four to five awards (of $100,000 to $300,000 each) were anticipated for cities having a population of at least 100,000 persons. LEAA differs from other agencies in that it focuses on improving the functioning of the criminal justice system. A wife abuse program desiring LEAA funding may submit a proposal which sets forth a workable, well-constructed plan for ameliorating the battered woman's plight through coordination and linkage with one or more components of the criminal justice system: the police (for example, early case finding and referral) and courts or prosecutor's office (for example expeditious processing of criminal complaints against the abusive male).[3] Grants

---

[2]Reprinted from the *Foundation News*, July–August, 1978, p. 3, with the permission of Marianna O. Lewis, editor of *The Foundation Directory*.
[3]For further information on the Family Violence Program, including deadline dates and application materials, contact: Program Manager, Family Violence Program, Special Programs Division, Office of Criminal Justice, Law Enforcement Assistance Administration, 633 Indiana Avenue, N.W., Room 700, Washington, D.C. 20531; (202) 376–3550.

may also provide for a wide range of mental health and social services for family victims of violence.

State Funding

Many state legislatures have recently passed or are currently acting upon legislation on domestic violence. On May 28, 1977, the governor of Alaska signed into law an act providing a special appropriation of $216,000 to establish a shelter for battered women and their children in Anchorage. The funds provided for "personnel, materials, and rental of space for the operation of a shelter." In 1978, the state appropriation had grown to accomodate five shelters located in Juneau, Fairbanks, Bethel, and Nome in addition to the original one in Anchorage. The total authorization for fiscal year 1979 is $475,000, and $503,500 has been requested for FY 80 (S. Haley, 1979).

In December 1978, Wisconsin passed legislation calling for a continuing grant appropriation of $1.5 million each fiscal year for the period 1979–1981. Of that amount, each year $525,000 will be used for existing shelters; $525,000 will go for private home shelter care (either new or existing); and $425,000 has been earmarked for provision of services which are not available through either emergency shelter facilities or networks of private home shelters. The legislation sets the maximum grant award for each organization at $100,000 annually or 70 percent of its operating budget, whichever is less (State of Wisconsin, 1978).

Miscellaneous Funding Possibilities

The survey respondents also mentioned, albeit to a much lesser extent than the aforementioned funding sources, the following sources: local mental health association (8 programs), community development council (5), and police department (2). In one case, a large state university provided a program's funding. The following organizations were each noted by 1 respondent: the Salvation Army, a local hospital, local banks, and a legal services agency. Finally, 1 program stated that fees are charged on an ability-to-pay basis to help offset the cost of running the shelter.

Multiple Funding

Just over half (46) of the programs indicated that the bulk of their funds came from one (16) or two (30) different sources (Table 4–1). Sometimes a small additional amount was generated through individual donations or fund raising. One program mentioned that it had been relying solely on CETA funds and was now faced with the dilemma of losing that source and

TABLE 4–1. Number of funding sources

Sources of Funding	Number of Programs
1	16
2	30
3	18
4	8
5	9
More than 5	7
Total	88
No response	1

seeking support from other organizations. The obvious danger of relying on just one source of funds is the panic that sets in if that one source dries up for political or any other reasons. If a battered women's program is fortunate enough to have its budgetary needs met by a sole source, it would still be wise to be aware of other possibilities—just in case.

At the other end of the spectrum are those 7 centers which reported having more than five sources of funds. The inherent problem with this type of multiple funding situation is that seeking, coordinating, and accounting for the various funds can become quite burdensome, and it diverts energy that could be devoted directly to the victims. Nevertheless, programs which have not been able to attract large grants from one or two sources have no alternative but to pursue every possibility.

Sample Grant Proposals

Domestic Assault Program: Proposal

Program Description

The Domestic Assault Program is a component of the Assault Crisis Center of the Kalamazoo YWCA.[4] (Its sister component is the Sexual Assault Program.) The major goal of the program is to meet the urgent needs expressed by individuals who request protection and assistance because they fear harm from a spouse, a former spouse or another individual with whom they have shared an intimate relationship. The corresponding primary objectives are to provide information to victims, to provide refuge for

---

[4]Published with the permission of Carolyn A. Krill (Coordinator, Assault Crisis Center, Kalamazoo, Mich., YWCA). This proposal was submitted to Michigan's Domestic Violence Prevention and Treatment Board in September 1979.

victims and their children and to enable dependent individuals to realize self-sufficiency through action.

Through public relations and community education the Domestic Assault Program will attempt to reach a larger portion of the community, making people aware of the program, its services, and the nature, dynamics and preventive necessity of domestic assault. In addition, its staff and advisory committee will attempt to influence policy at the county, state and federal levels toward the provision of services for victims.

Any person, regardless of race or economic status, can be a victim of domestic assault. The program is primarily designed to serve women, although our services are available to men as well. We have served and will continue to serve all people regardless of age, race, sex and economic characteristics.

The Domestic Assault Program began serving the needs of victims in June, 1976. It was funded and supported by the Kalamazoo Foundation from January, 1977 through December, 1978. Funding in 1979 was provided by the Kalamazoo Foundation, the Upjohn Community Trust, C.E.T.A., Federal Revenue Sharing, H.U.D. and the Michigan Domestic Violence Prevention and Treatment Board. The program enjoys a broad base of support in the community and has been a model for the development of shelters in Michigan and other states. Over forty inquiries for assistance and advice have been received from groups throughout the country who are attempting to organize similar programs. It was the first shelter to open in Michigan. To date it has provided direct service to over 600 women. Quarterly reports for January through June 1979 are included on pp. 69-72.

Program Objectives

The objectives of the Domestic Assault Program are as follows:

client	1.	To provide facts about options for victims.
need	2.	To provide shelter.
related	3.	To promote self-sufficiency by giving the victim space and time to decide her own direction.
program	4.	To assess the unmet needs of assaulters, victims and their
need		children.
related	5.	To secure on-going funding of services to victims.
	6.	To influence public policy toward responsibility for provision of services to women who have been dependent.

Methods

The activities in relation to the three client objectives for providing factual information, protection, and self-sufficiency occur in different units with overlapping functions. Please refer to the program chart [Table A].

TABLE A. Program chart

Needs	Objectives	Methods	Evaluation
Client			
A. Information	to provide the facts regarding options for the victims	•by 24 hours crisis telephone •by crisis counseling •by legal information •through community education	# of calls received # of sessions # of requests for service # of mass media exposures # of community groups contacted
B. Protection	to provide refuge	•secure shelter for abused women and their children	# of clients, # of nights of service
C. Self-sufficiency	to promote self-sufficiency to giving the victim the space to decide her own direction	•offering short term housing and emergency food •case management to connect victims with continuing resources •support groups	incidence of use client contract, service plan, case management interviews # of sessions held, # in attendance
Program			
D. Involvement	to assess the unmet needs of assaulters victims and their children	•record gaps in service •identify barriers •advocate through local agencies	quarterly and annual reports # of requests for shelter denied success in altering local policies
E. Continuance	to secure on-going funding of service to victims	•prepare quarterly reports for feedback and improvement of the system •prepare proposals and present to funding sources	reviewed by the YWCA Board of Director, Administrative Committee and YWCA Executive Director on-going funding achieved each year
F. Public Acceptance	to influence public policy toward responsibility for provision of services to women who have been dependent	•maintain an exchange of information with local DSS and DVPTB •communicate information on program needs to Domestic Violence Board and Michigan Legislature •participate in MCADV	updated policies copies of letters dues paid and meeting attended offices or committee positions held

Crisis Phone—Information

The victim enters the service system initially through the 24 hour crisis line. Clear information regarding service options and careful listening are the tasks of this unit. Hopefully, this results in more crimes being reported as well as more victims receiving attention to their urgent needs.

The Program Director will provide information outreach through community education, in-service training and consultation services.

Emergency Shelter with Crisis Counseling

The central and most costly task of the program is providing shelter. In-kind or volunteer workers are available 24 hours a day to admit women to the shelter. A wide range of services is available to the victim—counseling, legal information, criminal justice advocacy, financial assistance, medical assistance, employment information, school intervention for her children, and/or child care while she makes arrangements. The program staff assists her in securing in-house and community services.

Support Services

For those battered women who remain in their homes or those who have become independent, there are a variety of services available. In addition to counseling services offered by the program staff, agencies such as the Kalamazoo Consultation Center and Family and Children's Services are utilized as referral sources for longer term follow-up counseling with the assaulter, victim and/or families. The Kalamazoo Consultation Center will continue to develop and facilitate support groups for the victims. A cooperative arrangement with Legal Aid allows the program to refer up to 6 cases per week for initiation and divorce proceedings.

The program staff became cognizant of gaps in service through interviews with clients and by experiencing barriers in obtaining adequate referral services. These occur primarily in the criminal justice system and the area of on-going housing. Identifying these problems is the first step in playing an effective advocacy role in the community.

The securing of on-going funding is time consuming and complicated. Although local support has been positive to date it is essential that vigorous and intensive efforts are applied to insure that the program receives continued funding. The program must be monitored, updated and improved to insure that it is service responsive and cost effective.

This same effort must be extended to keep the problem of domestic assault from being ignored by policy makers at the local, state and national levels. Two excellent avenues have been opened with the formation of the Michigan Coalition Against Domestic Violence and the creation by the legislature of the Domestic Violence Treatment and Prevention Board. Documentation of experience in the Kalamazoo program must be communicated and publicized to insure effective influence. Cooperation with these and other groups will help to bring about changes in public policy and improved services for domestic assault victims.

Data Collection and Evaluation

Data is collected for each face to face contact in the following ways:

1. A crisis contact card is filled out for each person who receives service listing demographic information, a profile of the abuse, and services requested and provided. (See p. 73)
2. An intake form designed by the Domestic Violence Prevention and Treatment Board is filled out for each client. A copy of this form is sent to the Board when the case is closed. (See pp. 74-79)
3. A fact-sheet intake interview form is completed with summarizes pertinent information. (See p. 80)
4. Release of Information forms are obtained before contact is made with other agencies. (See p. 81)
5. A client contract is completed for each client obtaining shelter services. (See pp. 82-83)
6. Within three working days following admission to the shelter a client service plan is drawn up.
7. Records are kept of subsequent case management interviews.
8. Health forms are obtained for all individuals residing in the shelter.
9. A brief assessment is made at the time a case is closed and/or reopened.

This information is used:

1. To monitor program usage;
2. To insure a program of effective service for each client;
3. To measure progress toward goals;
4. To gather data necessary for future program development, especially in the areas of prevention and treatment;
5. To gather statistical information for the purpose of reporting to the YWCA Board of Directors and to funding agencies.

Service Areas

1. Crisis and Support Counseling for Victims of Domestic Violence and their Dependent Children

Crisis and support counseling is provided both by phone and at the shelter facility for all victims, whether or not they make use of the emergency shelter. Staff members are available to women in the shelter without an appointment. The crisis line is open 24 hours a day with the evening and week-end hours covered by volunteers or mental health counselors. Women requiring long-term therapy are referred to one of several counseling agencies in the community who have indicated a willingness and the capability to assist with the unique problems of victims. In addition, a support group meets weekly for any victims, regardless of previous contact with the Program.

Children who require counseling are referred to one of two agencies who are experienced in dealing with their problems.

2. Emergency Health Care Services

Women in need of emergency health care are referred to one of the two hospital emergency rooms or, on occasion, to a private physician. Transportation is provided by staff and funds are available for treatment and/or subsequent medication, wound dressings, etc. Victims who seek emergency room treatment are often referred to the Program by hospital personnel. Private physicians have also referred women. On at least one occasion a staff member was provided time and space by a private clinic to interview a victim who was receiving medical treatment unrelated to injuries received in her abusive situation.

3. Legal Assistance

Legal assistance is procured in one of several ways. A unique agreement with Legal Aid allows the Program to refer for immediate appointments up to five clients per week whom the staff feel are in a dangerous situation. This by-passes the standard Legal Aid procedure of requiring a three month separation and making appointments only every two months on a specific "call-in" date. The Legal Aid Office frequently refers victims to the Program for screening and referral back to them for the "priority" appointments.

Women who cannot meet Legal Aid eligibility requirements are referred to a public interest law clinic. The attorney there gives special attention to clients referred from our Program and charges minimal rates for his services. Both he and the Legal Aid attorneys have made themselves available to the staff to answer legal questions and to suggest alternatives for prompt legal action.

Victims who wish only to obtain legal information and advice are referred to Lawyer Referral Service. Funds are available to assist them with the nominal consultation fee.

The Program works closely with the Prosecuting Attorney's Office to facilitate prosecution, obtain maximum bond and sentencing, and to further protect the victim by enforcing conditions of probation or parole. A member of their staff has been assigned as a contact person and member of the Advisory Committee.

In addition to providing an officer as contact person, the Kalamazoo Police Department cooperates by providing escorts for victims to obtain personal possessions from their homes, accompanying them to the Prosecutor's Office, or enabling them to leave the shelter safely on business. They respond quickly to calls involving assaulters who harass victims, the Program and its staff, and they frequently refer victims for shelter or other services.

Transportation to legal services is frequently provided by staff. Some offices are within walking distance, but may include a staff or police escort.

4. Financial Assistance

A cooperative arrangement with the Department of Social Services enables women who live in the shelter to obtain A.D.C. benefits. This is made possible by the Department's recognition of the shelter as an address for these women. In this way they may obtain food stamps, Medicaid, and a support allowance for themselves and their children while at the shelter. Victims make application for benefits soon (frequently one day) after arriving at the shelter. Transportation to D.S.S. is frequently provided by staff as well as assistance in making application.

Funds are available from the Program to enable victims to cover expenses until they receive A.D.C. benefits or to assist women without children. This may include such items as public transportation fees, personal needs, food, medical expenses, children's needs, etc.

5. Housing Assistance

In addition to the Program shelter, back-up housing is provided for short periods of time in motels, the expense of which is covered by emergency funds. Other emergency shelter is available on referral at a local church affiliated mission.

Women who are ready to leave the shelter are assisted in locating housing and furnishings by the Program staff. Volunteers provide transportation and supportive service in viewing and obtaining housing.

6. Transportation Assistance

Transportation is provided to clients to reach the shelter, to return home for clothing and personal belongings, to obtain medical services, to attend appointments which are not within walking distance, and occasionally for group shopping.

When staff is not available or the situation is such that it is not deemed safe to send staff, the woman may be transported by cab. An arrangement with the cab company allows Program staff to charge the fare by giving a series of code letters to the dispatch.

The Program also provides bus fare for clients to appointments and for children to school when school bus transportation is not available.

7. Child Care Services

Child care is provided primarily by women in the shelter. They are paid by emergency funds to care for children when victims are gone for short periods of time to attend specific appointments in the community. Day care is obtained by Program staff through cooperation with the Department of Social Services and Community Education for Young Women. Summer day camp programs, offered by the YWCA, are available to children residing in the shelter. Volunteers provide activity programming for the children, using the facilities of the YWCA.

The YWCA as Sponsoring Agency

The YWCA is a particularly appropriate place to house this program. The YWCA has a long history of commitment to meeting the needs of women and their families. The Domestic Assault Program has been operating in the YWCA since 1976.

The YWCA residence provides emergency shelter for women and their children in addition to long-term housing for women in transition.

Location of the program in the YWCA offers the following advantages:

1. Staff experienced with the program and committed to its goals.
2. Central location with convenient access to other resources.
3. Relatively secure facility, close to the police station.
4. Space, equipment, and toys for children.
5. Completely furnished rooms, with access to kitchen facilities and household items.
6. Child care available.
7. Telephone lines and other office equipment already in place.

Community Service Integration

While the goal of Domestic Assault Center is to provide supportive services and advocacy for victims of domestic assault, these goals can only be met in so much as close relationships are maintained with other community service providers. The program fills needs previously unmet until its establishment but requires cooperation from other agencies to give complete and comprehensive service. In addition to direct service through the use of an extensive referral system, other service providers contribute the following:

1. Representatives from some of the major service providing agencies serve on the Advisory Committee.
2. The Kalamazoo Consultation Center provides a staff person to facilitate the support group.
3. Gryphon Place Mental Health professionals provide after hour crisis phone and shelter access which is supplemented by volunteer workers.
4. Legal Aid accepts referrals on a priority basis.

Volunteer Training Program

We encourage all interested persons in the community to work with our program. All volunteers are required to be 18 years of age and successfully complete our training program. Prospective volunteers submit an application which is followed by an interview. The 30 hour Training Program covers empathy skills, crisis intervention techniques, factual information related to domestic assault victims and orientation to the Domestic Assault Program. A packet of information is given to the trainees to facilitate the skills taught and for their use as volunteers in the program activities.

Volunteers who successfully complete training are assigned to handle crisis calls and provide access to the shelter facility during evening and week-end hours.

All volunteers are required to attend a general monthly meeting for brush-up training which includes special speakers, updated factual information, educational materials and interaction with other volunteers and staff. Scheduling and program policy dissemination is also done at this time.

Newsletter

Published in cooperation with the Sexual Assault Program, the Assault Crisis Center newsletter distributes criminal assault information to volunteers and community agencies. This includes changes in hospital, criminal justice and human service agency policies and/or procedures. The newsletter also includes notification of meetings and other program activities.

Role of the Advisory Committee

The Assault Crisis Center Advisory Committee holds a responsibility to the two program divisions, i.e., Domestic Assault and Sexual Assault. Representatives from the legal, criminal justice and human service systems along with community volunteers comprise this group which meets once a month to:

1. facilitate coordination of services;
2. discuss program procedures;
3. make recommendations of program policy to the YWCA Board of Directors;
4. plan and implement goals;
5. evaluate effectiveness.

Fiscal and Administrative Responsibility

The YWCA is a membership organization and the voting members are responsible for electing a Board of Directors. Included in the responsibilities of the Board of Directors are: (1) determining and carrying out the policies and program of the Association; (2) controlling operating funds and capital assets. The YWCA President, with the Treasurer, sign all leases and other contracts of the Association. The Board of Directors, employs the Executive Director, who is responsible for the execution and administration of policies and programs approved by the Board. An organizational chart is included.

The YWCA is a Michigan Non-Profit Corporation with January 12, 1884 as the date of incorporation. Each year an Annual Report Form CS-2000 is filed with the Michigan Department of Commerce.

1980 Program Staffing

The Domestic Assault Program Staff shall consist of a Coordinator at 3/4 time, a Program Director at 3/4 time, two half-time Victim Support Workers, two Live-in Shelter Workers, a half-time Clerical Worker, and a Housekeeper at 3/4 time.

Although the Coordinator has responsibility for the entire Assault Crisis Center (including the Sexual Assault Program), the on-site location of the shelter and the case load of the Domestic Assault Program requires that a greater share of this worker's time be given over to this program. A proportionately higher budget for this division also requires that more time be spent in fund seeking, and the larger staff of the Domestic Assault Program requires a greater share of supervisory time.

The Domestic Assault Program Director shall bear the responsibility for the development, promotion and delivery of service to the program's clients. This includes management of the shelter and supervision of the individuals housed there.

The Victim Support positions may be utilized in a number of ways to accomplish the objectives outlined in the job description. The specific emphasis of these job components will be determined by the program needs, but will retain as its priority the best use of time and personnel to meet the needs of the clients.

Two Live-in Shelter Workers will provide supervision for the shelter at night and on weekends. They will be available for support counseling, to admit women and to insure efficient functioning of the shelter. It will be their responsibility to respond to emergencies and to provide guidance and direction to the residents.

The Clerical Worker will be assigned to the Domestic Assault Program by the Coordinator on a half-time basis. In addition to performing routine office procedures, the worker will assist in improving training and community education materials.

Job Descriptions
Program Coordinator

A. Facilitate funding and develop grant proposals.
B. To develop, coordinate, and promote functions related to the total Assault Crisis Center.

C. Supervise and evaluate the Program Director related to this program.
D. Interpret the Domestic Assault Program in the community.
E. Facilitate community service inter-agency co-operation.
F. Develop and monitor the budget.
G. Maintain and coordinate necessary records and office responsibilities.
H. Implement/expand workshops, community education, and supportive services.

Accountability: Is directly responsible to the YWCA Executive Director.

Domestic Assault Program Director

A. To develop, coordinate and promote functions related to the Domestic Assault Program component.
B. Provide up-dated information to maintain awareness of volunteers regarding domestic violence.
C. Evaluate the Domestic Assault Program component in areas of responsibilities.
D. Maintain and coordinate necessary records and office responsibilities.
E. Provide counseling to the victims who request shelter for themselves and their children and secure necessary resources of other agencies such as financial, legal aid, prosecution, and health services.
F. Assure the continued functioning of the support groups.
G. Assist with workshops, community education and support services.
H. Supervise and evaluate all staff related to this program.
I. Provide information, referrals and crisis counseling to all victims who request service.
J. Perform related functions at the Program Coordinator's request.

Accountability: Is directly responsible to the Program Coordinator.

Victim Support Workers

A. Direct service in the assigned program area: the Program Director to determine the appropriate area according to skills and experience.
B. Assist/provide 24 hour coverage of the program.
C. Assist with counseling and referral services to victims of criminal assault and their families.
D. Assist with coordination of volunteer training and activities.
E. Provide information and community education on the problem and the services available.
F. To be an advocate for victims going through the criminal justice system.
G. Assist with data collection.
H. Develop and implement follow-up procedures for victims receiving services from the assigned program components.
I. Perform related functions at the Program Director's request.

Accountability: Is directly responsible to the Program Director.

Shelter Workers

A. Provide supervision of the shelter from 9:00 P.M. until 9:00 A.M. Monday through Friday and from 9:00 P.M. Friday until 9:00 A.M. Monday.
B. Provide supportive counseling to shelter residents during the above hours.
C. Admit victims and their children to the shelter during duty hours.
D. Monitor and enforce rules, policies and procedures of the shelter.
E. Respond appropriately to emergency situations in the shelter area during duty hours.
F. Consult with Program Director and Victim Support Workers regarding clients in the shelter and their related needs.
G. Assist with data collection.
H. Perform related functions at the Program Director's request.

   Accountability: Is directly responsible to the Program Director.

Clerical Worker

A. Handles correspondence, public contact (phone/in person) filing, typing (45 wpm) and operates business machines.
B. Typing duties include: Volunteer packets, training manual, volunteer lists, grants, new releases and statistical reports.
C. Required to successfully complete the Volunteer Training Program.

   Accountability: Is directly responsible to the Program Director.

Housekeeper

A. Perform general housekeeping tasks, including the following:
   1. Laundering of residence linens.
   2. Cleaning kitchen, restrooms and residence rooms.
   3. Window washing, defrosting refrigerators, emptying trash.
   4. Maintenance of walls, floors and woodwork and moving furniture.

Minimum Qualifications for Staff

Program Coordinator

   Master's degree in human service area with experience in grant writing, program supervision and administration.

Domestic Assault Program Director

   Master's degree in counseling or social work. Minimum of three years experience in counseling or case management. Supervisory experience desirable.

Victim Support Workers

Minimum of bachelor's degree in human service area. Master's degree desirable. Counseling or case work experience desirable.

Shelter Workers

Bachelor's degree desirable but may substitute experience as residence assistant or similar position. Need listening skills and ability to deal with interpersonal interactions.

Clerical Worker

High school graduate with human service agency experience. Must be able to file, complete statistical reports and type 45 wpm. Knowledge of copy machine and offset press desirable. Must have ability to deal with people in crisis.

Housekeeper

High school diploma or equivalent. Ability to follow written directions. Knowledge and skill in cleaning techniques and the ability to work without direct supervision. Must sometimes meet tight schedules in getting residence rooms ready to meet emergency situations. The ability to work with people of diverse backgrounds and experiences is required as well as good physical health.

Budget Narrative

The 1980 budget reflects minimal increases in costs and salaries well within the guidelines suggested by government. Capital improvements to be completed in 1979 have been eliminated from the 1980 budget. No further expansions or improvements are planned at this time.

Building

The cost of the shelter space is based on a square footage rate, taking into consideration such items as utilities, maintenance, upkeep and other overhead.

Pool, gym and playroom facilities are used by the women and children housed in the shelter. These are effective in providing worthwhile leisure activity, in developing skills and providing relief from anxiety. Some victims are fearful of leaving the shelter area and it is important that some activity be available. Children are frequently placed in the summer day camp program sponsored by the YWCA.

Office space cost includes the use of two offices for administrative and counseling purposes. The YWCA provides minimum furnishings.

Staff Salaries

Salaries are in line with present YWCA pay ranges. The Coordinator position is figured at 3/4 as an approximation of the division of time spent between the Sexual Assault and the Domestic Assault Programs. This rationale has been developed more fully in the section on program staffing. Job descriptions for all positions have been included.

Administrative Costs

The YWCA assumes ultimate responsibility and supervision for the program. The Board of Directors, the Executive Director and the accounting staff all contribute time, experience and expertise to the operation and continuation of the program.

Office Needs

This item includes printing, postage and office supplies for the program. The printing facilities of the YWCA are made available at cost. Some public relations materials must be printed commercially.

Community Education

This will continue to be a vital component of the program and will include the updating and expansion of materials to increase public knowledge and awareness of domestic assault. An informational library will be established to provide access to materials to interested citizens, including students and other human service agencies.

Transportation

Transportation reimbursement will be provided to staff for transporting clients, procuring services, and on a limited basis, for other program related business.

Training

Training materials for trainers and volunteers are purchased from several sources. These include materials on empathy skills, crisis intervention techniques and factual information related to domestic assault.

Emergency Fund and Miscellaneous

The emergency fund provides small amounts of money to victims to cover the cost of emergency medical needs, food, personal items, public transportation, child care, etc. The cost averages less than $20.00 per client.

Telephone

The 24 hour crisis line is essential to the service provided to the community. The program office handles day-time crisis calls. After 5:0 0 P. M. the calls are taken by qualified Mental Health workers or volunteers. The cost for this service is based on figures quoted by Michigan Bell Telephone Company.

Answering Service

The Domestic Assault Program assumes 1/4 of the cost of an answering service employed primarily by the Sexual Assault Program. Because of the related nature of the program the answering service takes many domestic assault calls and refers them to the appropriate crisis line.

Calculation of In-Kind Contributions

Group counselor. The Kalamazoo Consultation Center provides the services of a therapist with a Ph. D. in Psychology to conduct a group session for 2 hours each week.

Night and weekend workers. These individuals, all qualified counselors at the M.A. level, provide complete coverage, including admission to the shelter from 5:00 P. M. until 9:00 A. M. week-days and from 5:00 P. M. Friday until 9:00 A. M. Monday. Of that time approximately 11-1/2 hours per month are spent in actual counseling. The remaining hours are calculated as crisis phone work. These individuals are currently provided by the community Mental Health Board. They will gradually be replaced by volunteers.

Donations. Individuals and groups from the community donate food, clothing, linens, diapers and personal items to the shelter. These items are not covered in the budget.

DOMESTIC ASSAULT PROGRAM
Quarterly Report

Period of Time: January 1 - March 31, 1979

Active Cases Carried Over: __22__   Total Number of New Cases: __51__

Age: Marital Status:
  15-19 __2__   35-40 __5__   Married   __33__
  20-24 __19__ 41-45 _____   Single   __9__
  25-29 __13__ 46-50 __2__   Divorced   __3__
  30-34 __7__   50+   _____   Separated   __6__
         Unknown __3__

Racial Origin:
  American Indian _____   Hispanic __4__
  Asian   _____   White   __40__
  Black   __7__   Unknown   _____

Time of Contact: Regular __47__   After-hour __4__

Source of Referral:
  __3__ Dept. Social Services   __1__ Van Buren Co.
  __1__ Kal. Couns. Center   _____ St. Joe County
  __3__ Pros. Att. Office   _____ Allegan Co.
  __1__ Mental Health Board   __2__ Barry Co.
  __3__ Police   _____ Calhoun Co.
  _____ KADAC   __10__ Self, Friend, Relative
  __1__ Gryphon Place   __10__ Other (specify) __see *__
  _____ Fam. & Child. Ser.   __5__ Unknown
  __9__ Legal Aid
  _____ Red Cross
  _____ Borgess Hospital
  __2__ Bronson Hospital

Source of Financial Support:
  Self __12__ ; Other Person __18__ ; Public __15__ ; Unknown __6__ .

Relationship of Assaulter:
  Husband-Living with __33__   Boyfriend   __9__
  Husband-Estranged   __6__   Former Boyfriend   __1__
  Husband-Former   __2__   Other   _____

Types of Assault:
  __5__   1. Pushed, threw objects, slapped.
  __17__ 2. Threats or emotional abuse.
  __25__ 3. Punched, kicked, pushed down, hit with hard object.
  __4__   4. Choked, stabbed, shot.

Duration of Abuse:
  1 month __7__ ; 6 months __10__ ; 1 year __6__ ; over 1 year __20__ ; unknown __8__ .

Type of Service Provided:
  __23__ Crisis Phone Counseling
  __20__ Shelter: No. Adults __20__ , No. Children __33__
  __22__ Carry-over Cases Sheltered: No. Adults __22__ , No. Children __56__

(continued)

Type of Service Provided: continued

    1620 Total No. of Nights of Shelter
      33 Legal Information
      12 Food
       5 Money
       3 Transportation
      44 Counseling
       4 Clothing
       2 Child Care

Support Group: No. Held   14   No. Attending 63

Referrals:

7	Dept. of Social Services		Kal. Coun. Center
	Health Department	1	Borgess Hospital
2	Pros. Att. Office	2	Bronson Hospital
2	Mental Health		Operation Turnaround
3	Police		KADAC
5	Mike Slaughter		Fam. & Child. Ser.
	Red Cross	16	Legal Aid
	Salvation Army	5	Other (specify) see **
	Gospel Mission		

       Legal Consultation (on contract)

Emergency Funds Expended: $115.94

Number of Families denied shelter because of lack of space: 15 .

Community Presentations: 11
   Where: Church Women United
             Women in Transition
             W.M.U.
             Operation Turnaround
             Stockbridge Methodist Church
             Van Buren Co. Parent Aides
             Portage Central High (2)
             Bronson Nurses Alumni
             First Presbyterian Youth Group
             Battle Creek Family & Children's Services

----

* Sojourner Truth Center	** Lawyer Referral
Kalamazoo Ghild Guidance Clinic	Kalamazoo Public School
Every Women's Place	Voluntary Action Center
School Counselor	City Probation
St. Joe Lodge	
City Housing Office	
McKinley School	
City Hall	
United Migrant Opportunity	

(continued)

DOMESTIC ASSAULT PROGRAM
Quarterly Report

Period of Time: April 1 - June 30, 1979

Active Cases Carried Over: __34__   Total Number of New Cases: __42__

Age: Marital Status:
   15-19 __2__   35-40 __3__   Married   __33__
   20-24 __11__ 41-45 __3__   Single   __3__
   25-29 __14__ 46-50 _____   Divorced   __2__
   30-34 __7__   50+   __2__   Separated   __4__

Racial Origin:
   American Indian _____   Hispanic __1__
   Asian   White   __36__
   Black   __4__   Unknown   __1__

Time of Contact: Regular __34__   After-hour __8__

Source of Referral:
   __4__ Dept. Social Service   __3__ Van Buren Co.
   _____ Kal. Coun. Ct.   _____ St. Joe Co.
   _____ Pros. Att. Office   _____ Allegan Co.
   _____ Mental Health Board   _____ Barry Co.
   __2__ Police   _____ Calhoun Co.
   _____ KADAC   __3__ Borgess Hospital
   __1__ Gryphon Place   _____ Bronson Hospital
   _____ Fam. & Child. Serv.   __13__ Self, Friend, Relative
   _____ Red Cross   __7__ Other (specify) __see *__
   __9__ Legal Aid

Source of Financial Support:
   Self __9__ ; Other Person __11__ ; Public __18__ ; Unknown __4__ .

Relationship of Assaulter:
   Husband-Living with __32__   Friend-Living with __3__
   Husband-Estranged   __3__   Friend-Not living with __1__
   Husband-Former   __2__   Other __1__ (Stepdaughter)

Types of Assault:
   __6__ 1. Pushed, threw objects, slapped.
   __11__ 2. Threats or emotional abuse.
   __23__ 3. Punched, kicked, pushed down, hit with hard object.
   __2__ 4. Choked, stabbed, shot.

Duration of Abuse:
   1 month __1__ ; 6 months __6__ ; 1 year __5__ ; over 1 year __27__ ; unknown __3__ .

Type of Service Provided:
   __19__ Crisis Phone Counseling
   __20__ Shelter: No. Adults __20__ , No. Children __38__
   __11__ Carry-over Cases Sheltered: No. Adults __11__ , No. Children __22__
   __2270__ No. of Nights of Shelter - Total
   __1__ Child Care

(continued)

71

Type of Service Provided: continued
  _7_ Clothing
 _39_ Counseling
 _11_ Food
 _20_ Legal Information
  _6_ Money
      School Intervention
  _1_ Transportation

Referrals:
  _7_ Dept. of Social Services   _1_ KADAC
      Pros. Att. Office   Kal. Coun. Center
      Mental Health   Borgess Hospital
      Police   Bronson Hospital
      PCOC   _1_ Operation Turnaround
  _1_ Fam. & Child. Ser.   Family Divorce Coun.
  _1_ Red Cross   _5_ Other (specify) _see **_
 _10_ Legal Aid

No. of Families denied shelter because of lack of space: _28_ .

Community Presentations: _8_
  Where: Ladies Library
           Welcome Wagon
           WKZO
           W.M.U.
           K.V.C.C. Women's Festival (2)
           First Congregational Church
           Kellogg Community College

----

* Att. Joe Miller   ** Gryphon Place
  Pediatrics Intervention   Mike Slaughter
  Dr. Kinsey   YWCA Battered Women's Shelter,
  Kalamazoo Child Guidance   Grand Rapids
  DARE (Port Huron)
  Grand Rapids YWCA
  Michigan Economics

DOMESTIC ASSAULT PROGRAM

DATA CARD

Case No._____

Name: _____ Date:_____

Address:_____ Phone:_____

Age: _____ Sex: _____ Marital Status: M__S__D__Sep.__ No. Children:_____

Referred by:_____Intake Worker:_____

Racial Origin:
  Amer. Indian _____ Asian _____ Black _____ Hispanic _____ White _____ Unknown _____

Income: Self _____ Other Person _____ Public _____

Relationship of Assaulter: _____

Nature of Assault: _____

Duration of Abuse:
  1 month _____ 6 months _____ 1 year _____ 2-5 years _____ over 5 years _____

Shelter	Dates
DAP	
REF.	
Motel	

□ 1

CASE INTAKE FORM

□□ 3 AGENCY

□□□ CLIENT CODE
   6

□ 1. WHAT IS THE VICTIM'S SEX?
 7
       1 = Female   2 = Male   3 = Unknown

□ 2. WHAT IS THE VICTIM'S RACE?
 8
       1 = White   2 = Black   3 = Other   4 = Unknown

□□ 3. WHAT IS THE VICTIM'S AGE?
9 10
   4. NUMBER OF CHILDREN BY AGE: (Enter number of each) 9 = Unknown

11 □   AGE THREE OR LESS

   □   AGE FOUR TO SIX

   □   AGE SEVEN TO ELEVEN

   □   AGE TWELVE TO SEVENTEEN

15 □   ADULT CHILDREN

□ 5. VICTIM'S APPROXIMATE NET INCOME:
16
       1 = Less than $200/month   4 = $601-$800
       2 = $201-$400   5 = $801 or more
       3 = $401-$600   6 = no income
                                     7 = unknown

□ 6. SOURCE OF VICTIM'S INCOME:
17
       1 = Victim's employment   4 = Victim's employment and public ass't.
       2 = Public assistance   5 = Other: _____
       3 = Social Security (SSI)   6 = Unknown

□ 7. VICTIM'S EDUCATIONAL LEVEL:

18   1 = Less than high school   4 = College degree
       2 = High school diploma/GED   5 = Unknown
       3 = Some college

□ 8. SOURCE OF VICTIM'S CONTACT WITH DOMESTIC VIOLENCE PROGRAM:
19
       1 = Telephone   2 = Walk-in   3 = Referral from: _____

(continued)

74

9. HAS THE VICTIM BEEN TO YOUR SHELTER BEFORE?

20

1 = Yes, once   4 = Yes, four or more times
2 = Yes, twice   5 = No
3 = Yes, three times   6 = Unknown

10. IS THE ASSAILANT THE PARENT OF ANY OF THE VICTIM'S CHILDREN?

21

1 = Yes   2 = No   3 = Unknown

11. HAS THE ASSAILANT EVER PHYSICALLY ABUSED ANY OF THE CHILDREN?

22

1 = Yes   2 = No   3 = Unknown

12. WHAT IS THE RELATIONSHIP OF THE ASSAILANT TO THE VICTIM?

23

1 = Spouse   5 = Ex-boyfriend/girlfriend
2 = Ex-spouse   6 = Friend
3 = Relative   7 = Other
4 = Boyfriend/girlfriend   8 = Unknown

13. WAS THE VICTIM LIVING WITH THE ASSAILANT AT THE TIME OF THE ASSAULT?

24

1 = Yes, 1 year or less   4 = No, never lived with assailant
2 = Yes, more than 1 year   5 = Unknown
3 = No, but did in past

14. IF YES, HAS THE VICTIM INITIATED SEPARATION?

25

1 = Yes, divorce   5 = Permanent injunctive order
2 = Yes, legal separation   6 = Yes, Other: _____
3 = Yes, informal separation   7 = No
4 = Temporary injunctive order   8 = Unknown

15. WAS A WEAPON USED IN THE ASSAULT?

26

0 = No weapon   5 = Hands, fist, feet
1 = Handgun   6 = Chemical/poison
2 = Long gun   7 = Explosive
3 = Cutting instrument   8 = Other: _____
4 = Blunt weapon   9 = Unknown

16. WAS THE VICTIM INJURED IN THE ATTACK?

27

0 = No injury   3 = Incapacitating injury
1 = Possible injury   4 = Fatal injury
2 = Non-incapacitating injury   9 = Unknown

17. WHERE DID THE ASSAULT OCCUR?

28

1 = Victim's residence   4 = Victim's place of employment
2 = Assailant's residence   5 = Other: _____
3 = Mutual residence   6 = Unknown

(continued)

75

18. WERE THE POLICE CONTACTED REGARDING THE ASSAULT?

□ 29

1 = Yes, victim did
2 = Yes, shelter did
3 = Yes, other party did: _____
4 = No
5 = Unknown

19. HAS THE VICTIM PREVIOUSLY CONTACTED THE POLICE REGARDING A DOMESTIC VIOLENCE PROBLEM IN THE PAST YEAR?

□ 30

1 = Yes, specify how many times: _____
2 = No
3 = Unknown

20. DID THE VICTIM ATTEMPT TO PRESS CHARGES AGAINST THE ASSAILANT?

□ 31

1 = Yes, pressed charges
2 = Yes, but attempt blocked by external control
3 = No
4 = Unknown

21. WAS THE ASSAILANT ARRESTED?

□ 32

1 = Yes   2 = No   3 = Unknown

22. HAS THE VICTIM EVER SOUGHT HELP FOR THIS PROBLEM BEFORE?

□ 33

1 = Yes, medical   5 = Yes, counseling
2 = Yes, financial   6 = Yes, Other: _____
3 = Yes, legal (civil)   7 = No
4 = Yes, legal (criminal)   8 = Unknown

23. WAS THE VICTIM UNDER THE INFLUENCE OF ALCOHOL OR DRUGS AT THE TIME OF THE PRESENT ASSAULT?

□ 34

1 = Yes, drugs   4 = No
2 = Yes, alcohol   5 = Unknown
3 = Yes, both

24. DOES THE VICTIM USE ALCOHOL/DRUGS FREQUENTLY?

□ 35

1 = Yes, How often? _____
2 = No
3 = Unknown

25. A. WAS THERE PHYSICAL ABUSE BETWEEN THE VICTIM'S PARENTS?

□ 36

1 = Yes   2 = No   3 = Unknown

B. IF YES, DID THEY SEPARATE OR DIVORCE AS A RESULT OF PHYSICAL ABUSE?

□ 37

1 = Yes   2 = No   3 = Unknown

(continued)

76

26. WAS THE VICTIM PHYSICALLY ABUSED AS A CHILD?

☐ 38   1 = Yes   2 = No   3 = Unknown

27. HAS THE VICTIM EVER PHYSICALLY ABUSED HER/HIS CHILDREN (IF ANY)?

☐ 39   1 = Yes   2 = No   3 = Unknown   4 = No children

28. WHAT IS THE ASSAILANT'S SEX?

☐ 40   1 = Male   2 = Female   3 = Unknown

29. WHAT IS THE ASSAILANT'S AGE?

☐ 41 ☐ 42

30. ASSAILANT'S APPROXIMATE INCOME:

☐ 43
          1 = Less than $200/month   5 = $801-1,000
          2 = $201-400   6 = $1,001-1,500
          3 = $401-600   7 = $1,501 or more
          4 = $601-800   8 = None
                                         9 = Unknown

31. SOURCE OF ASSAILANT'S INCOME:

☐ 44
          1 = Assailant's employment   4 = Assailant's employment and public
          2 = Public assistance   assistance
          3 = Social Security (SSI)   5 = Other: _____
                                         6 = Unknown

32. ASSAILANT'S EDUCATIONAL LEVEL:

☐ 45
          1 = Less than high school   4 = College degree
          2 = High school diploma/GED   5 = Unknown
          3 = Some College

33. WHAT IS THE ASSAILANT'S RACE?

☐ 46
          1 = White   3 = Other: _____
          2 = Black   4 = Unknown

34. HAS THE ASSAILANT EVER SEEN A COUNSELOR?

☐ 47
          1 = Yes, mental health   4 = Yes, other: _____
          2 = Yes, religious   5 = No
          3 = Yes, social services   6 = Unknown

35. HAS THE ASSAILANT EVER BEEN CONVICTED OF A CRIME?

☐ 48
          1 = Yes, specify: _____
          2 = No
          3 = Unknown

(continued)

77

36. A. WAS THERE PHYSICAL ABUSE BETWEEN THE ASSAILANT'S PARENTS?

49

        1 = Yes   2 = No   3 = Unknown

    B. IF YES, DID THEY SEPARATE OR DIVORCE AS A RESULT OF PHYSICAL ABUS

50

        1 = Yes   2 = No   3 = Unknown

37. WAS THE ASSAILANT PHYSICALLY ABUSED AS A CHILD?

51

    1 = Yes   2 = No   3 = Unknown

38. DOES THE ASSAILANT USE ALCOHOL/DRUGS FREQUENTLY?

52

    1 = Yes, How often? _____
    2 = No
    3 = Unknown

39. WAS THE ASSAILANT UNDER THE INFLUENCE OF ALCOHOL OR DRUGS AT THE TIME THE PRESENT ASSAULT?

53

    1 = Yes, drugs   4 = No
    2 = Yes, alcohol   5 = Unknown
    3 = Yes, both

40. HOW MANY DAYS WAS THIS VICTIM IN RESIDENCE?

54 55

    00 = No in residence, otherwise, record number of days,
        e.g., 03, 10, etc.

41. WHEN THE VICTIM LEFT THE SHELTER, WHERE DID SHE(HE) GO?

56

    1 = Previous residence, probably now safe.
    2 = Previous residence, probably still unsafe.
    3 = New residence, probably safe.
    4 = New residence, probably unsafe.
    5 = Other: _____
    6 = Unknown

42. FOR EACH OF THE FOLLOWING SERVICES, HOW MANY UNITS OF SERVICE DID THE VICTIM RECEIVE?

            CRISIS SUPPORT COUNSELING: 58

            EMERGENCY HEALTH CARE: 60

            LEGAL ASSISTANCE: 62

            FINANCIAL ASSISTANCE: 64

            HOUSING ASSISTANCE: 66

            TRANSPORTATION ASSISTANCE: 68

(continued)

78

42. continued...

CHILD CARE SERVICES: ☐☐ 70

INFORMATION AND REFERRAL: ☐☐ 72

☐ 73

43. WERE THERE ANY SERVICES THAT THIS VICTIM NEEDED FROM YOU WHICH YOU WERE
UNABLE TO PROVIDE?

1 = Yes, _____
2 = No

☐ 74

44. DURING THE TIME THAT THE VICTIM WAS IN RESIDENCE, WERE THERE THREATS
OF A PSYCHOLOGICAL NATURE? (i.e., custody, property, reputation, counter-
claims of violence, etc.)

1 = Yes   3 = Unknown
2 = No   4 = Not applicable

☐ 75

45. DURING THE TIME THAT THE VICTIM WAS IN RESIDENCE, WERE THERE INSTANCES
OF THREATENED ASSAULT FROM THE ASSAILANT?

1 = Yes   2 = No   3 = Unknown   4 = Not applicable

☐ 76

46. DURING THE TIME THAT THE VICTIM WAS IN RESIDENCE, WERE THERE ANY INSTANCES
OF PHYSICAL ABUSE FROM THE ASSAILANT?

1 = Yes   2 = No   3 = Unknown   4 = Not applicable

☐☐   ☐☐ 80
Day   Month

79

DOMESTIC ASSAULT PROGRAM

INTAKE INTERVIEW

NAME_____ DATE _____ CASE NO. _____

REFERRED BY _____ AGE _____

ADDRESS_____ PHONE _____

EMERGENCY CONTACT_____ PHONE _____

CLIENT EMPLOYMENT _____ OTHER INCOME _____

CHILDREN(S) NAMES _____ AGE _____

_____ AGE _____

_____ AGE _____

NAME AND ADDRESS OF ASSAULTER _____

_____

Relationship to Client _____ Length of Relationship _____
Place of Employment _____

DATE AND DESCRIPTION OF LAST ASSAULT_____

_____

	YES	NO
POLICE CONTACTED		
CHARGES FILED		
ALCOHOL		
DRUGS		

DURATION AND NATURE OF ABUSE _____

_____

CASE SUMMARY _____

_____

_____

_____

NEEDS AT INTAKE_____

_____

ACTION AT INTAKE _____

_____

_____ CONTRACT SIGNED
_____ NEXT INTERVIEW APPOINTMENT
_____ DATA CARD COMPLETED

INTAKE DONE BY _____ 7/79

80

DOMESTIC ASSAULT PROGRAM

RELEASE OF INFORMATION

I, _____, hereby give my permission for
release of information relevant to providing services and meeting my needs to
the staff of the Domestic Assault Program. As of this date for a period of
ninety days.

_____ Michigan Department of Social Services

_____ Kalamazoo County Legal Aid

_____ Kalamazoo County Prosecutor's Office

_____ Other: _____
              (Fill in)

_____   _____
(Client signature)   (Staff signature)

_____   _____
(Date)   (Date)

Original to be kept with case record.

Copies to be sent to referring agency.

DOMESTIC ASSAULT PROGRAM

CLIENT CONTRACT

I, _____, am a client of the Domestic Assault

Program, YWCA. I understand that I must follow the rules listed below in order

to reside in the shelter. FAILURE TO ADHERE TO THESE RULES CAN RESULT IN MY

LEAVING THE SHELTER.

KEYS

1. I will never give or loan my keys to anyone.
2. All keys will be turned into staff when leaving the residence for more
    than 48 hours.
3. All keys will be turned into staff when moving out of the residence
    permanently.

LENGTH OF STAY

1. I will try to limit my stay to no more than three to four weeks; for
    longer stay I must get written staff approval.
2. If I am no longer staying in the residence any personal items left at the
    residence will be disposed of after 6 weeks from the date I leave.

CHILDREN

1. If my children are sick I will seek aid in obtaining medical help.
2. At no time will I leave the residence without taking my children or
    arranging for their care.
3. I will follow the bedtime schedule as outlined in the General Information
    sheet.

KITCHEN

1. I will use only my own food.
2. I will clean up whatever I or a member of my family use.

ALCOHOL AND DRUGS

1. I will not bring any alcohol or illegal drugs into the YWCA.
2. I will not use any alcohol or illegal drugs in the YWCA.

PERSONAL

1. I am required to attend the Support Group sessions while a resident
    in the shelter unless excused by staff.
2. I will keep appointments made for me by staff.
3. I will not at any time give out any information concerning another
    resident.

(continued)

PERSONAL, continued

4. I understand and agree to sign, if necessary, a release of information form.
5. I will make the required appointments for progress interviews. Frequency of these interviews will be determined by staff members.

BUILDING SECURITY

1. The residence floor is not open to the public. Visitors will be met on the main floor.

WAIVER

1. The DAP and YWCA does not assume liability for any personal property or injury.

GRIEVANCE

1. A formal grievance in writing many be filed if desired with the YWCA Executive Director.

SERVICE PLAN

1. I will abide by the Service Plan set up by myself and staff.
2. This initial Service Plan will be formulated within three working days following admission to shelter and is subject to revision.

I have read and understand this client contract. Any violations may be reported by DAP or YWCA staff and will be discussed with me.

_____   _____
(Client Signature)   (DAP Staff Signature)

_____   _____
(Date)   (Date)

Proposal Narrative: Jackson County
Task Force on Household Violence

General Purpose

The purpose of the Jackson County Task Force on Household Violence is to provide shelter, counseling, and referral services for those persons seeking safety from household violence.[5]

Specific Goals

1. To provide shelter and supportive counseling to victims of household violence;
2. To provide a self-development program for the victims that will encourage their self-determination;
3. To increase public awareness of the problem of household violence and the need for the support of the public and private sector;
4. To impact change within the existing public agencies that are in a position to respond effectively to the victims of household violence.

This project is the only one of its kind in Jackson County. We see it as an important project because it serves the needs of low income persons, in particular, and establishes a working network among the social services of the county.

Objectives

Performance objectives for the program for the calendar year 1978 are:

1. To provide shelter for 102 persons (52 adults, 50 children) who are seeking safety from household violence;
2. To provide personal counseling to 52 victims of household violence (52 adults of the 102) as well as referral (inter-agency) services;
3. To establish a working network within the social service agencies to provide complimentary services to the victims of household violence;
4. To make a minimum of 25 presentations to agencies and police departments regarding the problem of household violence.

History

On January 10, 1977, a workshop was held on the Southern Oregon State College campus on the subject of "Household Violence: Help for Battered Women and Children." Four hundred persons shared a full day of discussion and panel presentations on this subject of household violence as a problem, both nationally and locally.

[5]Published with the permission of Rosemary E. Dalton (Chairperson, Jackson County Task Force on Household Violence, Ashland, Ore.). This narrative was part of a 1978 application for funding submitted to the Campaign for Human Development in Washington, D.C.

As a result of this conference, battered women began to emerge. Unfortunately, they were coming out to a community that didn't know what to do with them. It was then that the Jackson County Task Force on Household Violence was formed. A group of about fifteen people gathered together to begin planning, brainstorming and struggling with what could be done for these women.

We began by educating ourselves about the problem of household violence. We discovered these alarming facts:

• Approximately one-fourth of all murders in the United States occur within the family. Half of these are husband-wife killings.

• One-fourth to one-half of American couples engage in an episode of violence during their relationship.

• At least 10% of children who witness parental violence eventually become adult batterers themselves.

• In 1974 one of every five police officers who lost their lives did so while trying to settle a family fight.

• Only 2% of the men who beat up their living partners are ever prosecuted.

• Family violence cuts across race and class background. It occurs as often among the upper middle class as among the lower.

• Sex role stereotyping in our society often socializes men towards violence and to view women as property, and reinforces attitudes of women as victims.

• FBI statistics tell us that there is at least one incident of wife abuse taking place every 18 seconds.

• A Kansas police department study found that in 85% of the cases of domestic homicide, the police had been called at least once before the murder took place, and in 50% of the cases, they had been called five times or more before the homicide occurred.

• Boston police received 45 calls a day in 1976 pertaining to domestic violence.

Locally, we gathered the following information:

• In a county of approximately 119,000, the largest city of Medford, with a population of 37,200, police reported at least 560 cases of "household beefs" in 1976. Only eight of these cases were actually arrested, and only two of these cases went to court.

- Attitudes of workers in many community agencies, i.e., police, mental health, legal services, showed an ignorance and/or indifference of what to do with women who are abused.

- There was a general lack of awareness in the community at large about the problem of wife-beating.

- There was no place for women to go for shelter and protection.

The Jackson County Task Force on Household Violence has been operating without a permanent shelter for one year. We receive an average of one call per week for shelter and twenty calls for supportive, advocacy and referral services. Presentations for funding have been made to local churches, Junior Service League, Dental Wives Assoc., Business and Professional Women, Assoc., of University Women. This fundraising is a consistent endeavor for the Task Force and results are pending.

Program Description

Services

A person who contacts the Task Force can expect to talk with a specifically trained counselor who will help her assess her most immediate needs and assist her in finding ways to address those needs.

Short term counseling includes not only helping persons with the emotional crisis at hand, but also involves practical problem-solving such as checking on employment, welfare, child care, vocational and educational opportunities, legal options and temporary emergency housing. The counselor will also meet with the battered woman and her husband or living partner if he is willing to come for counseling.

Advocacy services may include accompanying the person to the hospital, police station and through court proceedings if she wishes. Since people are often not aware of their legal rights and what protection and services they may realistically expect from the police and courts, we seek legal information for them in these areas.

Barriers that exist for victims of household violence are: (1) lack of money, no job skills: (2) no place to go, no transportation; (3) worries about the children; (4) fear of the unknown; (5) not knowing what the next step is.

Shelter for victims of household violence will be provided for a maximum of three weeks. Decisions regarding the operation of the house and house rules will be made by the enrollees and director. The shelter house is to be under the direction of the House Director, who provides direction and supervision over all house activities. She will be guided by the Board of Directors, which is responsible for hiring and policy decisions.

Goals of the shelter are to facilitate the personal growth and parenting skills of the shelter enrollees. Group meetings will be held each week that will be designed to develop self-determination, decision-making and parenting skills. Because the enrollees are victims of poverty, we feel this is an essential component to the program. Services will include group and individual counseling, liaison between enrollees and social services, transportation and general advocacy services.

Needs Assessment

The demographic variables of Jackson County are an important factor in the consideration of this project. The county is experiencing relative economic deprivation. Unemployment is a significant problem. While the nation volleys between a 6 to 7% unemployment rate, Jackson County suffers from almost 13% unemployment in a general *rural* environment where the raw products are principally pears and timber. Seasonal employment is the norm which poses additional problems in the unemployment calculations. We can see that poverty, high unemployment rates and household violence are highly correlated in that the head of household generally experiences continual frustration stemming from economic instability (Jackson County average income for a family of four is just over $4,000.00). When a man cannot provide for his family there is an atmosphere for household violence. In addition, alcohol often plays a role in that the man is frustrated, turns to drink, then will abuse his family. About 80% of the cases involved alcohol.

Last year, approximately 52 persons sought shelter (not counting offspring) from household violence in Jackson County through the Task Force on Household Violence. While we have had to provide very short term shelter, we are in need of a permanent shelter location in order to continue serving this clientele. Household violence most often victimizes the poor in that these persons are not in a position to supply their own resources that would facilitate a goal of autonomy.

Evaluation

Records related to date of inquiry, date of entry into shelter, services provided participants, and follow-ups regarding status of victims at date of withdrawal from the program will be provided at the term ending of one year to date of funding. Feedback forms will be required from each participant. A cost analysis will be incorporated into the evaluation of the project. Quarterly reports will be available.

Personnel

Board of Directors

A board of low-income community citizens and professional persons consisting of at least nine persons will be maintained. The board is responsible for all policy, employee and fiscal decisions related to the functions of the Task Force and the shelter facility. Staff openings will follow affirmative action guidelines for hiring purposes.

House Director

This person is responsible for the operation of the shelter, its employee maintenance, and service of the participants in the shelter. The Director is accountable to the Board of Directors. Administrative and community related activities required. Degree preferred.

House Assistant

This person is the assistant to the house director and serves as an advocate for the house participants. House rules supervision will be the responsibility of the house assistant.

Consultant

Counselor. Crisis intervention, group facilitation to develop the capacity for those participants of the program to begin their own problem-solving as well as to help facilitate their decision-making regarding the operation of the shelter. 3 hours a week @ $15 per hour @ 52 weeks per year = $2,340. BS or BA required, as well as experience in counseling and group dynamics.

∎5
Coordination with Criminal Justice Agencies

Ideally, the criminal justice system should provide services and support to victims of spouse abuse. When a woman is assaulted by her husband or boyfriend, she should be able to report this crime to the police and receive emergency police assistance. Victims of violent crimes such as physical assault may need police protection, transportation, emergency medical care, and/or shelter. Because of the 24-hour mobile nature of police operations, victims of wife abuse can receive timely assistance from the police. However, in practice, individual police responses to calls from battered women vary considerably.

This study revealed that several police departments provide rapid intervention in wife-battering cases. Police officers from these more responsive departments are trained in crisis intervention techniques; and accordingly, they often provide necessary protection, transportation to the hospital, and understanding to battered women. Conversely, some police officers take the side of the abusive male. This type of officer may imply that the woman "deserved" the beating to "keep her in line"; he may refuse to arrest the abusive husband and may lecture the woman for calling the police altogether.

The findings reported in this chapter reveal that a number of battered women's shelters have gradually developed good communication links with the police. Several battered women's centers are beginning to realize the valuable role that concerned police can play in assisting battered women. Likewise, police in certain jurisdictions are relieved that they can rescue a severely abused woman and her children and bring them to a safe place—the local battered women's shelter.

The response of the courts is also difficult for abused women to predict. Some judges are sympathetic to the problems of seriously injured women, while other judges are apathetic and ignorant of the woman's plight. Family court magistrates and prosecutors often exercise wide discretion in their handling of cases. The battered woman's decision to pursue a legal remedy, whether it be separation, divorce, criminal prosecution, or an order of protection, is a difficult one. The experiences reported by the 89 respondents to this study document the positive and negative practices of local courts toward battered women. Equitable courses of legal action for victims of wife beating are beginning to emerge through new legislation and changes in police and district attorney policies. The findings reported in this chapter reveal the roadblocks awaiting those pursuing justice for abused women on a local and national level.

Role of the Police

The police can play an important role in crisis intervention work with battered women by providing emergency transportation to the nearest shelter or hospital, accompanying the victim to her home to retrieve personal belongings, and/or rescuing the abused woman from a violent male. Since many of the domestic relations calls that police receive involve spouse abuse, it is important for the police to be aware of the services provided by their local program for battered women. Similarly, when a violent husband is threatening to kill his wife or is holding his wife as a prisoner against her will, the police can accompany the hotline worker to the home to protect the woman from further injury.

The effectiveness of a particular wife battering program depends, in part, upon the cooperation of local community agencies. When it comes to providing safe passage out of the abusive home, the local police or sheriff's department has the potential for being one of the most significant community agencies. Staff members of battered women's programs should be engaged in such activities as meeting with their local police and providing them with orientation seminars on their crisis intervention service. In addition, tours of their shelter, training workshops, and sensitivity training on the dilemma of being a battered woman should be planned. By the same token, staff members at programs for abused women need to be sensitive to the danger and frustration police often encounter when responding to domestic disturbance calls. We are learning that police and counselors of battered women share a common concern: finding a safe and secure environment for the innocent victim of wife abuse. By working together, these human service workers can provide the emergency services battered women cry out for.

To ascertain the role police have played in assisting and rescuing battered women the following information was solicited: "Briefly describe the role that local police have played (positive or negative) with regard to your clients." There was wide variation in the responses. Of those 79 programs which responded to this question, 34 described generally positive experiences with the police, 10 had had negative experiences, and 35 discussed mixed experiences.

The following situations are illustrative of those reporting positive experiences:

- Police accompany client to her home to get personal belongings.
- Police help transport client to a battered women's shelter.
- Police refer clients to a battered women's center.
- Police respond immediately to a center's request for assistance.

From the programs which elaborated on the positive relationship they and the police department had established came high praise, for example:

- The police have worked very closely with us. One is an advocate. They are very supportive and call us at any time day or night. We also get a daily incident report (Austin, Minnesota).
- The police publicize our program by leaving a card with our phone number at all domestic disturbance calls (Montgomery County, Maryland).
- Local Sheriff Department deputies have been terrific—sensitive, supportive, informative, action-oriented. They have allowed our community educator to provide in-service training during briefings (Fresno).
- The police have been extremely supportive. They transport women, make referrals, stand by when women need to get belongings from home, etc. (Pocatello, Idaho).

The negative role of the police (10 responses) was described in terms of a police demeanor which seemed cold, impersonal, and apathetic toward battered women. Several programs characterized the police as extremely insensitive to the victims' plight. Examples of derogatory statements made by such officers include: "Wife abuse doesn't exist"; "Women need a good whipping once in a while"; and "A weekly beating keeps a girl in line."

More detailed descriptions of negative police encounters are as follows:

- Police often are abusive and insulting to the woman when she calls them to come to her house. The police do not feel they need to be educated on the issue (Somerville, Massachusetts).
- Police were invited to an open forum on the subject of wife abuse. They did not attend, responding: "Don't you know there's no such thing as wife abuse?" Also, when battered women ask police for transportation to the hospital, the police have told them to go alone (Traverse City, Michigan).
- Police . . . very unresponsive—they know the abuser well and are unwilling to intervene in family disputes. [They have the] man's home is his castle and kingdom attitude (Charleston, West Virginia).

Thirty-five respondents indicated that the role of the police had sometimes been positive while at other times it was negative, depending upon the police department and the individual police officer handling the call. In general, younger officers who had received some training in crisis intervention theories and techniques were reported to be more responsive to victims of wife abuse. Another common response among those who had had "mixed" experiences with the police was to distinguish between the attitude and reliability of two separate police units—one providing good to excellent support, the other acting negatively. Thus one California program reported that the city police were supportive but the county sheriff's department was not. A respondent from a southeastern state mentioned that "local police are good but State Police are not cooperative." In contrast, a program in New York State reported that "the State Police are supportive, but city police are unfeeling."

The following is a selection of the comments made by additional respondents who had had both positive and negative encounters with the police:

- We get good and bad reports from our clients; it seems to depend a lot on the individual officer (Seattle).
- [They] deal with us on an individual case-by-case approach and are basically cooperative but an ingrained prejudice always handicaps proper accessibility to clients (Lawrence, Massachusetts).
- If a woman says she is with our program, the police give a positive

response. If women don't mention our program, services are denied or are poorly delivered (Columbus, Ohio).

- Individual clients report bad experiences with police; however, when staff at our shelter have asked for assistance police have been cooperative (Eau Claire, Wisconsin).
- Police have been very helpful in offering police escorts. . . . Also good when needed at the house (shelter). However, they do not always make an arrest when there is an assault, which is an Oregon law, and sometimes they are impatient with the women (Portland, Oregon).
- On the whole the response is positive due to our extensive training and education with the police. However, it can be negative depending on the individual officer or, in some cases, the client (Brattleboro, Vermont).
- For the most part, in the past, they have denied that there is a problem, but now as they get to know us, they are beginning to make referrals (Ashland, Oregon).

Also included in this category were three respondents who stated that the police were cooperative in protecting the safety of the women once they had been admitted to the shelter but were not helpful when called by nonresidents to intervene in an assault at home.

This section documents the importance of and need for conducting police training workshops and forums on wife abuse to sensitize the police to the need for and purposes of crisis intervention services. Police departments as well as battered women's programs need to commit themselves to strengthening interagency cooperation.

Role of the Court

The development of a productive working relationship with the courts is seen as vitally important to facilitating legal protection for battered women. However, much work remains to be done to pave the way for a constructive working relationship between wife abuse programs and the courts. It is necessary for programs and centers for battered women to be knowledgeable about the legal rights of their clients and about the procedures for such basic legal remedies as filing a criminal complaint, obtaining a temporary restraining order from a judge, or obtaining a vacate order so that the abuser can be evicted from the home. There are, however, very real backlog problems which plague many court systems, and staff of battered women's programs would do well to recognize this fact.

To determine the role that the courts have played in protecting abused women, the respondents were asked to describe the role of their local court with regard to their clients. The marked variation in responses indicates that a battered woman who had suffered severe injuries would, in some cities, be encouraged by the prosecutor to drop the charges, while in other locations she would receive full cooperation from the prosecutor. Of the 74 centers answering this question, 33 (44.6 percent) described generally negative experiences with the courts; 28 (37.8 percent) had had positive experiences; and 13 (17.6 percent) referred to mixed experiences.

Many of those programs which commented favorably on their relationship with the courts pointed to a legal advocate (paid or volunteer) on their staff who helped smooth the way. A comment typical of this type of arrangement is as follows (from a Massachusetts program): "Having a legal advocate is a must. His contacts with the court have made personnel more aware and receptive." There was also this response from a Michigan center: "Because the assistant prosecuting attorney is part of our program, we have a lot of influence with the local court." And a center in New York State had this to say: "Magistrates are receptive to our presence. Our physical presence in family court was initially questioned but it is now accepted and sometimes requested by attorneys."

Those who had negative comments about the role of the court felt that the difficulties were the result of one or a combination of the following factors: (1) the court's ignorance of and insensitivity to the plight of battered women, (2) the court's heavy backlog of other cases, and (3) the court's inability to do much because of inadequate state laws. In addition, some felt that the district attorney's office actively discouraged women from seeking protection from the court. Selected examples which illustrate the problem areas are cited below:

> [Our relations are] very poor. Judges have shown little regard for the women. [They] tend to favor the male.

A center in Minnesota complained that in custody cases, the "rights" of the father superseded the safety of mother and child. From a center in New England came this response:

> This [role of the court] is one of the most frustrating areas. The court system is small, backed-up, male-oriented, and very ignorant in dealing with domestic violence.

As mentioned previously, not all of the responses judged the court system as either "good" or "bad." A total of 13 centers described "mixed" encounters. An Oregon program stated that local judges were found to be good in handling civil matters but not very responsive with criminal charges. Another Oregon center reported having been involved in only three court cases: In two cases (which involved divorce proceedings) the judge sided with the women. However, in the third case, a battered woman was on trial for having killed her husband in self-defense. She was found guilty and given a 20-year prison sentence. Another program responded: "Our local court is concerned with severity of injuries rather than frequency of beatings. They are effective with severe cases." Finally, an Ohio program described having gone to great lengths to educate judges on domestic violence issues. The outcome is that a woman who has been involved with that Ohio program and who tells the court of her involvement is afforded good treatment by the court. But women who are not involved with the center reported receiving mediocre services.

The battered woman must be helped to assess her marital situation, including the anticipated outcomes and consequences of legal action. When it is in the best interests of the woman to utilize the courts, she should do the following:

1. File a complaint as quickly as possible after the abusive act(s).
2. Go to the hospital for a complete examination, including X rays to reveal any fractures or other internal injuries.
3. Request that an advocate from the local battered women's program accompany her to the prosecutor's office.

Prosecutors are likely to be more receptive to assisting victims who have already obtained a police and/or hospital report and who have photographs or X rays of injuries made soon after the most recent beating. To illustrate, District Attorney Daniel La Rocque of Marathon County, Wisconsin, has suggested that "all victims should file a complaint immediately so that evidence may be gathered . . . while the details are fresh. . . . Quick reporting also increases a victim's credibility" (Abused Women's Project, 1978, p. 6).

The legal avenues available to abused women include: (1) seeking a separation or divorce; (2) filing for a temporary order of protection or an order of protection; (3) signing a criminal complaint against the abuser; and (4) postponing legal action by leaving the home, finding temporary shelter, and then assessing the legal options with an attorney.

Initiating a separation or divorce proceeding does not, of itself, provide a legal means for ending the abuse. Sometimes an abusive man becomes enraged when he learns that his wife is leaving him and the assaults increase. Therefore a woman contemplating separation or divorce should also consider the legal remedies discussed below.

A temporary order of protection is an order from a judge which can be obtained (in some jurisdictions) by battered women who have proof of serious injuries which were inflicted by an abusive husband. The "proof" may be in the form of visible injuries and/or X rays which show internal injuries. A temporary order of protection should be sought when a trial date has been set (usually 10 days to 2 weeks away) and the woman believes that during the interim the man will try to harm her again. It orders the male not to harm the woman and is in effect until the trial date.

At the court hearing, the judge hears testimony from the husband and wife, and the judge makes the decision as to whether the woman gets an order of protection and what it will say. The court may, in addition, order that the abuser be evicted from the house. An order of protection can be of any duration up to 1 year but is commonly not longer than 6 months. Since this is a civil court process, the abuser does not receive a criminal record and is not given a jail sentence unless he violates the order.

An abused woman may want to file a criminal complaint as well as a protective order. Neither procedure will have any effect on the other, since the former is a criminal process and the latter is a civil process. Depending upon the severity of abuse, commonly used criminal charges may range from harassment to simple assault to aggravated assault. The legal definitions of these terms are as follows:

> *Harassment*—A person commits a summary offense when, with intent to harass, annoy or alarm another person:
>
> 1. he strikes, shoves, kicks or otherwise subjects another to offensive physical contact, or attempts or threatens to do the same; or
> 2. he follows a person in or about a public place or places; or
> 3. he engages in a course of conduct or repeatedly commits acts which alarm or seriously annoy such other person and which serve no legitimate purpose. (LaFave, 1978, p. 645)
>
> *Simple Assault*—A person is guilty of assault if he:
>
> 1. attempts to cause or intentionally, knowingly or recklessly causes bodily injury to another;
> 2. negligently causes bodily injury to another with a deadly weapon; or
> 3. attempts by physical menace to put another in fear of imminent serious bodily injury
>
> Simple assault is a misdemeanor of the second degree unless committed in a fight or scuffle entered into by mutual consent, in which case it is a misdemeanor of the third degree (petty misdemeanor).
>
> *Aggravated Assault*—A person is guilty of aggravated assault if he:
>
> 1. attempts to cause serious bodily injury to another, or causes such injury purposely, knowingly or recklessly under circumstances manifesting extreme indifference to the value of human life; or
> 2. attempts to cause or purposely or knowingly causes bodily injury to another with a deadly weapon.
>
> Aggravated assault under paragraph (1) is a felony of the second degree; aggravated assault under paragarph (2) is a felony of the third degree. (LaFave, 1978, pp. 624–625)

For increased credibility, it is important for the battered woman to file a criminal complaint against the abuser as soon as possible while the details of the incident are clear and the injuries apparent. Many women who sign a criminal complaint against their abusive husbands change their minds and the charges are dropped before the trial. As a result of this lack of follow-through on the part of battered women, the courts are often reluctant to prosecute.

The victim who wants to file criminal charges should realize that she may face the following difficulties:

1. The magistrate often advises the woman not to press charges because "it's just your word against his." However, in many court cases, a decision is reached based on one person's word over another's. It is the responsibility of the judge or jury to hear both persons and decide whom to believe.
2. A magistrate may tell the woman that she cannot bring criminal charges against her husband. This is simply not true. The definition of a crime is a behavior which is illegal, and it does not matter who the victim is.
3. The attitude of court officials may thwart the efforts of a woman who is not knowledgeable of her legal rights. Typical in this regard is the example of a Massachusetts court clerk who refused to issue a complaint against an abusive husband telling the woman: "I push my wife around sometimes too. It doens't mean anything. It's a trivial domestic matter." (Robinson, 1978, p. 20)

The victim of wife abuse needs assistance from an attorney and court personnel when initiating dissolution proceedings, obtaining child support, seeking an order of protection, and prosecuting on a criminal charge. Since public defenders and Legal Aid attorneys usually defend indigent persons accused of a crime, it is sometimes difficult for battered women to qualify for this form of legal assistance because their financial status is based on their husband's income. Thus it is vital for battered women's programs to continue their efforts toward providing free legal services for the victims who cannot afford to pay.

Navigating the court system is generally a time-consuming, confusing, and frustrating ordeal for anyone no matter what background he or she has. But for a woman who has been the victim of brutal assaults inflicted by a husband, ex-husband, or boyfriend, the thought of going to court may be so intimidating that no effort is made to get legal protection, and the abuse continues as before. *A Handbook for Beaten Women*, by Fields and Lehman (1977) is an informative guide for abused women. It provides a clear, concise, and realistic account of a woman's rights and options in dealing with the police and courts. The handbook was developed specifically for battered women, and the authors' intention of clarifying and explaining the legal procedures involved in lay terms comes through clearly. The handbook is compact, measuring 4" by 5½", and is contained in 29 pages so that it fits easily into a purse or any personal "hiding place" around the home. It was published by the Brooklyn Legal Services Corporation B and contains a number of references to New York City and State. However the basic facts are applicable to abused women everywhere, and a universal version is offered here as Chapter 7 of this book.

The intent of the guide is stated in the first paragraph:

> This booklet tells you what you can do if you are threatened by your husband or boyfriend. It is a self-help guide. You must be ready to do something for yourself if you want the threats and beatings to stop.

A balanced view of the legal system and its red tape is presented so that a woman can decide for herself whether she wants to proceed. There are no rosy predictions that going to court will be the hoped-for panacea. In fact the booklet cautions the woman that, after following all the procedures and stating her case, the judge may side with the husband:

> Some judges are very sympathetic to battered wives, but there are other judges who blame women for starting the fights in which they get hurt. This is the gamble whenever you go to court. The judge has complete control.

■6
Study Conclusions

Many battered women need a safe place to stay while they recover from violent beatings and make plans for their future. Yet, until the mid-1970s secure shelters to serve abused women were largely unknown. Now the battered women's shelters that do exist are overcrowded, resulting in their being unable to accommodate from one-half to three-quarters of the spouse abuse victims who contact them.

With the possible exception of those shelters that are linked to a well-established organization such as the YWCA or the Salvation Army, most hotlines and shelters suffer from a severe shortage of funds. The result is that a number of newly established shelters have been forced to close their doors within a short time or to function without sufficient paid counseling staff. The ongoing clinical supervision which is provided to counselors, social workers, and psychologists at psychotherapy institutes and family service agencies is practically nonexistent within shelters for battered women.[1] A further result of insufficient funding is the lack of individual and group therapy for the vulnerable children of battered women.

A battered woman is likely to encounter many problems if she confronts the criminal justice system. In particular, some battered women who have requested the protection of local police have been confronted

---

[1]See Carlton E. Munson (ed.), *Social Work Supervision: Classic Statements and Critical Issues* (New York: The Free Press, 1979); and Munson, "Supervising the Family Therapist," *Social Casework*, March, 1980, 131–137, for guidelines that can facilitate the acquisition of good supervisory practices.

with police officers who have had no specialized training in crisis intervention and who are unwilling to provide safe passage out of a violent home. Some progress is being made toward educating and training police on appropriate methods of defusing volatile family conflicts. In 1978, the 112th General Session of the Ohio legislature passed an act which requires all peace officers to complete "a minimum of 15 hours of training in the handling of domestic disputes." The Special Committee on Domestic Violence of the Wisconsin Legislative Council recommended that the 1979 legislature of the State of Wisconsin increase the training requirement of all law enforcement officers from 240 to 245 hours and that 7 of these hours be specifically focused on methods of handling domestic violence incidents. The course content must be prepared in cooperation with agencies or programs that work with victims of domestic violence. Nebraska now requires all law enforcement agencies in the state to provide police officers with training on "the problems of domestic abuse, procedures to deal with such problems, and the services and facilities available to abused family and household members." Staff development and training of police officers in crisis intervention and conflict resolution should be instituted nationwide to sensitize these individuals to the critical needs of battered women.

It has been reported that a major weakness of shelters for abused women is their failure to prepare women to live independently. Women with children who cannot find a job may feel that they have no alternative but to return to their abusive mate. The entire area of vocational preparation is of extreme importance if the woman is to have the opportunity to create a new life for herself and her children. For some women this means career counseling, a scholarship, and encouragement to enroll in a two-year or four-year college program; for others it means a vocational evaluation, training, and placement program; for still others it may mean a refresher course to polish job skills which were used many years ago. A comprehensive job preparation program can prepare battered women for the role change from dependent housewife to independent wage earner. By bolstering the resources and skills of women in crisis, it is hoped that they will ultimately gain the self-esteem necessary to break the cycle of being a spouse abuse victim.

The study, based on 89 programs distributed throughout the United States showed that most victims who seek assistance from a battered women's program make their first contact through a crisis telephone line. Generally these hotlines are operational on a 24-hour 7-day-a-week basis and are staffed by volunteers or CETA workers. The primary objective of the line worker is to determine if the caller is in immediate danger and to make arrangements for shelter or other emergency services if needed.

Emergency services for spouse abuse victims have been developed only recently. Of the 89 programs, 45 (slightly over 50 percent) indicated that they had been in operation for 1 year or less. Only 13 of the programs reported being operational 4 years or more. If the rapid growth rate of these programs continues, we may have 500 such intervention services by the mid-1980s. This projection takes into account the fact that over 10 percent of the new programs close their doors within 1 year primarily due to a lack of funds. The plight of abused women is presently in vogue, as were the suicide prevention movement and youth hotlines for drug and alcohol problems in past years. There is always the danger that citizens' and professionals' concern for these victims may reach a crescendo and then fade as another long overlooked social issue comes to the fore. Therefore, it is important to develop standards and master plans, mobilize resources, and implement comprehensive service delivery systems now while funding priorities are ripe for responding to the urgent needs of battered women.

This study's findings revealed that over 110,000 women seek the aid of crisis hotlines and shelters for battered women annually. The majority of the programs (65 percent) reported that they operated a 24-hour hotline so that women who had been beaten could receive timely assistance any time of the day or night. Due to limited budgets, most of the other programs operated a hotline from 9:00 A.M. to 5:00 P.M., with an answering service or patch system used during the evenings and on weekends.

With regard to the busiest day of the week for callers, 38 of the 73 programs (52 percent) responding to this question reported that Monday was the busiest day for hotline calls. Friday was the second busiest day for callers; it was cited by 20 programs. One possible explanation for the high volume of Monday calls is that, since the husband is usually home on the weekend, there is a greater opportunity for activities which can lead to conflict and abuse and more time for beatings. Furthermore, because of the husband's presence on the weekend, it is more difficult for the abused woman to escape to a safe place to call for help. Monday calls may be a build-up of victims who were beaten at any time during the weekend. By the same token, Friday may be the second busiest day because of the wife's recollection of previous weekends and dreaded anticipation of the upcoming weekend.

The organizational structure of centers and programs for battered women consists of a board of directors, a director-coordinator, and a staff of volunteers and CETA workers; in some cases there is a small corps of paid staff; and in a few cases programs reported having a highly professional staff comprised of counselors, social workers, and psychologists. The majority of programs are staffed by six or more volunteers and a minimum of three CETA workers. Undergraduate and graduate student interns are often placed at these programs to gain an on-the-job experience while providing free labor to the program. In addition, almost half of the programs said that they employ one or more counselors and formerly battered women. Only 29 (approximately one-third) of the programs had a full-time social worker on staff. Hardly any of the shelters reported having a vocational counselor, children's coordinator, training director, group leader, or researcher.

The physical setting of the shelters varied, with 48 (53.9 percent) of the programs located in a separate facility and an additional 19 (21 percent) using areas of their local YWCA residence. Several programs stated that they shelter battered clients in churches, motels, and hospital clinics; and 18 (20 percent) used private volunteer homes for emergency short-term shelter. Several of the aforementioned centers indicated that, if they were able to secure additional funds, they would rent a large private house or small building with more adequate space than that available through volunteer homes. In some cases, volunteer homes are used in conjunction with an actual shelter facility to house women during those occasions when the facility is filled to capacity.

Obtaining operating funds is one of the most significant problems facing these programs, many of which are getting by on shoestring budgets. Of all the funding sources, the most frequently cited source of funds was CETA (57 respondents or 64.8 percent). Following CETA funding, the most frequently reported funding sources were grants from private foundations (34, or 38.6 percent), individual donations (19, or 21.6 percent), and the United Way (17, or 19.3 percent). Local church and civic organizations represent an excellent (and often overlooked) source of partial support, providing not only some direct financial assistance but also valuable services such as transportation and needed items for the shelter such as food and used furniture.

The programs' self-evaluations revealed the following strong points that shelters for battered women have in common: the availability and security of their shelter or volunteer homes (32 respondents); the 24-hour round-the-clock nature of their hotline (25 respondents); and the dedication, commitment, and special skills of their staff (24 respondents).

The respondents also cited three major needs: 1) money to hire additional staff (60 respondents), 2) money for a separate shelter facility or a larger building (43), and 3) staff to organize and run outreach groups (9). The three most frequently cited problems faced by these programs were: 1) difficulty in securing adequate funds (58), 2) attrition of volunteers (26), and 3) the lack of cooperation on the part of local police (26).

Police and court personnel are in a position to provide critical services and support to victims of spouse abuse. Unfortunately, positive encounters with the police were reported by only 34 spouse abuse centers. For the most part, these 34 programs reported good communication links with the police and timely police assistance to battered women in the form of protection, transportation to the shelter, and emergency medical care.

Another 35 respondents indicated that they had had both positive and negative encounters with the police. The need for careful screening and recruitment of humanistically oriented police officers was further demonstrated by the 10 programs which stated that they had had only negative police encounters (for example, the police officers with whom they had contact being uniformly insulting and deprecating to the female caller). The rate of programs having had negative experiences with court personnel was even higher than that reported for the police. Illustrations of the negative experiences (cited by 33 centers) are as follows: the district attorney's staff discouraging women from seeking the protection of the court; the heavy court backlog of cases and the insensitivity and hostility of court clerks and magistrates which led many women to decide not to file a criminal complaint for assault.

An alternative to the perpetuation of family violence can be provided through the development of comprehensive service delivery programs. First and foremost, these social service systems must provide safe shelter for battered women and their children. Of necessity, housing may at first be temporary and of an emergency nature. However, court advocacy, relocation counseling, and vocational rehabilitation must be provided so that battered women do not receive anywhere from 3 days to 3 months of shelter and welfare assistance only to return to an explosive and violent home environment. Federal and state funds will need to be allocated to provide shelter, individual and group counseling, family therapy, welfare advocacy, legal services, community education, police training, vocational services, and medical services.

Policy statements can provide frameworks for developing goals, objectives, and program plans. Antler (1980) addresses the need for developing explicit family policies which will support family life. Policies of this nature provide guidelines for the allocation of resources and services geared to helping families in crisis.

> Within the federal government numerous programs dealing with child abuse, spouse abuse, institutional abuse, sexual abuse, and juvenile delinquency collide with other efforts. The competing programs developed through the National Institute of Mental Health, and the Law Enforcement Assistance Administration are often uncoordinated and reflect differing views as to the substance of the problem of family violence. One view emphasizes treatment of family violence as a mental health problem requiring legions of therapists to provide continuing psychiatric treatment to violence-prone families, another sees it as a social problem of massive proportions reflecting the tensions experienced by a large and growing permanent underclass. Overriding these views are those of the law enforcement community, which, though reluctant to intervene in domestic matters generally, is seen as an important vehicle for controlling violence in the home.

Given the lack of credible evidence to support definitively any single view of these newly defined social problems, it is not surprising that there is no central focus for family violence programs. Yet there is a strong need to coordinate efforts and develop demonstration and research programs that can improve the technology of helping families involved in destructive and violent interchange.

Federal programs can offer some policy direction about family violence in four areas: (1) service accessibility and acceptability, (2) development of local-level coordination between drug and alcohol and family violence programs, (3) coordination between informal and formal service systems, and (4) training and sensitization of police and other law enforcement personnel in providing effective protection to abused family members:

1. Greater numbers of abused women are now able to request help through hotlines, the courts, and women's refuges. However, despite these new initiatives, women still experience considerable stigma when seeking help for violence-related domestic problems. Publicity and public information programs are needed to educate the public to reduce the shame attached to domestic violence. Such community education programs should be stimulated by the public sector, since informal and voluntary agencies rarely have the resources or skills to promote and implement large-scale publicity efforts.

2. Many of the new informal services which have emerged on the local level are not making use of the services of existing drug and alcohol programs in providing help to victims (and perpetrators) of domestic violence. Since alcoholism and violence in families are closely related, policy should provide incentives for these groups to work together on the local level.

3. Networks of community services offered by public agencies need to be linked to family violence programs offered both by professionals and volunteers. Facilitating coordination on the local level will provide access to income programs, health services, and child care resources to families requiring help. At present many of these newer programs are unaware of public services or find that obtaining them on behalf of their clients is unnecessarily complicated and subject to inordinate delay. Clients of these programs are often in crisis and require immediate material aid to assist in their transition.

4. The criminal justice system's response to family violence has been problematic for victims. For many years police refused to provide protection to family members. Currently, police attitudes are changing, and there is now greater willingness to provide help as new laws provide more specific boundaries for police intervention. Nonetheless there is need for more effective police training and better consultation with police departments in order to facilitate cooperation between local domestic violence agencies and to provide better protection for victims. The federal

government in particular can take the lead in developing training materials and in providing grants to police departments to take advantage of these programs.

Though programmatic improvements in services to victims of domestic violence are clearly needed, professionals and concerned citizens should not lose sight of the larger questions involved in services to families. During the past three decades the prime tendency in American social policy has been to develop new programs and policies in response to newly perceived problems. As a result each new problem generates its own professional and lay constituency, community advocates, and specialized technology. In the area of family services particularly, this has accelerated and energized continuing fragmentation of family-oriented services and has led to paralysis in the evolution of social policy for families. Comprehensive family policies, directed toward maintaining family well-being, appear to be the most appropriate vehicle for considering and meeting the needs of families.[2]

The National Association of Social Workers (NASW) has cogently affirmed the value of eliminating all forms of violence within society and family life. The 1979 NASW Delegate Assembly passed a domestic violence policy statement aimed at improving the quality of life for all individuals. It identifies the critical areas that must be addressed in order to develop comprehensive and feasible local and national policies:

The NASW Policy Statement on Family Violence[3]

Issues

The prevention and treatment of domestic violence is difficult because it is misunderstood, ignored, mythologized and condoned. Sex-role stereotyping, socialization, the tradition of patriarchy, and society's view of the family and domestic violence all contribute to the problem. Historically, domestic violence begins with the oppression of women in a patriarchal culture which considers the mate and the children as property of the man. They were expected to serve him, and he had a right by law to discipline them as he saw fit. The belief still is widespread today that a "man's home is his castle" and that outsiders are not to interfere in private family matters. The integrity of the family frequently receives more consideration than the safety and civil rights of its members.

The acceptance of violence as a way of life, particularly violence against women and children, is pervasive in American culture. Violence is sanctioned in child-rearing practices, as shown by the Supreme Court

[2]Dr. Stephen Antler, personal communication, January 30, 1980.
[3]Reprinted with the permission of the National Association of Social Workers, Inc., from *NASW News*, January 1980, p. 22.

decision on the use of corporal punishment in the classroom. The use of violence is found throughout literature, children's stories, theater, movies, athletic events, advertising, radio, and television.

Too many in the social work profession reflect societal attitudes toward women and toward violence. Too many professionals agree with an analysis which blames the victim, and many believe that the woman provoked or in some way is responsible for and deserves the beating. On the other hand, if she remains with the batterer, she may be considered a masochist who needs to be beaten or is pathological in some other respect. Too few social workers recognize the complex economic, emotional, and societal factors which serve to keep the battered woman in the battering situation.

Although expressing concern for the protection of human beings, a large number of social workers are poorly prepared by education or experience to work effectively with the multi-faceted nature of family violence. Schools of social work lack adequate curriculum in the area of family violence. Public and private social welfare agencies lack necessary policy statements, staff development and in-service training programs to provide the needed sensitive, relevant and adequate programs for both victims and perpetrators.

Policy Statement

I. Education and Prevention
   A. Work with schools of social work to develop curriculum materials that reflect sophisticated understanding of the dynamics of domestic violence. Encourage the development of experiential field training to prepare students to work in this area.
   B. Promote the development of social welfare agency in-service training and continuing education programs to increase the awareness of skills of social work practitioners in working with all forms of domestic violence. Encourage positive attitudes among social workers toward the treatment, prevention and eradication of domestic violence.
   C. Promote the development of inter-disciplinary training, education, and comprehensive services to link programs in the health, mental health, welfare, criminal justice, law enforcement and social services systems for effective treatment and prevention of domestic violence.
   D. Reassess and work to change attitudes, social policies, and practices which perpetuate domestic violence, such as those regarding child rearing practices, the patriarchical and sexist practices, and the nuclear family.
   E. Work to eliminate sexism, racism and homophobia in the social work profession and in society.
   F. Promote equality of respect for all family members of role or status.

G. Assess the role of the media in directly or indirectly encouraging domestic violence.

H. Develop programs to educate the public to: (1) recognize and reject myths and stereotypes that perpetuate domestic violence, (2) be aware of financial and emotional costs of domestic violence, and (3) hold accountable those who promote or perpetuate violence.

I. Develop programs to teach children and adults the use of non-coercive mutual negotiation skills for conflict resolution and improved communication skills.

J. Work to improve reporting mechanisms within agencies serving victims of domestic violence.

K. Work to make the social policy changes needed to enable this society to deal with economic problems which result in poverty, unemployment, and economic dependence and perpetuate family violence.

II. Legislation

A. Work for the strengthening and enforcement of legislation that protects individuals from all forms of violence.

B. Work for legislation to protect individuals in the home and to provide for the legal rights of family members, e.g., making it illegal to commit assault or rape against a mate.

C. Work for legislation which funds needed programs and services for victims and perpetrators, including the necessary resources and prevention programs to enhance the individual's well-being, free of violence in our society.

D. Work for legislation to provide for diversified and alternative sentencing programs for perpetrators to encourage redress and self-responsibility.

III. Funding

A. Work toward increased joint funding, by public and private sectors, of programs to deal with all forms of family violence.

B. Support funding for multi-lingual shelters, telephone hotlines, drop-in centers, self-help groups and other resources needed for crisis intervention, and support for persons engaged in family violence.

C. Work for the expansion of agency programs to include services for victims and perpetrators of violence within the scope of regular services. Specialized services should be integrated into a wide spectrum of services for all members of the family. Specialized treatment and preventive services should be developed to respond to the various forms and stages of family violence.

D. Work to change policies and practices of public and private social welfare agencies to provide for improved financial, legal, and emotional assistance and alternatives.

108 : : *Sheltering Battered Women*

E. Seek funding and support for research of all forms of family violence to examine assessment procedures, dynamics, and causality, treatment and prevention programs.
F. Support adequate funding for a federal Office of Domestic Violence to provide grants, to serve as a resource for information on programs and research, and to provide leadership within the federal government for changes in national policies, attitudes and programs.
G. Work toward the implementation of a full employment policy and a national system of income support.

While new, sorely needed centers for abused women are being developed across the country, there are no standards to guide their development. Hardly any evaluation studies have been undertaken on the effectiveness of different social service programs with battered women. The findings of this study provide the initial blueprints for developing standards for battered women's intervention services.

■ two
GUIDE TO PROGRAM PLANNING AND RESOURCES

7
Guide for Beaten Women: How to Get Help If Your Husband or Boyfriend Beats You

by MARJORY D. FIELDS and ELYSE LEHMAN

This chapter tells you what you can do if you are threatened by your husband or boyfriend. It is a self-help guide. You must be ready to do something for yourself if you want the threats and beatings to stop.

Your husband or boyfriend has no right to hit or injure you. It is against the law for a man to beat or threaten his wife or girlfriend. Unfortunately, the police and the courts often do not believe that fights between couples are serious. As a result of this attitude, many court officials and police officers discourage women from bringing their cases or continuing with them after complaints have been filed. Many times women give up

Initially Marjory Fields and Elyse Lehman wrote a 26-page pocket-sized handbook to aid battered women which was primarily applicable to New York City residents. Following the popular reception of that handbook, Ms. Fields developed a version which is universally applicable to abused women. This universal version is published here with the permission of Marjory Fields, the Managing Attorney, Family Law Unit, and Brooklyn Legal Services Corporation B. She is a leader in the movement to provide justice for battered women.

111

because going to court takes so much time, work, and patience. Even a woman who has been badly injured must fight hard just to get her case before a judge, and then to get the judge to believe her instead of her husband. People often wait all day for their cases to be heard by the judge. There are many adjournments, which means that nothing happens, and you have to come back to court again. In fact, more than half of the women who complain to the courts of beatings or threats drop their cases or withdraw their complaints. Certainly, the hassles they face from the police and the courts contribute to the drop-out rate.

Before you start a court case you have to think about the time you will be able to spend. You also have to decide if taking the man to court will be the best way to get him to stop beating you; sometimes it is better to just move away and get a divorce. But there are times when court is the only answer because your husband or boyfriend still will not leave you alone; when that happens you should know how to get the court's help, which is why this guide has been written.

What to Do

Move Out

Move away with your children. Stay with a woman friend, or with relatives. Do not stay with a man who lives alone, unless he is your brother, father, or grandfather. It would appear as though you were committing adultery. This could cause a custody fight. You would certainly lose any chance of getting alimony. But if you have no children, and you are self-supporting, or do not need alimony, or you have no property, or your husband is not working, there is no alimony or custody to lose. Do not leave your children with your husband. You would seem to the court to be a neglectful mother who abandoned her children. This would give your husband a strong legal weapon to use against you. He could try to win custody of your children, or threaten to try to get custody. He could use this to force you to take less child support or alimony. It would make it difficult for your lawyer to get you as much as your husband can afford to pay.

Save Evidence

Try to get your friends, relatives, or the women at the shelter to take color pictures of your injuries as soon as you arrive. Save any torn or bloody clothing. The picture and clothing may be shown to the judge to support your explanation of why you left your husband. These will assist your lawyer in getting the best possible settlement in a divorce.

Go to an Emergency Shelter

A community group or your local government may have emergency housing for women and their children. This is new so you will have to look hard to find it. Call the local chapter of the National Organization for Women (NOW), or other women's organizations in your area. Try the YWCA, Salvation Army, Catholic Charities, or Department of Welfare. Ask a court clerk or officer; call the victims' assistance bureau or information operator. Many areas have plans to open emergency housing for women and children. Listen to reports on television, radio, and in newspapers for announcements of the opening of a refuge or shelter for battered women and their children.

Call the Police

You should call the police during or immediately after the attack or threat if you want the man who beat you arrested, or if you want protection so that you can leave.

Whether or not you are legally married to the man, if you are physically hurt you may go to the police and ask the police to arrest him. If the police refuse to arrest him, you have the right to make the arrest yourself. This is called a "civilian arrest." The police must assist you in taking the man to the police station and filling out the arrest forms. If the police say they cannot help you because the man is your husband, or the father of your children, write down the officers' names and badge numbers. Let them see you do this. Then report them to their commanding officer or the Civilian Complaint Review Board.

Immediately Go to Court or the Police Station

When no arrest is made, if you want the man who beat you arrested, immediately go to court or the police station, and explain that you want to make a complaint against the man who threatened or hit you. This complaint is the start of a criminal court case. The police or court clerk will want to know why you did not come sooner. You may have to return several times and wait all day. Courts are very busy. You must decide if you can spend the time, and if the court can give you the kind of help you need.

When a Court Can Help You

Court can help you if your husband or boyfriend does any of the following:

1. Places you in fear of physical injury

2. Threatens you
3. Attempts to injure you
4. Injures you

What a Family Court or Domestic Relations Court Can Do for You

This is a civil court. It may do the following:

1. Order your husband to stop threatening or hitting you (this is called an injunction or restraining order, or an order of protection).
2. Order your husband out of the house.
3. Order your husband to stay away from you and the children.
4. Give you the custody of the children.
5. Set a time and place for your husband to visit with the children.
6. Order your husband to give you support for yourself and the children.
7. Give you a divorce or separation.
8. Order child support even if you are not married to the father.
9. Give you your share of the family property if you are married.
10. Order you and your husband to have counseling.

Get a Lawyer

In most states you will need a lawyer to prepare court papers for a civil court order. The lawyer will ask you to sign the petition and swear to the truth of what it says. Read it carefully, and tell the lawyer of any mistakes you see in it.

Court Tips

You will be asked when your husband or boyfriend hit or threatened you. If you have waited more than a few days before coming to court, you may not get an emergency injunction or restraining order. Because you did not come to court immediately after the attack, the people at court will believe that you are not in danger. If you are in need of immediate protection while you wait for the court hearing date, you must explain why it took so long to get to court. You must convince the judge that there was good reason for the delay: you were too badly hurt, or you did not know where to go, or you were getting medical treatment. They do not understand that you felt guilty and ashamed (even though you had no reason to feel that way) and that you tried to forgive and forget the previous attacks.

We know that it takes a long time for a woman to get the courage to seek help from a court. Sometimes people at court think that if a woman has put up with beatings in the past she does not really need the court's help. You have to let them know that this unspoken belief is not true. You must tell them that you are in need of their help and that you will return for appointments. The fact is that many woman do not return for court appointments. They get scared and decide to try to make peace at home. People at court often give this as a reason for not seriously considering a woman's request for protection.

Court Hearing

Your husband or boyfriend must come to court in the court date set in the summons. (The summons is a court order telling him to appear in court.) If he does not, your case will be adjourned, and you will be given a new court date. Ask the judge to issue a warrant for your husband's arrest by the police. Wait to get a copy of the warrant. Ask how it is given to your husband or boyfriend. Follow the instructions. You may have to take the warrant to the local police and take them to where your husband or boyfriend lives, works, or can be found so that they can arrest him.

The clerk, prosecutor, and judge will ask if this was the first time your husband attacked you. They may not take your complaint seriously unless you point out that this attack was worse than the previous ones, that you were hurt and made fearful. If it was the first time, they will try to get you to forgive him. But that is your decision.

Even if your husband or boyfriend does appear in court, the case may still be adjourned to permit him to get an attorney. (He has a right to a court-appointed free attorney, but you do not). You should have your own lawyer present. You will have to pay your lawyer unless she or he is a Legal Services or Legal Aid attorney.

Be ready on every court date, even if your husband or boyfriend said he would not be there. You want to impress the judge, so dress neatly as if it were a job interview. Your sworn statements will be good proof of your case, but if you have witnesses, your lease or house deed, medical reports, and photographs, bring them with you. show them to the judge at the hearing but not if a new date is being set. Show them only if the judge asks you to tell your story.

At the hearing the judge will try to determine what happened between you and your husband or boyfriend and will decide whether or not to sign an order for you. Everything depends on how well you present your story to the judge. Do not shout but speak loudly, slowly, and clearly. Practice with a friend. Tell what your husband or boyfriend did to you. Tell of your injuries and fear. Tell how the beating affected your children and if your husband hurt them too. Make it short. Answer the judge's questions briefly. Do not show anger with what the judge asks or says. If you get upset, don't be ashamed to cry. Talk only to the judge. Your husband or boyfriend will tell his side. Do not get angry and do not fight with him or answer him back. Do not interrupt your husband no matter what he says. When he is done, you can tell the judge your side of the story.

Some judges are very sympathetic to battered women; but there are other judges who blame women for starting the fights in which they get hurt. This is the gamble whenever you go to court. The judge has complete control over whether you get any relief. If the judge believes your husband or boyfriend and decides that you provoked him or attacked him first, your case may be dismissed.

Enforcing an Order of Protection or Injunction

If you get an order of protection and your husband violates any part of it, you may do either of two things:

1. Call the police and have your husband arrested. The police are supposed to arrest him if you tell them what happened and show them your order of protection. If the police officer refuses to arrest your husband take his or her badge number and write it down. This may force him or her to help you. Your husband will be arrested and taken to the police station. In most cases, the police will tell him to show up at court the next morning (or on Monday if he is arrested over the weekend), and shortly after the arrest he will be released.

2. Call your lawyer, after you call the police or even if you do not call the police.

There will be a hearing just like the one you had when you got the order. Prepare the same way: bring witnesses, photographs, and medical records. You must convince the judge that your husband violated the order and you got hurt or scared. Your husband will have a right to an attorney. You should have your own lawyer if you can afford to pay one or can get a Legal Aid lawyer. After the hearing, if the judge believes you, the judge may impose strict orders such as ordering your husband out of the home, or putting him in jail.

What Criminal Court Can Do

1. Set criminal charges against your husband, ex-husband, or boy-friend.
2. Release him with or without bail on his promise to return to court for a hearing.

3. Adjourn the case on his promise not to hurt you anymore.
4. Order him to stay away from you.
5. Sentence him to jail or probation after a conviction.

Criminal court cannot decide property or money disagreements or give you support for your children. If the man who attacked you is the father of your children, you must go to a civil court to get child support. This is a separate case and has nothing to do with the criminal court case.

What Happens at Criminal Court

If your husband or man friend was arrested for beating or threatening you, the district attorney will present your case to the judge. You must follow the arresting police officer's instructions about when and where to go to court. If you are not sure, ask the officer questions, or call the district attorney's office the next morning at 9:00 A.M. Tell them the name of the person arrested, and ask when you should come to court.

Some district attorneys are not interested in family violence cases. You must show that you are interested. Show your evidence. If you have trouble getting the district attorney to prosecute the case, get help from the victims information bureau or victims assistance project, located in the criminal court building, or from the local chapter of NOW, or from the people at a refuge for battered women, if there is one in your area. The final decision about whether to prosecute is up to the district attorney. If the district attorney takes your case in criminal court, the criminal court judge can order the man who hit or threatened you to stay away from you, but you must tell the district attorney that you need it. The district attorney should then request the order for you. If the district attorney says that your case cannot be won, or your evidence is too weak, he or she may refuse to prosecute the case.

If the man who threatened or beat you is not arrested you can go directly to criminal court to make a sworn complaint. There you may receive a summons ordering the man to come to court. This must be given to your husband or boyfriend. Follow the instructions the court clerk gives you. Ask questions if you do not understand. You may have the help of a police officer to give your husband or boyfriend the summons.

You will see a judge on the date set in the summons. If the man who beat you does not come to court, the judge will listen to you and decide whether or not to issue a warrant for his arrest by the police. If the man involved comes to court, the judge will listen to both of you and decide if either of you should be charged with a crime or if the case should be dismissed.

It is important that you present your case well. Do not shout, but speak loudly, slowly, and clearly. Practice with a friend. Tell what the man did to you. Tell of your injuries and fear. If it was not the first incident of beating, tell them you have been beaten before. Show pictures of your injuries. Tell how the beating upset your children. Make it a short story.

Answer the judge's questions briefly. Do not show anger with what the judge asks or says. If you get upset, do not be ashamed to cry. Talk only to the judge. The man who hurt you will tell his side of what happened. Do not get angry with him. Do not fight with him or interrupt him no matter what he says. When he is done, the judge will let you talk again.

You must help the district attorney and show that you will stay interested in the case. You must come to court on time each day the case is being heard. You may have to go before the grand jury if a weapon was used or if your injuries were very bad.

What You Can Do for Yourself

If you are not married, you may leave your boyfriend and take your children with you. You may apply for welfare, and you may go to the civil court to seek an order of filiation or paternity, which states that your boyfriend is the father of your child and orders him to pay child support.

If you are married, you may leave your husband and take your children with you. You may also apply to welfare for assistance and to civil court to get support for yourself and your children. No one can say you abandoned your husband if you have "good cause." If your husband was physically or mentally cruel to you with his threats, you do not have to continue to sleep or live with him, and you do not lose your rights to alimony and child support by leaving.

You may also sue for divorce or separation either while you are still living with your husband or after leaving him. Go to a Legal Aid or Legal Services lawyer for free advice and assistance with the divorce if you have no money. If you can pay a lawyer or your husband has a good income and a steady job, you should hire a lawyer. In some states the lawyer can get his or her fee from your husband if your husband has the money.

Questions You Should Ask When Retaining a Lawyer

Many people are disappointed with lawyers. This results from expecting too much and not having the right tools for choosing a lawyer. A lawyer is not a social worker, psychologist, or confessor. But an understanding lawyer can refer you to counselors or psychologists to help you through the stress of divorce or family legal problems. These are some questions you should ask the lawyer before you decide whether or not to hire him or her:

- How much do you charge by the hour? For a first meeting?

- What is your minimum fee for my kind of case?
- What is covered by your fee?
- How many negotiating sessions are included?
- How many court appearances are included?
- What is your rate for appearance in court?
- Do you have a written retainer agreement that I can sign and a copy of it for me to keep?
- Can you suggest a divorce counselor, or social worker, or psychologist?

After telling the lawyer the facts of your case and how much money you have, ask:

- How much money and/or child support can I expect to receive?
- What property settlement can I expect?
- What part of your fee will my husband have to pay?
- Are you willing to seek and enforce temporary support orders?
- Are you willing to enforce final orders and judgments of divorce?
- What are your fees for enforcement? Hourly rate for enforcement?
- Will you seek modification of final orders and judgments if changes in circumstances justify modifications?
- What are the practical limitations on enforcement?

Also ask:

- What should I do to help you with my case?
- What do you expect of me?
- What papers, documents, and witnesses should I assemble for you?

If you have doubts about the quality of the lawyer's responses, or the style of the lawyer, shop around. There is no absolutely right approach for a lawyer to take. You should select a lawyer whose values and attitudes are similar to your own. This choice should be made before the start of your case and before you hire a lawyer. Don't be afraid to look for another lawyer if you do not like the first one you talk to. But make your choice before the case begins; people who change lawyers more than once after the start of a divorce, or any other lawsuit, hurt their own chances of being believed by the judge and make a good settlement or a successful trial more difficult. Evaluation of the attorney you select to represent you should be made before you decide to retain him or her. But if you must change lawyers, do so quickly and only once in the course of the case. Make sure that your new lawyer has a clear picture of why you changed. This will avoid repeating your previous mistake and will give your new lawyer weapons with which to defend your change of lawyers.

There are so many lawyers practicing that you do not have to hire one you don't like. Ask friends for the names of lawyers they like. If you take the time to choose, you should be able to find a lawyer you trust and respect.

How to Get on Welfare

In order to receive welfare you must fill out an application form and have proof that you are eligible.

Application

Go home and fill out the application form and gather the necessary documents to prove eligibility. Return to the center for your interview on the date set. You will see someone in the center's application unit who will check the form and documents. If everything is filled in properly and you have the necessary documents, the worker will make a recommendation to the supervisor. The application supervisor, in turn, should issue a final written decision not later than the following working day. A copy is mailed to you, together with a statement of the aid you will receive if the application is approved.

A decision on the application may be delayed if you need to bring more documents, but the decision must be made within 30 days after the agency receives the application (the date of your interview). In case of immediate need, you should receive temporary aid. This is generally referred to as a "predetermination grant."

What You Can Get

Welfare gives you a budget for food, clothing, and rent and gives you free medical care. If you have some income, you may be able to get a supplement, Medicaid (free medical care), and food stamps. Even if you are not eligible for welfare, you may be able to get Medicaid and/or food stamps. Moving expenses, furniture grants, and rent security deposits are sometimes available.

Delayed Appointments

Although your interview appointment should be no more than 5 days after you pick up the application, many centers exceed that limit. The only remedy is to ask to speak to the supervisor. The office manager and center director can help.

Table 7–1. Documentation

Documents You Will Need	Alternatives
Your birth certificate	Baptismal certificates
Your children's birth certificates	Passports, school records
Apartment lease	Rent receipts
Mortgage bill or statement from bank	Affidavit by person with whom you are living or to whom you are paying rent
Unemployment insurance book	Your affidavit of your past and present income
Disability award letter	
Pay stubs	Letter from your employer
Income tax forms for last year	
Court support order	
Court statement of arrears—unpaid support	

Documentation

According to regulations, basic facts of eligibility—the applicant's identity, family size, residence, rent, and income—must be verified by documentary evidence "wherever possible" (Table 7–1). Thus an application may be denied because all birth records are in another state and therefore identity has not been verified. Bring originals and photocopies whenever possible. Give the worker the copies and keep the originals. If you have originals only, the worker will copy them while you wait and return the originals to you.

Documentation hassles often arise from repeated requests for the same proof. Worker A will demand a birth certificate and, upon returning with the documents, the applicant is rebuffed by Worker B, who demands a baptismal certificate or school record. Get the names of workers with whom you talk so you can protect yourself. Again, make vigorous complaints to the supervisors.

As a general rule, aid should not be withheld because of inadequate documentation when there is emergency need. Also, documentation should not be required from the applicant when there is good reason why it is not available, for example: your husband or boyfriend will not give them to you and the originals are in another state or country; you lost them or they were burned in a fire; you do not have the money to pay the fees to get new copies.

Past Maintenance

A special documentation problem called "past maintenance" arises from a requirement that you prove how you have lived in the past. This is easy for someone who has been laid off, payroll stubs should be adequate proof of past maintenance. Problems arise when an applicant has been borrowing from friends or relatives, and a welfare worker insists on proof of past maintenance for several years past. All too often applicants are rejected despite actual need solely because of technical failure to verify past maintenance. The proper interpretation of this policy is that you need only furnish a reasonable explanation and proof of the manner in which you are maintaining yourself and have maintained yourself in the *recent* past.

Processing Acceptance

Because of the paper work involved, it can take some time before you actually receive money. You may be told orally or by letter that you have been accepted, but it may be 2 or 3 weeks before you get a check. If you can prove that you have an emergency, you may receive the money sooner.

Look for the local chapter of NOW, any women's groups, hospital emergency rooms, or mental health clinics, victims information bureau, Legal Aid Society or Legal Service, lawyer referral service of the county bar association, Salvation Army, YWCA, and Catholic Charities. If you are unable to find any group to help, try the telephone information operator, or a rape crisis telephone hotline.

■8
Investigation
of Wife Beating

by THE INTERNATIONAL ASSOCIATION
OF CHIEFS OF POLICE, INC.

Despite the many complications that surround wife beating cases, one fact should always remain clear and should be the basis for police action. The wife has been physically assaulted and must be treated as a victim of a crime. The husband is a violent lawbreaker who should not be shielded from legal action.

Intervening in wife assault cases is a formidable task. The police officer is exposed to the threat of personal injury every time he responds to a family disturbance call. He witnesses and becomes a part of personal tragedy that frequently involves not only a husband and wife but also their children.

Initial Response

Although assaults on wives occur as a result of a variety of circumstances, there are a few characteristics that point out the seriousness of wife beating and should influence the police response. A prevalent factor that surrounds wife beating is alcoholic intoxication. In a majority of cases, the abusive husband is drunk when he assaults his wife. This is not surprising since overconsumption of alcohol and violent crimes of all kinds are closely linked. What it means to the officer is that the victim is in real danger and the suspect typically is not in a condition to accept a reasonable resolution of the situation. The intoxicated man who has already acted violently is a threat not to be underestimated. This applies especially to the victim as well as the police officer. Supporting this view is the fact that homicides occur in a significant number of homes where wife beating is chronic. The husband may increase his violence to the point of murder or the wife's felt need to protect herself may lead to homicide.

In 1975, murder within the family made up approximately one-fourth of all murder offenses and over one-half of these family killings involved spouse killing spouse. The wife was the victim in 52 percent of these murder incidents and the husband was the victim in the remaining 48 percent. Police officers must be aware of the danger involved in disturbance calls. Since 1966, 157 officers have lost their lives responding to disturbance calls.[1]

Receiving the Complaint

The dispatcher can contribute significantly to the safety of the victim and police officers. He has an opportunity to obtain from the caller valuable information concerning the nature of the assault and the emotional state of the parties involved. Failure to obtain such information makes the responding officers' task more difficult and more dangerous.

In a wife beating case, the dispatcher should try to keep the calling party on the phone and instruct the person to keep the telephone lines open even after the officers arrive. By keeping the telephone line open, the dispatcher can monitor the assault and provide additional information to the responding officers as the situation changes. Once the officers are inside the residence, the dispatcher can continue to monitor the activities and maintain communication with the responding officers.

In questioning the caller, the dispatcher should attempt to determine the extent of the injuries and what type of medical assistance is needed. The dispatcher should ask whether or not any of the parties are armed, and if so, with what kind of weapon, where the parties are located, and what they are doing. In agencies that maintain a cross reference file of incidents by names and addresses, the dispatcher should check it to

[1]*Crime in the United States—1975*, The Uniform Crime Reports (Federal Bureau of Investigation; Washington, D.C.), pp. 18, 19, 22.

determine previously reported incidents involving the same parties and the probable danger involved.

By listening to the background noises, as well as the complainant's description, the dispatcher can make further determinations about the extent of the danger. Threats, screams, breaking glass and furniture or shots indicate the seriousness of the incident. In some cases, the dispatcher may urge the wife to leave the residence and meet the responding officers outside.

Arriving at the Scene

Officers should approach the residence from a direction which offers the greatest protection from an attack. When a house is the incident location, the officers should stay close to the residence and pass beneath windows. Since the officers will not know exactly what is taking place inside, whether the incident scene is a house or an apartment, they should stop and listen to determine if the disturbance is in progress and to pinpoint the location of the parties involved. Persons encountered in the hallways of an apartment building should be briefly questioned about the incident and the parties involved.

The officers should also try to view the inside of the residence before announcing their presence. Such observations of officers, when made without unusual action such as standing on top of boxes to peer through a window, fall under the plain view doctrine and can be used to establish probable cause that a crime has been committed.

When the officers reach the door, one officer should position himself near a window where he can observe the person who answers the door. The officer at the door should stand to the side to avoid gun fire or other attack. He should be prepared for any circumstance when the door is opened since he is often met with hostility or violence.

Gaining Entry

When conditions permit, the officers should introduce themselves, give an explanation of the police presence, and request that they be invited into the home. If entry is refused, the officers should calmly explain that they understand the citizen's feelings, but that they must make sure there is no serious trouble inside.

The emergency nature of the complaint and the refusal of the citizen to allow the officers into the home may require them to make a forced entry. Whenever practicable, a warrant should be obtained before entry is made. However when it can be reasonably believed that the reported victim is in danger, the process of obtaining a warrant may prove to be too time-consuming, and the officers may lawfully force an entry into the home. Among the circumstances that can provide the officers with the necessary probable cause to force an entry include cries for help, weapons displayed, obvious signs that a struggle occurred and an eye-witness account that a felony occurred and the victim is still in the home.

Establishing Control

Nothing positive, not even rendering first aid, can be achieved until the police officers have the emergency situation under control. The officers should immediately locate all parties, determine whether they are armed, and determine the extent of their injuries. The parties should be separated so that they are out of normal hearing range of each other but within continuous viewing range of the officers. The kitchen area should be avoided because of the manay potential weapons located there. Children or others not directly involved should be separated from the parties and kept out of hearing range so that their witness status will not be compromised.

In these incidents, the parties frequently make spontaneous statements to convince the officers that they are blameless and the other person is at fault. The officers should not discourage such statements; in fact communication of this sort can serve to distract the parties while being separated. It is appropriate for the officers to encourage initial comments by simply asking "What happened?" Any incriminating answers would be considered as volunteered or "ResGestae" statements. Volunteered statements are those made without police questioning, therefore, when a person becomes the target of direct questioning or when he begins to incriminate himself beyond a spontaneous statement, he should be stopped and advised of his rights.

Protecting the Victim

Police officers need to protect the victim from further battery and administer first aid where required. Use of physical force to protect the victim is not typically required since the assault will usually have stopped by the time the officers intervene; however, the police officers must always be prepared to counter violent resistance. The officers should determine the extent of injuries suffered by the victim and obtain the necessary medical aid.

Battered wives frequently sustain internal injuries to the stomach, breast area, portions of the head covered by hair, and the back. Pregnant women are often hit or kicked in the stomach. The absence of external injury, therefore, does not mean that the victim has not been assaulted.

Officers should always ask the victim if she has sustained injuries that do not show.

In some incidents where the wife is obviously hurt, she may refuse medical attention. The officer should tactfully determine whether she is rational, the injury is obvious, or the victim is unable to care for herself. It is the police officer's responsibility to obtain the proper medical attention for her, even if she protests receiving it.

The Investigation

Proper investigation of a marital assault requires that the officer establish that a crime was committed and that the elements of an offense are present. The circumstances of each case affect the officer's determination of the type of offense, if any, that has been committed. Each assault category has specific elements that must be present to constitute a crime. For example, to charge a person with assault and battery with intent to kill, the officer must determine that the means of force used was capable of causing death.

Interviewing the Victim

Throughout his contact with the victim, the officer should display concern for her physical and psychological well-being. The victim should be permitted to wash or care for other needs before being interviewed.

The victim should be given an opportunity initially to relieve her emotional tension. The officer should be aware that during this "ventilation" period, the trauma of the assault and stress she has suffered may distort her self-image. She may talk and act as if she were helpless. If this occurs, the officer should offer the victim encouragement and assure her that she is now safe.

After the ventilation period, the victim should be allowed to describe the incident without interruption. The officer's actions here can either discourage the victim or build her confidence in his sincerity to help her. The officer should be attentive and utilize the types of positive verbal and nonverbal communication techniques that encourage the victim to give him the information he needs.

Critical to the success of an interview is the manner in which the officer shows interest in the victim's account and predicament. This requires effective listening, and effective listening demands concentration, an understanding of what is being said, and an awareness of the importance of nonverbal communication.

Eye contact is an important nonverbal communicator. To maintain good eye contact, the officer should look at the victim in a spontaneous manner. Natural glances that express the officer's concern and interest will reassure the victim. Head and facial movements are also important nonverbal communicators. A slight nod demonstrates interest and encourages the speaker to continue the conversation.

Verbal responses of the officer also greatly influence the interview's success. The officer should use neutral words and phrases to encourage further statements. Phrases such as "yes," "oh," "I see," and "please continue" will encourage communication yet will not interrupt the person's thought. When the victim needs to be prompted to continue the statement, the officer should repeat the victim's last phrase in a questioning tone.

The physical violence and emotional stress suffered by victims of marital violence are manifested in various verbal styles and emotional states. The physically abused wife's verbal pattern can range from quiet to talkative. Some wives find it difficult to discuss the incident and may omit embarrassing details. Others are relieved to have the opportunity to discuss the incident. It is not uncommon for a victim to "substitute" her true feelings with laughs or smiles or, at the other extreme, with highly controlled behavior which hids her stress. Some victims will graphically express their reactions through verbal and physical behavior, displaying fear, rage, and anxiety.

When the victim has completed her account of the incident, the officer should ask about details of points he needs clarified and then summarize her communication. Summation gives the victim a chance to point out statements that she feels were misunderstood and may help her to better understand her situation.

Interviewing Witnesses

Witnesses to the assault—typically children, other family members, or neighbors—should be interviewed as soon as possible. The statements of witnesses who are related to or are friends of the victim or assailant must be carefully evaluated for bias. Such witnesses may well be under significant emotional stress that influences the accuracy or truthfulness to their accounts.

It may be necessary to conduct a neighborhood canvass to locate witnesses. During this canvass, officers should not overlook the possibility of witnesses providing information about prior assaults that can establish a pattern of chronic abuse.

The officer should remember that a witness's knowledge of an offense must be based on one of his physical senses. In wife-beating cases, the senses of sight and hearing would be most applicable. At times some individuals have a tendency to tell what they believe occurred, not what they observed or heard; therefore, the officer should verify whether a witness could physically experience what he claims.

Interviewing the Assailant

The interview of persons at the scene, which may include the assailant, consists of the general on-the-scene questioning as a fact-finding process and the interrogation of the assailant as a criminal suspect.

Most states have held that general "on-the-scene" questioning is not interrogation within the meaning of the Supreme Court decision in the Miranda and Escobedo cases. Since the officers need to determine if the incident is accidental, a matter of self-defense, or criminally committed, general questioning of all persons, including the husband, at the scene is part of the fact-finding process. However, if the purpose of the officer's questioning is to elicit incriminating information, it is assumed the questions constitute "interrogation." Officers will find themselves in the area known as "threshold confessions" in many family-related offenses. Such confessions are made at the beginning of the police involvement and are usually in response to an innocuous inquiry, such as "What's wrong here?"

When the interview has progressed to the point that the husband is a criminal suspect, and he will be interrogated for incriminating statements, then he must be advised of his Constitutional rights. Before interrogating the suspect, the officer must review all available information.

The officer must be alert to both what the suspect says and what he avoids relating. During the interview a sudden silence, shifting of conversation, or a sudden outburst of indignation or anger on the part of the suspect will indicate that the officer is discussing a sensitive area that should be explored. At such an opportunity, the officer could remain silent and use the long-pause technique to make the suspect feel obligated to continue the statement. If this fails, the officer should review the sequence of the discussion to the point where it became uncomfortable for the suspect.

Gathering Evidence

Physical evidence typically takes three forms in cases of wife assault: the injuries of the victims; evidentiary articles, such as a blood-stained blouse or weapon, that substantiate the attack; and the crime scene itself. The victim's account of the injuries sustained can be corroborated by a doctor. Information about the injuries should be obtained from him, including descriptions of the location, shape, size, and direction of all cuts and bruises. Whenever feasible, photographs of the injuries should be made. The officer should remember that any part of the female body that is normally covered cannot be photographed without the victim's written consent. Photographs should be taken under the direct supervision of the examining physician, whose testimony the photographs are intended to illustrate. Besides photographing external injuries, the officer should either photograph the crime scene to show that a struggle occurred or make a written description of it. All articles of evidence should be collected as in other investigations.

The Arrest

The decision to arrest depends on whether the specific elements of an offense are present. The officer is typically concerned about "false" arrest. However, charges of neglect of duty can result if the officer fails to make a necessary arrest.[2]

It is recognized that without victim cooperation wife beating cases are difficult to investigate. However, if strong circumstantial and physical evidence exists in felony cases, the officer can conduct an investigation under his own authority and can make an arrest without the wife's cooperation when probable cause exists.

In misdemeanor cases that do not occur in the officer's presence, the victim will have to secure the arrest warrant. In this situation, the police investigation can serve to validate or disprove the complaint.

As with all arrests, the officer should try to avoid the use of physical force. The arrested person should be given the opportunity to accompany the officers peacefully. Any action which may provoke a violent response from either spouse should be avoided.

Exploring Alternatives

For a variety of reasons, many battered wives will not proceed criminally against their husbands. The officer's only positive course of action in these cases is to explain to the victim the types of noncriminal assistance that are available locally. The primary concern of the officer in suggesting alternatives is the future safety of the victim.

Social Service Agencies

Although only a few communities have agencies that deal specifically with battered wives, most social service agencies offer a wide variety of services that may be useful to the victim. Unfortunately, these services are fragmented, and often it is difficult to sort out what help is actually available. In addition, there is the ever-present problem of the agencies being open only from 9 to 5 during weekdays.

[2]State v. Lombardi, 8 Wis. 2d 421, 99N.W. 2d 829 (1960). In this case, a sheriff was found guilty of willful neglect of duty when he did not pursue an investigation, at the request of the victim, against the victim's father.

To make a proper referral, the police officer must be provided with the information that both he and the victim need to identify the assistance available. Crucial information needed by the police officer to provide to physically abused wives includes how to obtain financial aid, legal assistance, and counseling.

Civil Action

Rather than pursue a criminal charge, the victim may choose a divorce or legal separation. The wife should obtain the assistance of a private attorney or Legal Aid Agency when initiating a separation. At the same time she may also wish to secure a peace bond or restraining order—court orders directing the assailant not to interfere with the wife.

Another alternative for the battered wife is to seek a mental illness commitment of her husband when he is mentally ill and dangerous to himself or others. If this course is followed, the wife will need to enlist the services of mental health agencies. A psychiatric assessment and court action are needed to determine whether the abusive husband is mentally incompetent and should be institutionalized.

Emergency Housing

Women's task forces across the country are presently establishing refuges for battered wives. The goal of these shelters is to provide 24 hour housing to battered wives. In addition, many of these shelters have developed general education efforts to inform the public about the problem and to make women aware of the shelter. Some shelters provide a telephone hot line, counseling, and legal services.

It is necessary for the police, social service agencies, or women's groups to survey each community to determine what facilities are available and what are needed. Survey results should be passed on to all officers so that they are aware of the services available.

Separation

Where an arrest cannot be made and the victim wants to leave the premises, the police officers should remain to ensure her safety. Most abusive husbands are extremely possessive and may try to prevent their wives and children from leaving. The potential for violence in these situations is real. Officers should try to explain to the husband that a temporary separation is in the best interests of the family. Officers should also be prepared to meet any violent resistance.

Officers should not assist the wife in packing or removing articles from the home. Officers should advise the wife that she can remove property which she alone owns and common property that the husband agrees to release. Officers should advise the wife not to take property owned solely by the husband. The officers may wish to remind the wife of items, such as birth certificates, insurance policies, and identification cards, that she may overlook when leaving under emergency conditions.

The procedures followed when the husband leaves the home are essentially the same as when the wife departs. Officers should ensure that the husband takes with him all property that he will need for a reasonable length of time so that he cannot return under the pretext of having "forgotten" articles such as a razorblade.

Explaining Responsibility

Many victims of marital assault choose to stay with their husbands. Their reasons for doing so may be sound or frivolous. Regardless of the case, it is not the job of the officer to judge the victim; it is his duty, however, to explain that at a given point his responsibility stops and hers begins.

When a victim continually refuses to take legal action against her spouse and displays an indifference toward seeking other remedial alternatives, the police officer should explain that he cannot be her personal bodyguard. The officer should assure the victim that his assistance during emergencies will always be forthcoming. However, the victim must be made to understand that, by refusing to pursue a solution to the problem, the beatings may continue to occur and may become more severe. The victim must be made to realize that ultimately she is responsible for seeking her own safety.

∎9
Woman Battering
and the Church's Response

by ANNE McGLINCHEY

Although many people deny its existence and others try to minimize its extent, the problem of battered women is present throughout our society, touching all classes and ages of people. Examples of woman battering can be found in all periods of recorded history. It is a multifaceted problem which includes sociology, psychological, and religious dimensions. In this chapter I want to explore the religious guilt and alienation from the church experienced by many battered women. I also want to suggest ways the institutional church can more positively respond to women in this situation and help combat the problem itself.

I believe the religious dimension has been largely ignored by those writing on the problem of battered women because they themselves have left the institutional church in despair of it ever dealing with its complicity in women's oppression. However, the problem still exists. Many of the women who have talked with me blame themselves for what is happening or has happened to them, and they have been reinforced in this belief many times by their church. They have internalized the guilt bestowed on all women by a patriarchal theology derived from a biased interpretation of

Ann McGlinchey holds a master's degree in theology from New York's Union Theological Seminary. Ms. McGlinchey, a former nun, is currently the Coordinator of Women's Survival Space, a shelter for battered women in New York City.

the first three chapters of Genesis and the letters of Paul. This theology supports our society, which, as Straus maintains, "actually has rules and values which make the marriage license also a hitting license" (1977/1978, p. 195).

The power of religious legitimation of our societal values cannot be ignored. Even women who have left the institutional church or who never attended one are still subject to the societal values sanctioned in part by religious institutions. Thus if the church intends to delegitimate this license for men to batter their wives or partners, it must get involved in helping women with the resources it has available: buildings for shelter; emergency money for food, clothing, rent; the power to advocate for them with the police, the courts, and social service agencies.

Women's Guilt and the Church's Complicity

Anne's husband had broken her jaw in one of their many fights. . . . She decided to talk to a minister she had met. However, the conversation did not help her. She explains: "Gradually, the tone of our conversation shifted. We had drifted away from the problem of my survival—of what I could do to try and maintain my sanity and my health while living with a man who liked to beat me—to what I was doing to cause all this trouble. . . . He didn't believe me either. . . . He was a clergyman, but nevertheless, a man first. He had the same attitudes of the society at large, that I was here to serve my husband, and if I got slapped around some, I ought to search my soul and find out what I was doing wrong. . . . I was betrayed by God's minister. I had put out my hand for God's help and received a male reprimand." (Langley and Levy, 1977a, pp. 90–91)

For seventeen years "Dorothy" was married to a man who beat her. She had two children, few job skills, and too much middle class pride to admit what was happening. "I had gone to a minister, a priest, and a rabbi, and they all told me that was my lot in life and I had to suffer." (Stephen, 1977, p. 15)

These are not isolated incidents but examples of what many battered women are told when they ask for help from a minister or priest. I became aware of this problem in counseling women on the crisis hotline and in a weekly support group. This is not to say that some ministers and priests are not becoming sensitized to this problem and want to help the women who approach them. But the number is very small at present. Many clergy who want to help have neither the understanding of the problem nor the resources to refer the women to someone who can help. Instead, they send the women back to their violent situations. The knowledge, too, that other women have received bad advice from the clergy, has kept many women from even asking any kind of help from the church. For these women it reinforces their belief that the church as God's representa-

ive sees women as "other Eves"—"weak, deceived, sinful, the eternal
eductress" (McGrath, 1972, p. 42).

Some battered women go to a social worker, psychiatrist, or other
type of counselor for help and are reinforced in their guilt here too. The
counseling or therapy may be directed toward getting rid of the woman's
"masochism," or helping her identify how she "provokes" the beatings.
Other women aware of this counseling bias are offering help which recognizes the many ambivalent feelings which women who are battered experience. "Women have been raised and socialized to believe they must make
their husbands happy . . . So, they not only take the beatings, they tend to
feel responsible for them. Their guilt feelings prevent them from getting
out" (Gingold, 1976, p. 52). In a counselor training manual for domestic
violence counselors, Mindy Resnik explains:

> It is very important to help the victim to express the anger and to get it
> focused in the proper direction, that is, at the assailant. If this is not done,
> the victim may well internalize the anger, getting angry at herself instead of
> the assailant, thus leading to feelings to guilt and self-blame. . . . Guilt also
> arises from some all too commonly held beliefs, that if a woman gets beaten
> she deserves it; therefore, it goes that she must be a bad woman, wife or
> mother. Another belief is that women are by nature masochistic and thus
> expect and enjoy physical abuse. It is important to explore these beliefs and
> misconceptions with the victim to let her know that her counselor doesn't
> believe these things are true. (1976, p. 6)

For many women, a counselor working from the above perspective may be
the first person who has ever told her that it wasn't her fault. I have had the
experience many times of women saying to me, "No one ever believed me
before," or "No one has ever shown me a way out." For some it was the
point at which they began to take control of their own lives.

In many cases, the fact that I was perceived as a church person
helped the woman admit her feelings of guilt which were reinforced by a
minister or priest. If the woman asked me what kind of work I did, I would
explain that I was a seminary student and former Roman Catholic nun. This
usually brought out a story about going to a clergyman for help. In talking
about this to a friend who is a social worker, she commented that the
women she had contact with did not mention having a problem with the
clergy. I suggested that she let the woman know in some way that she was a
regular churchgoer. A few weeks later, she told me that she had explained
that she went to church regularly and then a couple of women described
similar experiences with a minister or priest. It was knowing that the other
person would understand their reliance on the church, I think, which
enabled the women to open up to the counselor. It is one aspect of the
battering problem that social workers, who are seen as part of a secular
agency, may rarely uncover. But it is present.

The church has a great deal to do with the guilt women experience, precisely because it has helped legitimate a society which fosters this guilt. Sociologists and anthropologists have documented how religious institutions in each society sanction the values of that society. The history of our patriarchal Western civilization contains ample proof of the Christian church's complicity in subordinating women by legitimating the societal values which allow this. One example of this is the fact that women are socialized into believing they are best suited for careers as wives and mothers. Sermons in church support this idea with Scripture references and devotional jargon. Women are praised for their nurturing, their spiritual capacity, their selflessness and spirit of sacrifice. When they complain of injustice, they are reminded to sacrifice themselves as Christ sacrificed himself for them.

Part of the problem has been that up to now women as a whole have accepted this definition of themselves. Those who resisted were burnt as witches or, in more modern times, forced to leave the institutional church. But it is hard to escape the church's influence. Ruether, a feminist theologian, believes that

> Religion has been not only a contributing factor, it is undoubtably the single most important shaper and enforcer of the image of women in culture and society. . . . It has been religion that has been the ideological reflection of this sexual domination and subjugation. And it has been religion, as a social institution, that has been its cultural sanctioner. (1974, p. 9)

Changing the Role of the Church

What can the church do? I see three main areas in which the institutional church can have significant positive impact on the problem of battered women: offering sensitive counseling based on an unbiased theology; giving practical aid by utilizing available resources; becoming an advocate for battered women with the legal system, the police, and social service agencies.

In the area of counseling, much can be done to guarantee sensitive and sympathetic treatment for the victims of battering and also realistic counseling for the men who batter. As has already been noted, the churches are accessible to many women, and this may be the first place they turn for help. Poor advice can be harmful. If the minister or priest, whom the woman looks upon as God's representative, rebuffs her or tells her she is responsible for the violence, this guilt often becomes internalized, and the problem is exacerbated. Many clergy commiserate with the woman but cannot offer any solutions; so the woman must return to the violent situation or seek help elsewhere. Educating ministers and priests about this problem and the help that is available is important.

A more enlightened seminary education, which includes more women in faculty positions, can expose the biases against women in the Christian tradition. Continuing education programs and workshops for clergy already working in churches or counseling agencies are necessary. More imput on the problem of battering should be given in clinical pastoral education studies and pastoral counseling institutes. At the present time, one pastoral counseling institute in New York City refers victims of battering to a counseling program for battered women. However, unless the counselor there has some experience with the religious dimension of this problem, the woman may be helped with legal advice, possible shelter, and counseling, but the religious aspect of her problem will not be dealt with. It would be another example of the church rejecting the woman.

Individual churches and church agencies can hire more women who are trained in working with battered women and who have some background in theology. Many battered women would prefer to speak with a woman in this crisis. Also it gives the woman a chance to make contact with another woman whom she can trust and treat as a friend, not as a competitor or enemy as she may have done previously. In some churches the pastoral staff works as a team. In these situations a woman counselor with experience in dealing with battered women could certainly add a needed dimension. Besides helping to sensitize the other staff members to this problem, she could work as a team with a male colleague in counseling couples who come for help. Having both a man and a woman counselor eliminates the "ganging up" problem of having the man feel intimidated by two women or the woman feel intimidated by two men.

The potential for the church in helping battered women with practical help is enormous. For many women, the counseling must wait until the immediate crisis is alleviated. This may mean she needs shelter, food, clothing, furniture, medical help, or money or transportation. One of the greatest needs is shelter, either long or short term. Church members could offer their homes for a few days. In the Park Slope section of Brooklyn, New York, the clergy association in conjunction with the Children and Youth Development Services, started a "safe homes" project. Women who go to the local hospital for treatment of injuries or who call the hotline number are seen by a counselor from the project. If a woman does not want to return home, one of the homes on their list is contacted and the woman and her children are sent there for 3 days with money for food. Within 3 days time a counselor talks with the woman and helps her decide what next step to take, whether to go back home with an order of protection from family court or criminal court or to seek long term shelter and then find an apartment on her own, get a job, and become self-supporting. The idea of this project is that people should not be asked to make long-term decisions in the midst of crisis. Taking a woman to another place where she is free from the threat of violence can give her an opportunity to think through her options and make an informed decision. The amount of danger to the people who take in these women and their children is negligible, since the husband's only contact is with the counselor, who will call him and explain that his wife and children are in a shelter. A safe home project could be set up by individual churches or groups of churches and could be autonomous or connected with existing organizations working with battered women. The organizing and training of counselors and host families is not an insurmountable task but one that churches could undertake with a minimum of financial outlay.

Many churches are presently dealing with the problem of what to do with some of the unoccupied buildings they own. Many of these residences could be turned into shelters. Convents, formerly used by Roman Catholic nuns, have been converted into housing for the elderly in some cities. Why couldn't some of these empty convents be used as shelters for battered women and their children? Many Protestant churches also have large parsonages that could be rented at low rates to local groups seeking shelter space. An ecumenical group in Sparkhill, New York, has set up a shelter in a former Presbyterian manse. Del Martin, in her book on battered women, lists specific suggestions about shelter possibilities:

> In San Francisco, for example, the Mary Elizabeth Inn was established to provide a low-cost residence for young working women and female students. The Inn was opened in 1914 when such a facility was necessary, but it is not used very much anymore. Recently, in fact, the Inn's administrators, the Board of Global Ministries of the United Methodist Church, sent a bulletin to all San Francisco Methodist parishes reminding them of the existence of the facility and encouraging them to use it. Surely some rooms in this residence could be reserved for battered wives who are presently dependent, but wish to acquire skills that will qualify them for work. The same applies to the Florence Crittenton Homes for unwed mothers. And it seems only logical that the YWCA Hotel should make one floor available to battered women in need of temporary shelter. Why couldn't facilities like these open their doors to the women who currently need them? (1976, p. 128)

Initial research would have to be done on the feasibility of using church buildings. Zoning regulations, insurance coverage, tax liability will have to be investigated. In some cases, if the church keeps the ownership of the building, many of these regulations would be handled by the church, eliminating problems for the shelter.

Offering shelter to victims of violence is a tradition that the church has pointed to with pride. Why not extend this tradition to help battered women? Can churches take seriously Christ's command to shelter the homeless, or is the image of woman as weak and prone to evil still part of the thinking of church people today?

Making food, clothing, furniture, and transportation money available to battered women and their children can also be done by churches. Many churches have funds set aside for such emergencies. Church groups hold benefits for various causes. Canned goods and clothing are collected around Thanksgiving and Christmas to be distributed to the poor. Bake sales and bazaars raise money for many charities both in the United States and overseas. Putting some of this money at the disposal of battered women who have had to leave home is not inconceivable. Every Catholic church has a Saint Vincent de Paul Society which distributes food, clothing, furniture, and money when necessary to needy families in the parish; Presbyterian churches have the board of deacons, which do the same; other churches have comparable groups. These groups could be used to help women from the church or from the community. It would entail no extra planning or budgeting, just a decision to make battered women and their children eligible for these services. The problem of battering must be seen as a problem that is the responsibility of the entire community, not just of the couple or the woman herself.

For this to happen, the clergyperson, staff person, or church member must bring this problem to the attention of the other church members. It must be seen as a social problem with religious dimensions. It is not just a personal problem, or something that the couple should work out for themselves. This kind of thinking isolates the woman from any help. Another way the church can help this situation is to take an advocate role. This means taking the woman's side when she has problems with city agencies, courts, or police and publicly working for justice for all battered women. Unless this is done, the problem remains on the personal level and reinforces the woman's guilt and powerlessness. The church can become the place where a woman knows she will be accepted for herself and where any act of violence against another person will not be tolerated.

Churches can begin with worship services around the theme of battering. This approach can make the clear connection between this problem and our Christian tradition of justice and charity. Having time after the service to talk about this issue also enables members of the congregation to address this as a religious issue and share their own experiences. This may lead to some of the members passing this information on to women who need it, and some may offer their homes for temporary shelters as part of a safe homes project.

Individual members can also help by accompanying women through the court procedures or welfare process. Both can be intimidating for the woman who is already shaken by the situation. But a great deal can be done by church bureaucracies in an advocacy role. They have the resources to bring this to the attention of the member churches and to support programs designed to help the battered woman. One example of a church using its resources to help is the Baptist churches in New York City.

The Reverend Sarah Darter has set up the Battered Women's Task Force for the American Baptist Churches. This group composed of women and men concerned about the issue, is focusing on educating church members, especially in the Baptist churches, on this problem. They ask to come to church groups to speak, either as part of the worship service or at church meetings. They distribute literature and hold discussions about what the problem is and how church members can help. Other denominations could start similar programs.

The American Friends Service Committee in New York City has taken battered women as a project. One of their staff members has been able to work on setting up conferences on this issue, one in February 1977, and another in February 1978. The outcome of these conferences has been the establishment of a coalition of groups working for battered women. All mailings and announcements are handled by the AFSC staff, and money comes out of their budget. Meetings of the coalition are held at the Friends' Meeting House. Without this help the coalition might never have been organized.

Finally, the church needs to be involved with other groups that are working to change societal attitudes and laws which oppress battered women. Many people who would not ordinarily pay attention to, or respond to, a feminist group, or a community group, will do so if the church supports it. The institutional church has political power and has used it for other problems. Churches have supported housing legislation, union organizing, and antipornography campaigns and, most recently, have been involved on both sides of the abortion debate. This kind of power can be tapped for advocating legislation, such as the class action suit against the New York police and family court by 12 battered women for failing to give proper assistance when they were beaten by their husbands. Or the church could work with community groups to get shelters set up in the city and more equitable welfare payments to these women. Projects such as these are certainly within the scope of individual churches, church agencies, and national church structures. The institutional church needs to recognize that there can be no neutral stand. If the church does not help to solve this problem, then it is supporting the status quo, which is oppressive to battered women.

The church has the structures and the resources to *act*. Up to now, for most social issues, the church has only *reacted* to societal pressures. It is time the church recognizes the universiality of this problem of battering, admits its complicity in supporting the structures and customs that have allowed this problem to exist, and resolves to help in solving this problem. It is time for battered women to be able to turn to the church for sensitive counseling, immediate practical help, and effective advocacy—to a church which reaffirms them as women and co-inheritors with men of God's promise on earth and in heaven.

■10
Selected Examples
of Shelter Procedures

Hotline Procedure for Crisis Calls

For purposes of this chapter we will define a *crisis call* as one in which the caller is in immediate danger or has just been abused and in which the volunteer must take action other than simply talking to the victim. In handling crisis calls, the focus is not as much on in-depth counseling as it is on gathering essential information as quickly as possible in order to take action to handle the crisis. Often a call will sound like a crisis at first, but as you ask the first few questions, you will find that the woman is not in immediate danger but feels very upset and needs to talk; this type of call then becomes a counseling call, and the volunteer can relax a bit!

The following procedure is your step-by-step guideline for handling crisis calls, from information-gathering to your conversation at the hospital and plans for follow-up.[1] However there are some calls in which the situation is so extreme or immediate that you cannot follow the procedure in an orderly way and must take action more quickly. These are also the most anxiety-producing types of calls for volunteers. We will call these *life-and-death emergencies*, and the procedure for handling those is listed after this section.

---

[1]Published here with the permission of the Marital Abuse Project of Delaware County, Pennsylvania; adapted from an unpublished training manual prepared by this project.

141

Step 1: Assess the Immediate Danger

Find out:

- Where she is (address and phone number, if she will tell you; if not, find out whatever you can)
- Where her attacker is
- Whether there is a weapon involved
- Whether she has been injured
- Whether her children are in danger
- Whether her husband has a psychiatric history

Tell her:

- To call police
- To get herself and her children to the safest place available and stay there till the police arrive
- That you will also contact police and find out where to meet her
- To get back in touch with you after calling police
- To ask the police to take her to the hospital if she has been injured

If she doesn't want the police:

1. Encourage her to make a police report even if she doesn't want to press charges—a police report now will help her get more protection later if she needs it.
2. Encourage her to go to the hospital, even if she thinks she has not been hurt "enough" to go to the hospital. She may have internal injuries. Also, a hospital report is important if she should decide later to press charges. Tell her you will meet her at the hospital.
3. Talk to her about her safety for the night, her options, and plans for follow-up (go to Steps 6, 7, and 8).

Step 2: Call Police

It is important for the victim to take responsibility for her situation as much as possible, so in most cases she should call the police herself. But if for any reason she *cannot* call them herself, you should do it and then call the victim back, or have the victim call you back. There may be situations in which you will think it is best to keep the woman on the line while you call the police on another line. If you have a second line in your house or if you have a close neighbor who wants to be involved, you could arrange with them to call police if you or a member of your family brings an emergency message to them. Otherwise, you will have to break your connection with the woman in order to call police—be sure to arrange how you will get back in touch with each other.

If the woman is calling the police herself, wait a minute or two to give her time to call. Then call the police yourself. Tell them that you are ___(name)___ from the Marital Abuse Project (MAP) and that a client of yours is calling them for assistance. Ask them whether you should meet her at the police station or at the hospital (if they don't know yet, ask them to call you back as soon as they know. If you haven't heard from them in a half hour, call them again and ask them what is happening.) Be sure to find out which hospital they are taking the woman to!

Step 3: Call Crisis Intervention?[2]

In some cases it may be appropriate to involve Crisis Intervention. They are on call daily from 5 P.M. until 8:30 A.M. and all weekend at (215) 565-4300. They should be involved in these situations:

- Suicide attempt
- Drug overdose
- Psychiatric emergency

Crisis Intervention and like agencies have authority to commit someone during the night and on weekends. If you think this might be necessary, call them and discuss it with them. They can be called for this kind of consultation without calling the police first.

Step 4: Meet Her at Police Station or Hospital

If you are going to meet the victim at the police station, be sure you are familiar with police protocol. Also, you need to be familiar with the procedure listed below for pursuing a complaint with the help of police. There are three situations in which steps can be taken that night to issue a warrant.

1. If the police witnessed the abuse personally, they may take the man directly to the magistrate and swear out a warrant. They are reluctant to do this, but if you are at the police station, tell her about this so that she can suggest it to them.

---

[2]The Crisis Intervention agency referred to here is based in the Philadelphia suburban area. Therefore, Step 3 is not universally applicable. However, there are similar agencies in many other cities.

2. The police may issue a warrant on information received. This is applicable if the woman has visible severe injuries which the police can see and if she is willing to sign a statement as to who injured her. In this case she bears all liability for false information and she can be sued if it turns out she is lying about who her assailant was. The volunteer can suggest this to the woman if it is appropriate.
3. The police can sign a warrant on the basis of the hospital report. If the hospital report shows internal or other nonvisible injuries, the woman can then ask the police to sign a warrant on the basis of information received from the hospital and from her statement as to who the assailant was. The volunteer may suggest this to her also.

Step 5: Make Sure She Has a Safe Place for the Night

It may be safe for the victim to go home. Always ask her if you can call someone such as a relative or friend to be with her at the hospital, to drive her home, to stay with her, or to let her stay at their house. Do not immediately suggest emergency housing. If she and her children have absolutely no other options and it is not safe for her to return home, follow the procedure for emergency housing placement.

Step 6: Discuss Her Options and Arrange Follow-up

Usually, your main role in crisis counseling will be to get the victim settled for the night and arrange for her to meet with you or someone at the office the next morning to plan the next steps. Most of the in-depth discussion of her situation and detailed planning will be done as part of the intake interview, and you normally will not be doing that at the hospital or police station. During the crisis, you should help her focus on her immediate safety and give her information about things she actually needs to act on that night, such as asking the police to sign a warrant and getting the hospital report. But you need to know what options are available to her and answer her questions. She will probably have enough to think about with the hospital, police, and magistrate and will be reassured to know that she can talk about welfare, lawyers, support, custody, and all those other confusing things in the morning.

In any case, her situation should not be discussed in detail in front of police or hospital personnel or in a public place such as the hospital waiting room. Also, you should not fill out any forms or write anything down there.

Get her to write her name, address, and phone where she can be reached, give her the flyer listing our services (or tell her about them, if you are talking on the phone rather than in person), and try to pave the way for her to contact the office by phone or in person the next day.

Step 7: Reporting

As soon as the crisis is over, the woman is settled, and you are alone, either in your car or at home, fill in all appropriate forms. Fill in an Intake Form with as much information as you can remember. If the office receptionist has not reached you by 10 A.M. the next morning, call the office, give them all the data, and get a number for the case.

If you have decided to follow through on the case yourself, you should still let the office know what is happening. Make sure that all court accompaniments that the woman has requested are recorded on the chart in the office, even if you are accompanying the woman yourself.

Procedure for Life-and-death Emergency

You will be most apprehensive about the most far-out life-and-death crisis you can imagine. What if the call is interrupted by screaming, sounds of struggle, or gunshots, or the phone goes dead, or the woman says she has just cut her wrists or taken 35 aspirin? Although this kind of situation will probably never happen to you, you will feel more comfortable about being on call if you know what to do. Also, all suicide threats and drug crises are not necessarily life-and-death emergencies.

The general guideline is: If a Life Is in Danger, Call the Police. If you have good reason to think that something is happening *right now* which is endangering a life, it is your responsibility to call the police. This is the only time that confidentiality does not apply. Of course, in most cases you will *not* be calling the police without the permission of the victim. Extreme emergencies in which you must act without the permission or knowledge of the caller will be *very rare*, but in case it happens, this is the procedure:

1. If you know the address or phone number, call the police immediately and give them all the information you have. If possible, call from another phone to keep the line open to the victim.
2. If you do not know the address and the phone line is still open, you can have the call traced. Leave your phone open, get to another phone, call the operator, and ask for the supervisor. Tell her or him the situation, and ask her or him to trace the call.

Provide any shred of information you may have which would help locate the caller, such as the name of the town, the first three letters of the phone number, whether it is a pay phone. She or he probably will not tell you any information but will call the police if she or he can locate the source of the call.

3. If the phone is dead or the woman has hung up, there is nothing you can do. If you have *any information at all* about her, call Crisis Intervention (or comparable agency). They may recognize her as a client of theirs and be able to help. At the very least, you will be upset yourself, and you can freak out to them; they are also on call all night and are very supportive.

Shelter Objectives and Telephone Contact Form[3]

1. To provide temporary lodging and food on a 24-hour basis, on request, for battered women and their children. Clients may be referred to the Shelter by law enforcement agencies, private and public helping agencies, or they may be self-referred. Admittance to the Shelter will be a function of Shelter policy and the woman's willingness to adhere to basic Shelter rules, regulations, and guidelines. In order to keep the Shelter from becoming a "revolving door," there will be a maximum length of stay and a maximum number of times a woman may come to the Shelter.

2. To provide referral for medical assistance and legal assistance. Coordination with area hospitals, mental health agencies, and other medical facilities will facilitate the smooth handling of clients' medical needs. Coordination with the Legal Aid Society and the statewide Lawyers Referral Number will fullfill a similar function for the clients' legal needs.

3. To provide a supportive community of women through advocacy and counseling services. The Shelter will have a fulltime counseling services administrator who will oversee all in-house counseling and advocacy activities as well as the personnel who conduct such activities. All advocates, paid and volunteer, will go through an extensive training program designed to prepare them for the intricacies of crisis counseling, child abuse, and spouse abuse. Further, it will provide guidelines for the constructive task of building the low self-esteem of abuse victims.

4. To provide social services information and/or referral. Shelter staff will guide the clients to those agencies whose services are appropriate, telephoning the agencies first if necessary to clear the way for the battered woman.

[3]Reprinted with the permission of Judith Kaufholz (Executive Director, Winston-Salem/Forsyth County Battered Women's Services, Inc., Winston-Salem, N.C.).

5. To provide housing information. Besides having local apartment guides available, the Shelter will coordinate on an information and referral basis with local agencies such as the Department of Social Services and the Housing Authority.

6. To provide an opportunity for growth, advancement, and independence for the clients. This objective will be accomplished via the following subobjectives:

a. To establish a fee scale for residents of the Shelter and their families, dependent on their ability to pay

b. To establish an in-house child care system, to be run by the residents

c. To provide assertiveness training via the counseling services administrator

d. To provide job or education guidance by coordinating with agencies such as Vocational Rehabilitation, local technical-vocational schools, and the Employment Security Commission

e. To provide financial and budgetary advice. Basic counseling will be handled by referral to the local consumer credit counseling service

In addition to providing needed services to the battered woman, there is the longer-term community objective:

7. To provide counseling for the battering mate. Working in conjunction with the courts, the Probation and Mental Health Departments, the program will provide court-imposed incentives for psychological counseling.

(*See* Telephone Contact Form on next page)

TELEPHONE CONTACT FORM

Time:_____

Name:_____Age:_____

Social Security#_____

Home Address:_____Phone:_____

Ethnicity:_____Occupation:_____

Employed?: yes_____ no_____ Income:_____Edu. Level:_____

Job Skills:_____

Marital Status:_____How long married or living together?_____

No. of prior marriages_____Partner's name_____

Employed? yes_____ no_____ Occupation_____

No. of Children_____Ages:_____Referral Agency:_____

Persons name:_____Phone:_____

Abuse Alcohol or Drugs?: yes_____ no_____Police Officer Involved_____

Volunteer Assigned_____

Immediate Needs_____

What was done for client?_____

_____

REMARKS:

Objectives, Policies, and Procedures of Family Violence Intervention[4]

1. *Aid to Battered Women* provides emotional support, information, emergency shelter, follow-up counseling, and referral for battered women.
2. Here is an example of our card:

> **Aid to Battered Women**
>
> **277-4735**
>
> **Confidential**
>
> **Help, Support, Information**

[4]Published here with the permission of Sharon E. Cook (Assistant Director, Department of Human Development, City of Cedar Falls, Iowa). Ms. Cook wrote these materials when the Family Violence Intervention program was called Aid to Battered Women.

3. When a battered woman is in need of emergency shelter, call our service and we will arrange shelter.
4. A counselor will meet the woman at the hospital or police station and escort her to the shelter.
5. Police will transport woman (and children) to the police station if transportation must be provided.
6. When a battered woman needs support, information, and/or counseling, refer her to our service.
7. We suggest our card be given to battered women for their reference.
8. We accept referrals from victims, friends or relatives of victims, hospitals, police, and other agencies.
9. *Aid to Battered Women* has 24-hour availability.

Objectives

1. Provide emotional support for battered women.
2. Provide information for battered women (legal options, alternatives, community resources).
3. Provide emergency shelter when needed.
4. Provide for follow-up counseling.
5. Provide referral to other agencies when appropriate, such as clergy, marriage counselors, etc.

Policies

1. Referrals are accepted from victims, friends or relatives of victims, the hospital, the police, and other agencies.
2. When receiving a referral from the hospital or police, counselor can meet the victim at the hospital or police station.
3. Counselor will not go to the scene of a domestic disturbance.
4. The drop-in-center has a list of available shelters.
5. These shelters are to remain strictly confidential. (The locations are not to be given to callers over the phone.)
6. When emergency shelter is necessary, counselor will call the shelter and make arrangements.
7. If transportation must be provided, police will transport woman (and children) to the police station.
8. Counselor will accompany woman (and children) to shelter from the police station or hospital.
9. Any caller under immediate threat should be urged to contact police.

10. Counselor should contact the department director or assistant director the next morning to insure follow-up counseling.

Procedure Narrative for Crisis Call

1. Counselor receives call from battered woman.
2. Counselor assesses situation.
   Is there immediate threat?
   Does woman need emergency shelter?
   Does woman need information?
   Does woman need emotional support?
   Does woman need medical care?
   Does woman need someone to talk to?
3. If immediate threat, counselor encourages woman to contact police.
4. If emergency shelter is needed, counselor explores alternatives: friend, relative, neighbors, drop-in-center.
5. If shelter is needed through drop-in-center, counselor makes arrangements with woman to meet her at police station.
6. Counselor calls Shelter to arrange for placement of victim.
7. Counselor meets woman at police station and accompanies to Shelter.
8. Next morning counselor informs director or assistant director of contact and follow-up is provided.
9. If there is no immediate danger and emergency shelter is not needed, counseling is provided over the phone and meeting arranged.

Procedure Narrative for Incoming Referral

1. Counselor receives battered woman referral from police or hospital.
2. Counselor assesses situation:
   Is there need for immediate intervention?
   Does woman need emergency shelter?
3. If shelter is needed, counselor explores options:
   Friend
   Relative
   Neighbor
   Counselor
4. If shelter is needed through counselor, counselor makes arrangements for placement in Shelter.

5. Counselor meets woman at the hospital or the police station and accompanies her to the Shelter.
6. Next morning, counselor informs director or assistant director of contact and follow-up is provided.
7. If immediate intervention is not needed, counseling is provided over the phone and meeting arranged.

FIGURE 10–1. Sample operational flow chart.

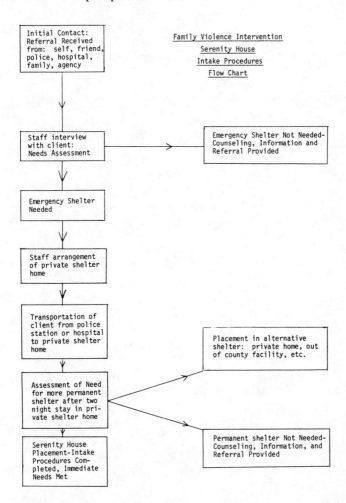

■ three
PREVENTION STRATEGIES

■ 11
Recommendations and Prospects for the Future

Too often crisis intervention is seen as the final rehabilitative step for battered women. On the contrary, intervention programs are only the beginning in the establishment of a comprehensive network of services for abused women. Battered women who take refuge at an emergency shelter have an important decision to make: Should they return to the abusive mate with the hope that it "won't happen again" or should they strike out on their own and make a fresh start? It is a difficult decision for them to make.

Emergency shelters are not (nor were they intended to be) a panacea for the victims of wife battering. Their stated purpose is to assure the victim's physical safety by providing a safe place to stay, crisis intervention services, and an opportunity to think about reorganizing her life. To be sure these are all essential. But one or two months of the most supportive environment is often not sufficient to provide the women with the self-confidence that their husbands tore away year after year, the self-confidence needed if women are going to become totally independent.

The impetus for developing shelters to aid battered women was generated by the following:

1. A growing sociopolitical awareness of the oppression of women, in particular, culturally sanctioned violence against women by their spouse or boyfriend.
2. Published articles and books on the causes, nature, and prevalence of wife beating, such as Gelles (1972), Pizzey (1974),

155

Martin (1976), Straus (1976/1977), Warrior (1976), and Roy (1977).
3. A growing awareness of the need for crisis intervention services for victims of wife battering. This was especially evident among rape crisis centers, women's groups, and voluntary organizations, such as YWCAs and the Salvation Army.
4. The availability of CETA funding to help fledgling programs get off the ground by paying staff salaries.
5. The passage of domestic violence legislation by a growing number of states, resulting in state appropriations for emergency shelters.

Preventive programs need to be developed around three goals:

1. The elimination of the conditions that lead to spouse abuse (primary prevention); instituting environmental changes that deal with the underlying causes of family violence
2. Early case finding and provision of services before the violence becomes severe (secondary prevention)
3. Providing women who have already been seriously beaten with a comprehensive treatment approach in order to prevent any further abuse (tertiary prevention)

Primary Prevention

Primary prevention of spouse abuse is exceedingly difficult to accomplish because it requires a change in attitudes and values of individuals, communities, and social institutions. However, if we are to work toward elimination of wife battering, this must be our approach.

Judge Lisa Richette gave testimony before the United States Commission on Civil Rights in 1978. She addressed the need for eliminating family violence through basic changes in educational and cultural spheres and through recognition of women and men as equals under the law. Richette made clear her beliefs that the *long-term solution* to wife abuse does not lie in the development of more shelters but rather in the elimination of the factors that lead men to use violence against women. In Judge Richette's words:

I think the shelters are extremely important. But shelters will just be underpinning to a decaying system. We will be giving not only a Band-Aid, but we will be giving conscience balm to a society which tolerates the oppression of women by the single response of funding these shelters; we must confront very clearly that all this occurs in a society because women are denied fundamental human and legal equality. It isn't that wife beating is misunderstood, it's a tacitly accepted custom in our society and it is a clear index of the devaluation of women. Now, the formal legal revisions, the tinkering with statutes will be of little avail if there are not parallel changes in the educational and cultural phases in American society. (1978, p. 128)

Efforts aimed at eliminating the conditions which breed wife abuse should include:

- Eliminating sex-role stereotyping
- Improving the quality of life for all families
- Providing family life education for children and adults
- Changing society's attitude toward violence through community education programs

Eliminating Sex-role Stereotyping

Straus considers "the sexist structure of the family and society" as being a fundamental cause of wife abuse. It follows, therefore, that, to eliminate this form of family violence, sex-role stereotyping must be ended. Straus suggests eight areas to pursue in the accomplishment of this goal. His recommendations are:

- Eliminate the husband as "head of the family" from its continuing presence in the law, in religion, in administrative procedure, and as a taken-for-granted aspect of family life.
- Eliminate the pervasive system of sex-typed occupations in which "women's occupations" tend to be poorly paid, and the equally pervasive difference between the pay of men and women in the same occupation.
- Reduce or eliminate the sex-typed pattern of family role responsibilities.
- Establish or subsidize a comprehensive and high quality system of day-care centers for preschool children.
- Full sexual equality is essential for prevention of wifebeating.
- As the society eliminates fixed sex roles, alternative sources of stability and security in self-definition will be needed.
- Parent-child interaction, parental expectations, and all other aspects of socialization should not be differentiated according to the sex of the child.
- Eliminate from the criminal justice system the implicit toleration of wifebeating which comes about through statutory and common law; the attitudes of the police, prosecutors, and judges; and through cumbersome and ineffective procedures which make even the available legal remedies and protection ineffective. (1977, p. 728)

Improving the Quality of Life

Our efforts to end domestic violence need to go beyond the limited scope of identifying psychopathology among batterers. We must acknowledge the broader social and economic variables that have such a significant impact on family life. This holistic view recognizes that counseling victims and perpetrators of wife abuse is not enough to eliminate this prevalent social problem. In order to deal with the mounting pressures of modern society that families encounter, national and local programs are needed which include full employment for all those able to work and a nonstigmatizing guaranteed income for those unable to work; a comprehensive system of support services for families, and equal access to the resources necessary for people to have satisfying lives.[1]

In summary, family stress, strain, and conflict would be considerably alleviated by:

1. A guaranteed minimum income provided to each needy family for food, shelter, and child care
2. Housing adequate for accommodating large and small families in optimal sanitary conditions
3. A comprehensive family health care program
4. Community-based recreational and cultural centers
5. Neighborhood family social service centers
6. Equal educational opportunities (Gil, 1970, p. 145)

Family Life Education

This area encompasses a wide range of educational and counseling programs designed to prepare individuals for their role as spouse or parent. Traditionally, high school curricula steered away from the real problems their students would be facing in future years. But the schools' reluctance to delve into family life stresses is changing.

It is a known fact that human beings tend to repeat in their adult lives what they learned as children. Aggressiveness, toughness, and violence are learned during childhood. Many abusive males were reared in homes where violence was commonplace. These males were often physi-

---

[1]For a comprehensive comparative analysis of the issues, costs, benefits, effectiveness, and values of the family policies in 11 Western and Eastern European countries, Israel, Canada, and the United States, see Sheila B. Kamerman and Alfred J. Kahn (eds.), *Family Policy: Government and Families in Fourteen Countries* (New York: Columbia University Press, 1978). Also see Kamerman and Kahn, "Comparative Analysis in Family Policy: A Case Study," *Social Work*, November, 1979, 506–512.

cally abused as children and may have had a male role model who beat their mother as well. A child raised in a loving and compassionate home has a good chance of becoming a loving and compassionate husband or wife. On the other hand, a child raised in a violent and unstable environment will be likely to resort to violence when pressures and frustrations become unbearable in adult life. The way to end the ongoing cycle of an abused child becoming an abusive husband and raising children who may then beat their wives is to develop family life education programs in every community. In other words, the purpose of family life education is to counteract the deleterious effects of one's own childhood as well as to educate persons who are unaware of appropriate child-rearing techniques. Menninger has aptly focused on the need to provide children with love and security:

> People repeat in adult life emotions they experienced in childhood. Many of the people whom I spent the last 30 to 40 years treating at so much per minute wouldn't have needed any treatment if they'd had the right kind of care as children.
>
> Most prisoners come from evil homes. . . . You can almost be certain that the man who commits violent crimes has been treated violently as a child. (Proctor, 1977, p. 25)

Day Care

Day care services are needed for young children whose mothers enter the labor force. These services can be especially useful to the former battered woman who leaves her abusive spouse and finds a job or enrolls in a full-time college or vocational training program. These women already bear a heavy financial burden, and quality day care services are often expensive unless they are subsidized by government agencies.

There are different types of day care services from which to choose, including licensed family day care homes, day care or child development centers, nursery schools, compensatory preschool education programs, and after-school programs. Quality day care is intended to be not just a babysitting service but an opportunity for children to gain an enriching experience under the supervision of trained and experienced child development specialists. At present, however, the reality of day care is too often at variance with the good intentions. Day care facilities are in short supply and are often staffed by workers who lack appropriate skills in child development. In order to promote the well-being of the children, the following elements should be included:

> An understanding of a child's individual needs and stages of growth, consistent nurture, supportive emotional response, attention to the child's health and physical progress, and a variety of stimulating experiences

which contribute to the child's cognitive and social development. In other words, day care must deal with the whole child in a well-rounded program. Children are not well cared for and protected if their need and capacity to learn and acquire competence are not given careful attention. Similarly their success in learning, even in carefully devised educational programs, is hampered if there is no appropriate response to their feelings and emotions. (Costin, 1979, p. 398)

As the number and variety of day care facilities expands, it will become even more important for the federal and state agencies concerned with children to prepare and disseminate day care standards, descriptions, and guides. These public education pamphlets would provide parents with a useful knowledge base in the selection of a high-quality day center for their children. Another important strategy for strengthening family life is parent education programs.

Parenting Education

Through classroom lectures, discussion groups, and media presentations, parent education programs present information about effective child-rearing practices. Parenting education focuses on teaching adolescents, parents-to-be, and those who already are parents about normal child care, the child's behavior at different developmental periods, listening skills, and appropriate nonviolent techniques for disciplining the child and setting limits on his or her behavior.

One of the most well-known family life education programs in the United States is Parent Effectiveness Training (PET), popularized by Dr. Thomas Gordon (1975). PET is taught in small groups of 15–30 one evening a week for 8 weeks. It transmits communication and problem-solving skills to parents to enable them to have better relationships with their children.

Prenatal classes have become increasingly popular and are attended by both the mother- and father-to-be. Usually conducted in the hospital where the baby will be delivered, these classes provide information on: the importance of proper nutrition and health care for the growing fetus; the stages of pregnancy, labor, and delivery; and basic care of a newborn. Perhaps the most valuable contribution of prenatal classes is preparing the new parents for the major life change that the baby will bring about. Couples have an opportunity to share their concerns and anxiety about parenthood. They learn what resources are available to help them if they have difficulty after the baby is born.

Beginning in 1972, the federal government through the Office of Child Development, started the Education for Parenthood Program for adolescents. This program is designed to aid schools and voluntary organizations in developing programs to train adolescents in the essentials of child care, to provide opportunities for the youths to work with young children, and to expose the youths to potential careers in the child care field.

There are only a small number of persons who are employed full-time as parent educators. However, I believe that by the year 2,000 high schools, nursing schools, and medical schools will have established regularly scheduled courses on early childhood development and child-rearing practices. Furthermore, libraries will become increasingly involved in family life education through their audio cassette and videotape centers. The ultimate goal is a better prepared and more effective generation of parents.

Changing Society's Attitude toward Violence

If we are striving to achieve an end to acts of family violence, society's attitudes toward violence must be changed. Stories about violent crimes, forced sexual acts, and other forms of brutality have become commonplace on television and motion picture screens throughout the Western world. It is the children who watch 40–50 hours a week of TV who are particularly impressionable in response to repeated viewings of violence. It is the parents' responsibility to decide what shows their children may watch and which ones are not acceptable. But it is difficult for a 9-year-old when programs filled with acts of brutality aired in the early evening are watched by other family members while she or he is prohibited from watching. Concerned citizens, parent-teacher associations, and women's groups are encouraged to mount an intense lobbying effort to persuade media tycoons to curtail the glorification and exploitation of violence. In addition, public television, which has proven its capability of producing high-quality, nonviolent programming for children, should receive increased funding so that it can offer youngsters expanded viewing both for educational and entertainment purposes.

Parents are well advised to encourage less television and more reading on the part of all family members. This can be accomplished by planning family reading periods and family book discussions, as well as encouraging children's participation at an early age in storytelling and reader's groups at local public libraries.

With proper programming, television can provide a variety of useful learning experiences for children and youth. For further information on the potential of television in socializing children see: Peter L. Klinge, editor, *American Education in the Electric Age* (Englewood Cliffs, N.J.: Educational Technology Publications, 1974); Eli A. Rubenstein, "Televi-

162 : : *Sheltering Battered Women*

sion and the Young Viewer," *American Scientist* (Nov./Dec. 1978); or write
to: the Division of Educational Technology, U.S. Department of Education, Washington, D.C. 20201; and the Association for Educational Communications and Technology, 1126 16th Street, N.W., Washington, D.C.
20036.

Secondary Prevention

Early intervention with domestic violence cases involves the identification
and treatment of couples who have the potential for violence. This early
phase is commonly referred to as early case finding or early detection. The
goal of secondary prevention is to nip the problem in the bud—to help the
woman in getting couples counseling or in leaving the marriage before
those first attacks become more frequent and severe. Early detection and
intervention should be the responsibility of all professionals who have
direct contact with couples: physicians, nurses, clergy, marital counselors,
social workers, psychologists, and psychiatrists. Early intervention is important with all types of clients, but it is especially crucial in wife-battering
cases where the woman's very life is in jeopardy when the violence goes
unchecked.

Social workers view a certain amount of family conflict as natural to
rational problem solving and growth. Conflict in this sense is viewed as
"the continual negotiation and renegotiation of values, beliefs, and goals"
(Eisenman, 1977, p. 138). There is a minimal amount of conflict in the daily
interaction of marital partners in the healthy family, but in problem
families destructive clashes are quite frequent. Men who have difficulty
controlling their frustration and rage may begin to resort to physical force
as an outlet for their anger.

When physical force such as a slap or a punch is used *for the first
time* the woman should take action to prevent it from ever happening
again. After that first incident, the woman is likely to be surprised, shock-
ed, and confused. She may feel that her action provoked the attack, and the
husband is likely to reinforce that notion by saying that she "made him hit
her" because, for example, she burned the dinner. This is the time for the
woman to make clear that no matter what she and her husband argue
about, there is never any justification for him to hit her and she will not
tolerate any further abuse. The man should be encouraged to seek professional help so that he can learn to express his pent-up hostility without the
use of physical force. If the relationship is worth preserving, the man and
woman should go for individual psychotherapy and marital counseling; if it
is not worth preserving, the woman should get away before the occasional
slap escalates into frequent and severe abuse.

In almost *all* cases, the abuse, though it may be mild at first, begins while the man and woman are dating or early in the marriage—before any children are born. Physical abuse becomes more severe during pregnancy and after the first baby is born. In Gelles's study of battered women he found that almost 25 percent of the victims were beaten while they were pregnant (see Gelles, 1972, 1975). Some women have felt that by marrying their boyfriend or by having a baby the assaults would stop. This is simply not the case and only serves to exacerbate the problem.

In addition to psychotherapy and marital counseling, another early intervention modality is the hotline. The hotline enables women who have been abused for the first time to contact someone who is a good listener and can provide information and referral suggestions in an accepting and nonjudgmental manner. For detailed information on the functions of hotlines as they presently exist for abused women, see Chapter 2 in this book.

As of this writing hotlines have been used only rarely to help the abuser and the potential abuser, but I believe that this is a valuable intervention tool and one that will receive widespread attention as more programs are developed to help the batterers. A man who felt that he could not control a violent impulse to hit his wife would be able to dial the toll-free hotline number—operational 24 hours a day—to receive immediate assistance from a male crisis counselor. The men's hotline would be staffed by experienced social workers or paraprofessionals trained in marital conflict and abuse intervention techniques. These emergency hotlines should be developed in every community under the auspices of a private organization or linked to a state or county family violence prevention project. One example of a hotline to help batterers is the Victims Information Bureau of Suffolk (VIBS); the VIBS program, which utilizes a hotline as one component of a counseling program for abusers, is described in the following section.

Tertiary Prevention

In addition to short-term emergency shelters for beaten women, tertiary prevention services should be aimed in two directions: The first is counseling for the abusive males to enable the majority of women who want to remain with their husbands to live in a nonviolent home; the second is for women who want to leave the batterer and start a new life—aftercare and support groups beyond the short-term services provided by most shelters.

Counseling the Abusive Male

What happens to the women after they leave an emergency shelter? In the majority of cases they return to their abusive partner. Their reason for doing so may be that they are afraid to leave their husband permanently, or it may be that they truly love him and have a good relationship when they are not being beaten. According to Janet Geller (1977), Clinical Director of the VIBS program, the overwhelming majority of their female clients resume the marital relationship after leaving VIBS.

While there are undoubtedly some abusers who are unable and are unwilling to alter their violent habits, social workers, psychologists, and psychiatrists are now recognizing that a significant number may be receptive to change. Social work professor Kim emphasizes the necessity for developing treatment programs for batterers:

> In those instances in which the woman chooses to remain with or return to her partner, the therapy provided must be mutually supportive of the two of them. We must move away from an adversary orientation toward a more collaborative effort; we must develop male consciousness-raising groups and treatment programs for men who have been involved in battering women. If we do not make a concerted effort to change male attitudes toward women and to alter their behavior toward them, then we will always be treating symptoms. Although it is certainly true that we must give priority to providing services to women who have been battered, we should also seek to reduce and eventually to eliminate battery, a goal which we can achieve only by effecting changes in male attitude and behavior. (1978, p. 137)

Counseling programs are based on the premise that the man and woman love each other and want to remain together and that the man resorts to violence because of his inability to deal with stress and anger in a nonviolent manner. Therapeutic programs for abusers provide an opportunity for the men to learn nonviolent ways of problem solving. As of 1978 there were only a handful of programs which counseled the batterer. By mid 1980 the number of programs had climbed to 67. Based on the acceptance of this treatment mode, such services are likely to be widely adopted in the future.

In 1977 EMERGE, a volunteer organization located in Boston, developed a program to help abusive males (Berg, 1979; F. Roberts, 1979). Group counseling is used to help the men explore nonviolent alternatives to handling stress. EMERGE views wife battering as an outgrowth of traditional societal pressure for men to be publicly "in control" of their emotions. Continually keeping one's frustrations and anxieties bottled up inside, the staff members believe, too often produces feelings of isolation and results in violent outbursts. Batterers come to EMERGE voluntarily. Their willingness to seek help may stem from the belief that their wives will leave them if they continue the abuse. EMERGE does not concentrate on reconciliation between husband and wife. Their emphasis is purely on helping the men to develop nonviolent methods of problem solving.

The VIBS program, based in Long Island, New York, takes a

different approach. As part of its therapeutic program for battered women VIBS provides couples counseling. This form of counseling is initiated by the wife, and the men who participate do so voluntarily because they recognize that they need help. However, in addition to the men who acknowledged that they have a problem, VIBS wanted to reach out to those men who refused couples counseling. They therefore initiated group counseling (the term *therapy* was never used as it would be too threatening), which was short term (10 sessions) and goal oriented. They reasoned that "the men needed a concrete goal and quick results or they would become impatient and discouraged with treatment" (Geller, 1977, p. 5). The initial group was led by a male worker, but later groups have incorporated a male and female therapist working together to serve as models of appropriate interaction. In an effort to provide immediate intervention and to aid the men in rechanneling their violent impulses, VIBS set up a hotline. The group leader suggested that, whenever the men felt they were going to abuse their wives, they call the hotline instead. Following the completion of the initial 10 counseling sessions, many of the men are ready to join VIBS' couples counseling group.

Another treatment program for batterers, one which has direct linkage with the criminal justice system, is called Therapy for Abusive Behavior (TAB), in Baltimore, Maryland (Center for Women Policy Studies, Oct. 1978). TAB serves as a resource for abusers who are brought to court; it has the support of the police and social service agencies in the area. The judge may require that the men participate in TAB's program as an alternative to further legal action. Men who do not comply with the judge's order are returned to court. This program teaches batterers more effective methods for handling personal relationships.

Chiswick Women's Aid in London, England, established in 1971 by Erin Pizzey, is recognized as the very first shelter for battered women. In 1976, Chiswick broadened its treatment goals when it secured a house for the purpose of establishing a refuge for abusive men. The men who participate in the therapeutic program have the choice of staying at the refuge or attending group therapy sessions while continuing to live at home. The two male therapists who run the program have found that most of the abusers have "come from backgrounds where violence was employed as a means of enforcing dominance or expressing a need" (Chiswick Women's Aid, 1977, p. 2).

In the United States, a structured short-term residential treatment program for batterers has been designed by Anne Ganey and Lance Harris, two psychologists in Tacoma, Washington (Center for Women Policy Studies, July 1979). The purpose of therapy is to have the men take responsibility for their own behavior and to realize that they are capable of breaking the cycle of violence. The reason for having a residential program is to focus totally on eliminating violence; if the abuser continues to live with his wife, the psychologists believe, he is likely to be diverted by concentrating instead on marital problems. Marital counseling is available only after the man has finished the 4-week program and has learned to control his violent impulses. While the men are receiving treatment, their wives are asked to join weekly group sessions. Aside from providing an opportunity for the women to discuss their problems, the group sessions are useful in verifying information about the men's violent behavior. Included in the program are physical activities (including relaxation training) designed to alleviate physiological tension. Ganley and Harris discovered that abusers tend to be loners; "often the batterer's only active relationship is with the victim, whom he often isolates from her other relationships." To counteract that, each participant must have close personal contact with an assigned "buddy" (important decisions cannot be made without first talking to his "buddy"). Known as the Domestic Assault Program, this innovative approach to treatment has been based at the American Lake Veterans Hospital in Tacoma. Unfortunately, the residential program ended in 1978 because of difficulty in filling the amount of beds mandated by the hospital, but the program has continued on an out-patient basis.

In summary, service delivery for batterers is beginning to emerge as an urgently needed form of treatment. Since the majority of beaten women who seek refuge at an emergency shelter ultimately return to their husbands, it is vital that abusive men become aware that: (1) hitting a woman is unacceptable behavior and there is no defense, excuse, or explanation which can make it justifiable; and (2) they can learn alternative ways of coping with stress and anger. It is hoped that programs for wife abusers will be developed at an accelerated pace to help the thousands of men who are capable of learning nonviolent methods of problem solving.

Vocational Services for Victims of Abuse

We should not underestimate the importance of providing vocational counseling and training to beaten women. Finding gainful employment is essential not just for the economic reasons but also to enhance a woman's self-concept as a productive and worthwhile human being. Generally the abused woman has endured years of physical and emotional battering before she seeks help. After years of hearing the husband criticize and berate her, a woman—even one who had been successfully employed at one time—comes to doubt her capability and competence. To a woman who has undergone years of pain and self-doubt, having a job is tangible proof of her worthiness.

We must keep in mind, however, that it is exceptionally difficult for an insecure woman who has no job skills to obtain a job on her own. Women who have never been beaten and who had held responsible positions 15 years earlier but who quit work to raise a family are finding it difficult to return to the world of work. So we must recognize the position of a battered woman lacking in job skills who is plagued by the fear of not being able to manage a paying job. If such a woman is merely told to get a job on her own, she is likely to be turned down—if she makes any attempts in the first place. Any attempts which are met with refusals will serve to reinforce what she was already thinking: "I am a failure."

It is recommended that all women who would like to seek gainful employment be given vocational counseling and evaluation and, where indicated, vocational training as well. Vocational evaluation is a highly specialized process and is usually best accomplished by referring the woman to a center which has expertise in vocational services. Vocational evaluation is defined as:

> a process designed to assess and predict work behavior and vocational potential, primarily through the application of practical, reality-based assessment techniques and procedures. It is the practical nature of vocational evaluation methodology that "sets it apart" from traditional programs of vocational assessment and establishes it as a unique entity. (Nadolsky, 1971, p. 1)

Most vocational evaluation programs incorporate a combination of various tests and worksamples. The worksample approach focuses upon the assessment of actual work skills related to specific types of jobs. Worksamples are concerned with different categories of work skills as performed in a simulated work setting. Standardized criteria for quality and speed of various tasks have been established and are used in rating the woman's performance in various areas. During worksample administration those difficult-to-measure qualities such as motivation, interest, and attitude are observed and contribute to the overall assessment.

A situational assessment (also referred to as an on-the-job tryout) may also be included in a vocational evaluation. A woman who is given a job tryout is working in an actual job setting for a limited period of time. A situational assessment is valuable for two reasons: (1) It provides an opportunity for the woman to decide whether she would enjoy that type of work; (2) it enables a woman who is highly anxious about the world of work to learn about a particular job in a protected setting. In that way, if she has any adjustment problems, they can be worked out with her vocational counselor before she is thrust into the regular labor market.

If the woman is interested in a college education, the vocational counselor can guide her in obtaining college catalogs, requesting old transcripts, making applications, helping to determine her eligibility for financial aid, and visiting local college campuses. Most colleges have developed support programs for women who are continuing their education after a hiatus of many years. Many women in this position prefer enrolling first in a 2-year or community college with the option of transferring to a 4-year college after obtaining an associate of arts (A.A.) or associate of sciences (A.S.) degree. There are two advantages to this route. First, community colleges generally have lower tuition and less stringent admission requirements than the 4-year schools. Second, upon completing a 2-year course of study, the woman will have a degree and will have acquired marketable skills, for example those of a social work case aide or a laboratory technician. If finances are tight, she would then be prepared to obtain a job in her field and could contemplate transferring to a 4-year program in its evening division.

A comprehensive vocational service agency should provide job placement and do follow-up. Any woman who has received vocational services should feel free to contact her counselor if problems, such as sexual harassment, arise on the new job.

All too often shelters are preoccupied with making ends meet and providing the necessary crisis intervention assistance. In most cases, shelter staff are not trained in or knowledgeable about vocational rehabilitation. One way for abused women to acquire the self-esteem that their husbands have destroyed is to become successfully employed. If battered women are to have a real opportunity to have a meaningful life free from physical abuse and the fear of abuse, they urgently need vocational guidance combined with preparation for independent living (which is discussed below).

Preparation for Independent Living

The women with the courage to leave the abusive relationship need far more assistance than that which is usually available at the shelter. The shelters which provide the essential crisis intervention services do recognize the need for long-term assistance, but most do not have sufficient staff to continue providing supportive services to all the women who need them.

Many women have returned to a refuge again and again each time their spouse launches an especially violent attack. For those women time spent at a shelter has not led to a cessation in violence at home; neither has it enabled them to feel capable of leaving the batterers permanently. With a more structured, comprehensive aftercare program (referred to as second-stage houses in England) such women might be able to achieve a satisfying life for themselves and their children away from the abuser.

Some shelters, overwhelmed by the demand for their service, have resorted to imposing a limit on the number of times a woman may be housed there. The frightening result is that women who are victims of brutal attacks, who are particularly insecure, and who need long-term support in order to establish their independence are the very women who may be turned away from this essential service on the grounds that "they have been here two times in the past year." Some shelters refuse to provide safe housing more than once. Martin presents a cogent argument against the rigid policy of allowing a beaten woman to receive shelter only once:

> Second thoughts and confused loyalties are in the nature of the battered woman's problem. Home ties are not easily broken and many battered wives return home after a few days. . . . Most people need time to make a final break from a job they should have quit or a personal relationship gone bad. When the battered wife makes the break, she often loses both at once: her "career" as a married woman and the most intimate relationship of her life. The reasons that operated to keep her home in the first place beckon her back once she leaves: hope that her husband will change, fear of the unknown, lack of financial resources. Vacillation is inevitable. . . . I cannot help but feel that the one-chance-only rule is too harsh and even a bit judgmental. Need is need, and the woman's safety has to be the prime consideration. (Martin, 1976, p. 237)

Funds need to be made available so that shelters can establish ongoing support for the women who do not want to return to their husbands. The way things are at present in the United States, the battered woman may spend years suffering—in silence—from repeated brutal beatings. She enters an emergency refuge with deep physical and emotional scars and finds a supportive, caring atmosphere where she can unburden herself from all the years of pain and torture with women who know exactly what she has been through. But following 1 month or 2 months (or in rare instances 3 months) of this protected environment the woman's choice is to return to her husband or become totally independent. What kind of choice is that for someone who may just be beginning to develop a sense of her own self-worth but who does not yet have the money, the job skills, or the confidence to be completely on her own?

In too many shelters either there is no aftercare program whatsoever or aftercare consists only of a support group once a week which the women are invited to attend. If a woman does not return, no one calls to inquire about the way she is coping or to offer further assistance. Has she returned home to a husband who prohibits her from attending the meetings? Has she returned home because of her husband's promise to attend a counseling program for batterers—a promise which was not kept? Has she attempted to be independent and been unable to find adequate housing and a job? Is she having difficulty handling her children who, having been exposed to the repeated violence at home, may be exhibiting acting out and other problem behaviors? In an attempt to escape from the abusive husband has she become involved with another man, one who beats her just as the husband had done? No one knows.

What is desperately needed is a network of second-stage housing, clusters of apartments where women and their children can live by themselves or with another former battered woman. The insecure once-abused woman has a better chance of carving out a new life by living in an environment with easy access to women who share her traumatic history and who understand the entirely new set of problems with which she is confronted.

Walker (1979) describes the innovative provisions for extended assistance to abused women which exist in England. The British have developed second-stage and third-stage housing options so that a woman can adjust to being independent of her husband gradually, not in just a few weeks, as most of the American shelters require. At Chiswick Women's Aid, for example, all abused women are first housed in a "crisis-oriented receiving center." The emergency refuge is intended as a short-term center much like the American shelters. However, when a woman leaves a shelter in the United States, in almost all cases she is totally on her own. Not so at Chiswick, where she may transfer to one of many second-stage houses located in London as well as in other cities. Most of the second-stage residences can house about 20 persons, although there is one residence, a former hotel, which has a capacity of 80. Women and their children are permitted to live at these houses until they feel ready to be on their own. Under the British social security system, these women are eligible for a financial allowance. The houses are run communally, and everyone is expected to do her share.

Third-stage housing is available for women who want the communal life on a more permanent basis. The people living in long-term third-stage housing are able to develop a real affinity for one another and exhibit a true sense of community. Walker was impressed by the way in which these housing options served to benefit this special population. She concluded: "I was struck by what a beneficial alternative to the nuclear family this arrangement was for these women and children" (1979, p. 195).

For some women, leaving the husband to set up a new home across town is no solution. Even with the legal remedies at her disposal, a woman may live in terror that the batterer—incensed over the fact that his "possession" has walked out on him—will track her down and carry out his threat to kill her.

During the Civil War between the states thousands of black slaves were brought to freedom by means of Harriet Tubman's "underground railroad." Similarly, in some cases the enslaved wife may need an underground railroad to transport her to a new city and a new life. Such a system was begun in 1976 in Tampa, Florida, reports Carol Evans, president of the Abused Women's Alternative Resource Exchange, Inc. (AWARE) in St. Petersburg. The 1970s version of the underground railroad "allows threatened wives to be moved secretly to cities far enough from their husbands that they can feel safe" (Evans, 1978, p. 20). Such networks need to be further expanded so that shelters coast to coast can communicate with each other.

Networks have been established in areas around the country to unite shelters and coalition groups which serve battered women. For the most part they provide information, referrals, technical assistance, and community education to the shelters within their region as well as legislative and lobbying efforts at the state and national level. Further information on state and regional networks can be obtained by contacting:

Carol Lopes or Terry Berman, Western States Shelter Network, c/o Women's Litigation Center, 1095 Market Street, Room 416, San Francisco, Calif. 94103.
National Coalition Against Domestic Violence (NCADV), 1728 N Street, N.W., Suite 201, Washington, D.C. 20036.
Carol B. Evans, Abused Women's Alternative Resource Exchange, Inc., AWARE, P.O. Box 3154, St. Petersburg, Fla. 33731.
Kathleen Fotjik, NOW Domestic Violence/Victim Assistance Project, 1917 Washtenaw Avenue, Ann Arbor, Mich. 48104.
Joan Swan or Yolanda Bako, New York Coalition on Battered Women, c/o American Friends Service Committee, 15 Rutherford Place, New York, N.Y. 10003.
Jackie Lynch, Dyan Oldenburg, or Bonnie Tinker, Oregon Coalition against Domestic Violence, P.O. Box 40132, Portland, Ore. 97240.
Pennsylvania Coalition against Domestic Violence, c/o Lancaster Women's Shelter, 110 N. Lime Street, Lancaster, Pa. 17602.
Washington State Shelter Network, 829 Broadway Avenue W., Spokane, Wash. 99201.
National Women's Aid Federation, 15 Chalcot Road, London NW 1, England.

Conclusion

Wife assault is a criminal offense just as rape, attempted rape, armed robbery, and burglary are criminal offenses. Equitable treatment and legal protection for battered women will require a joint effort on the part of the human service and criminal justice professions and the community. The human service agencies in each community should feel obligated to make every effort to provide health and social services to these victims. Likewise the criminal justice agencies should provide increasing legal protection to spouse abuse victims while being sensitive to the volatile and life-threatening situations these women experience.

This book has examined crisis intervention programs for battered women throughout the United States. The primary premise is that until such time as men stop victimizing their wives comprehensive social service programs for these women must be accepted as a legitimate need and established in every community nationwide.

Bibliography

Abused Women's Project, Marathon Health Care Center, *Project Report: Phase I* (Wausau, Wisconsin: Abused Women's Project), February 1978, mimeographed.

Ackerman, Nathan. *The Psychodynamics of Family Life*. New York: Basic Books, 1958.

————. *Treating the Troubled Family*. New York: Basic Books, 1966.

Adams, Wanda. "A Man's Voice, a Woman's Scream, a Silence," (Everett, Wash.) *Everett Herald*, April 5, 1978, p. 10.

Adorno, T. W., E. Frenkel-Brunswik, D. J. Levenson, and N. Sanford. *The Authoritarian Personality*. New York: Harper & Row, 1950.

Antler, Stephen. Personal communication, January 30, 1980.

Ball, Margaret. "Issues of Violence in Family Casework," *Social Casework*, January 1977, pp. 3–12.

Bard, Morton. *The Function of Police in Crisis Intervention and Conflict Management: A Training Guide*. Washington, D.C.: U.S. Department of Justice, 1975.

Bard, Morton, and Joseph Zacker. "How Police Handle Explosive Squabbles: New Techniques Let Police Settle Arguments without Force," *Psychology Today*, November 1976, pp. 71–74, 113.

Barkas, J. L. *Victims*. New York: Scribner's, 1978.

Berg, Frances. "EMERGE Helps Violent Men Who Batter Women," (Lowell, Mass.) *The Sun*, Jaunary 22, 1979, p. 14.

Berkowitz, Leonard. "The Case for Bottling Up Rage," *Psychology Today*, July 1973, pp. 24–31.

Bode, Janet. *Fighting Back: How to Cope with the Medical, Emotional, and Legal Consequences of Rape*. New York: Macmillan, 1978.

Brownmiller, Susan. *Against Our Will*. New York: Simon & Schuster, 1975.

Center for Women Policy Studies. "Response to Violence in the Family," *Center Newsletter*, 2(1) (Oct. 1978), pp. 1–8; 2(2) (Nov./Dec. 1978,) p. 3; 2(3) (Jan. 1979) pp. 1–4; 2(8) (July 1979); 1–8.

Central Pennsylvania Legal Services. *Domestic Violence*. Harrisburg, Pa.: Author.

Chapman, Jane Roberts, and Margaret Gates (eds.). *Women into Wives: The Legal and Economic Impact of Marriage*. Beverly Hills, Calif.: Sage, 1977.

Chesler, Phyllis. *Women and Madness*. New York: Avon, 1972.

Chiswick Women's Aid. *Battered Wives Need a Refuge*. (mimeographed description of Chiswick Women's Aid, 369 High Road, London W4, England), 1977.

Costin, Lela B. *Child Welfare: Policies and Practice*. New York: McGraw-Hill, 1979.

Davidson, Terry. *Conjugal Crime: Understanding and Changing the Wifebeating Pattern*. New York: Hawthorn, 1978.

Dobash, Russell, and R. Emerson Dobash. "Wives: The 'Appropriate Victims' of Marital Violence," *Victimology: An International Journal*, 2(3–4) (1977–1978):426–442.

Eaton, Joseph W. *Culture and Mental Disorders*. Glencoe, Ill.: Free Press, 1955.

Ehlers, Walter H., Michael J. Austin, and Jon C. Prothero. *Administration for the Human Services*. New York: Harper & Row, 1976.

Eisenberg, Sue E., and Patricia L. Micklow. "The Assaulted Wife: 'Catch 22' Revisited," *Women's Rights Law Reporter*, 3(3–4) (Spring/Summer 1977):138–161.

Eisenman, Elaine. "The Origins and Practice of Family Therapy." In Peter J. Stein, et al. (eds.), *The Family: Functions, Conflicts and Symbols*. Reading, Mass.: Addison-Wesley, 1977, pp. 135–145.

Elbow, Margaret. "Theoretical Considerations of Violent Marriages," *Social Casework*, November, 1977, pp. 515–526.

Etzioni, Amitai. "Violence." In Robert K. Merton and Robert A. Nisbet (eds.), *Contemporary Social Problems*, 3rd ed. New York: Harcourt Brace Jovanovich, 1971.

Evans, Carol B. "How to Start Your Own Spouse Abuse Shelter." In *Access*. Tallahassee, Fla.: Department of Health and Rehabilitation Services, 1978, pp. 19–21.

Field, Martha H., and Henry F. Field. "Marital Violence and the Criminal Process: Neither Justice nor Peace," *Social Service Review*, 47(2) (1973):221–240.

Fields, Marjory D. "Wife Beating: The Hidden Offense," *New York Law Journal*, 175(83) (April 29, 1976):1–7.

———. *The Battered Woman Syndrome: The Lawyer and the Psychologists* (mimeographed), 1977, 12 pp.

———. "Representing Battered Wives, or What to Do Until the Police Arrive," *Family Law Reporter*, 3(22) (Apr. 1977), Monograph No. 25, 5 pp.

Fields, Marjory D., and Rioghan M. Kirchner. "Battered Women Are Still in Need: An Answer to Suzanne Steinmetz," *Victimology*, 3(1–2) (1978):216–222.

Fields, Marjory D., and Elyse Lehman. *A Handbook for Beaten Women*. New York: Brooklyn Legal Services Corp. B, 1977.

Finkelhor, David. *Sexually Abused Children*. New York: Free Press, 1979.

Fleming, Jennifer. *Family Violence: A Look at the Criminal Justice System* (unpublished paper available from Women's Resource Network, 4025 Chestnut St., Philadelphia, Pa. 19104), 1978.

Flynn, John P. "Recent Findings Related to Wife Abuse," *Social Casework,* January 1977, pp. 13–20.

Fojtik, Kathleen M. *Wife Beating: How to Develop a Wife Assault Task Force and Project.* Ann Arbor, Mich.: Ann Arbor–Washtenaw County NOW Wife Assault Task Force, 1976.

Foundation News, 19(4) (July/Aug. 1978):3.

———, 20(1) (Jan./Feb. 1979):3–15.

Fromson, Terry. "The Case for Legal Remedies for Abused Women," *New York University Review of Law and Social Change,* 6(Spring 1977):135–174.

Geller, Janet A. *Reaching the Battering Husband* (unpublished paper available from Victims Information Bureau of Suffolk County, Hauppauge, N.Y. 11787) 1977.

Gelles, Richard J. *The Violent Home.* Beverly Hills, Calif.: Sage, 1972.

———. "Violence and Pregnancy: A Note on the Extent of the Problem and Needed Services," *Family Coordinator,* 24(Jan. 1975):81–86.

Gil, David G. *Violence against Children: Physical Abuse in the United States.* Cambridge: Harvard University Press, 1970.

Gingold, Judith. "One of These Days—POW Right in the Kisser," *Ms. Magazine,* August 1976, pp. 51–54.

Goode, William J. "Force and Violence in the Family," *Journal of Marriage and the Family,* 33(Nov. 1971):624–636.

Gordon, Thomas. *P.E.T.: Parent Effectiveness Training.* New York: New American Library, 1975.

———. *P.E.T. in Action.* New York: Wyden, 1976.

Haffner, Sarah. "Victimology Interview: A Refuge for Battered Women," *Victimology: An International Journal,* 4(1) (1979):100–112.

Haley, Jay. *Problem-solving Therapy.* San Francisco: Jossey-Bass, 1977.

Haley, Sharman. Personal communication, February 8, 1979.

Hankoff, Leon D. *Emergency Psychiatric Treatment: A Handbook of Secondary Prevention.* Springfield, Ill.: Thomas, 1969.

Hankoff, Leon D., and Bernice Einsidler (eds.). *Suicide: Theory and Clinical Aspects.* Littleton, Mass.: PSG, 1979.

Hepperle, Winifred L., and Laura Crites (eds.). *Women in the Courts.* Williamsburg, Va.: National Center for State Courts, 1978.

Higgins, John G. "Social Services for Abused Wives," *Social Casework,* May 1978, pp. 266–271.

Holmstrom, Linda Lytle, and Ann Wolbert Burgess. *The Victim of Rape: Institutional Reactions.* New York: Wiley, 1978.

Jobling, Megan. "Battered Wives: A Survey," *Social Service Quarterly,* 47(4) (Apr./June 1974):142–146.

Johns, Ray. *Executive Responsibility.* New York: Association Press, 1966.

Johnson, Carolyn, John Ferry, and Marjorie Kravitz. *Spouse Abuse: A Selected Bibliography.* Rockville, Md.: National Criminal Justice Reference Service, 1979.

176 : : *Sheltering Battered Women*

Kamerman, Sheila B. and Alfred J. Kahn (eds). *Family Policy: Government and Families in Fourteen Countries*. New York: Columbia University Press, 1978.

————. "Comparative Analysis in Family Policy: A Case Study," *Social Work*, November, 1979, 506–512.

Kim, Bok-Lim. "Response of Bok-Lim Kim." In U.S. Commission on Civil Rights, *Battered Women: Issues of Public Policy*. Washington, D.C.: The Commission, Publications Management Division, 1978, pp. 133–137.

Kliman, Ann S. *Crisis: Psychological First Aid for Recovery and Growth*. New York: Holt, Rinehart & Winston, 1978.

LaFave, Wayne R. *Principles of Criminal Law: Cases, Comments and Questions*. St. Paul, Minn.: West, 1978.

Langley, Roger, and Richard C. Levy. "Wife Abuse: Why Will a Woman Stay and Take It?" *New Woman*, July/August 1977, pp. 90–91.

————. *Wife Beating: The Silent Crisis*. New York: Dutton, 1977.

Lewis, Marianna O. (ed.). *The Foundation Directory*, 6th and 7th ed. New York: The Foundation Center, 1977 and 1979.

Mahaffey, Maryann. "Sexism and Social Work," *Social Work*, 21(6) (1976):419–420.

Martin, Del. *Battered Wives*. San Francisco: Glide, 1976.

McGrath, Albertus Magnus, Sr. *What a Modern Catholic Believes about Women*. Chicago, Ill.: Thomas More, 1972.

Michigan Women's Commission. *Domestic Assault: A Report on Family Violence in Michigan*. Lansing: State of Michigan, 1977.

Minuchin, Salvadore. *Families and Family Therapy*. Cambridge: Harvard University Press, 1974.

Munson, Carlton E. (ed). *Social Work Supervision: Classic Statements and Critical Issues*. New York: The Free Press, 1979.

————. "Supervising the Family Therapist," *Social Casework*, March, 1980, 131–137.

Nadolsky, Julian M. *Development of a Model for Vocational Evaluation of the Disadvantaged* (monograph, Auburn University), September 1971.

Nichols, Beverly B. "The Abused Wife Problem." *Social Casework*, January 1976, pp. 27–32.

Noe, Lee (ed.). *Foundation Grants Index 1977*. New York: The Foundation Center, 1978.

Office of Legislative Research. *Selected Report 78–30*. Hartford, Conn.: Joint Committee on Legislative Management, the Connecticut General Assembly, February 17, 1978.

"Pennsylvania Code, Chapter 35, Sections 10181–10190," *Family Law Reporter*, 3(8) (Dec. 21, 1976):3031.

Perkins, Carol. "Salvation Army Has Shelter for Abused Wives," *Seattle Post Intelligence*, March 26, 1978.

Pizzey, Erin. *Scream Quietly or the Neighbors Will Hear*. Short Hills, N.J.: Ridley Enslow, 1977.

Potter, Joan. "Police and the Battered Wife," *Police Magazine*, 1(4) (Sept. 1978): 40–53.

Proctor, Pam. "Dr. Karl Menninger Pleads: Stop Beating Your Kids," *Parade*, October 9, 1977, pp. 24–25.

Resnik, Mindy. *Wife Beating: Counseling Training Manual No. 1.* Ann Arbor, Mich.: Ann Arbor NOW Wife Assault Task Force, 1976.

Richette, Lisa. "Long Term Needs: Presentation of Lisa Richette." In U.S. Commission on Civil Rights, *Battered Women: Issues of Public Policy*. Washington, D.C.: the Commission, Publications Management Division, 1978.

Roberts, Albert R. (ed.). *Childhood Deprivation*. Springfield, Ill.: Thomas, 1974.

――――. "Police Social Workers: A History," *Social Work*, 14(2) (1976):98–103.

Roberts, Fletcher. "Woman Abuse Problem Faced," *Boston Globe*, January 22, 1979, p. 19.

Robinson, Walter V. "Help for Abused Springing Up," *Boston Globe*, June 8, 1978, p. 20.

Roy, Maria (ed.). *Battered Women: A Psycho-sociological Study of Domestic Violence*. New York: Van Nostrand Reinhold, 1977.

Ruether, Rosemary Radfird (ed.). *Religion and Sexism*. New York: Simon & Schuster, 1974.

Schickling, Barbara M. "Relief for Victims of Intra-family Assault—the Pennsylvania Protection from Abuse Act," *Dickinson Law Review*, 81(4) (1977):815–822.

Schuyler, Marcella. "Battered Wives: An Emerging Social Problem," *Social Work*, 21(6) (1976):488–491.

Sorenson, Roy. *The Art of Board Membership*. New York: Association Press, 1950.

State of Florida. "House Bill 74—Spouse Abuse"; "Senate Bill 409—Spouse Abuse Centers." *1978 Supplement to Florida Statutes*, effective October 1, 1978.

State of Maryland. "Article 88A and 101 Battered Spouses Shelter." *Annotated Code of Maryland, 1978 Cumulative Supplement*. Annapolis: General Assembly of Maryland, 1978.

State of Massachusetts. Chapters 447 and 209A, "Abuse Prevention Act." *Legislative Document of the Commonwealth of Massachusetts*, 1978.

State of Pennsylvania. "Act 218—Protection from Abuse Act." *Laws of Pennsylvania, 1976*.

State of Wisconsin. "WLCS: 132/1." *Domestic Abuse Act*, December 11, 1978.

Steinmetz, Suzanne K. "The Battered Husband Syndrome," *Victimology: An International Journal*, 2(3–4) (1977–1978):499–509.

――――. *The Cycle of Violence: Assertive, Aggressive and Abusive Family Interaction*. New York: Praeger, 1977.

Steinmetz, Suzanne K., and Murray A. Straus (eds.). *Violence in the Family*. New York: Harper & Row, 1974.

Stephen, Beverly. "My Husband Beats Me," *Sunday News Magazine*, September 18, 1977, pp. 15 & 17.

Straus, Murray A. "Sexual Inequality, Cultural Norms and Wife Beating." In Emilio C. Viano (ed.), *Victims and Society*. Washington, D.C.: Visage, 1976. (Reprinted in Jane Roberts Chapman and Margaret Gates (eds.), *Women into Wives*. Beverly Hills, Calif.: Sage, 1977.)

――――. "Societal Morphogenesis and Intrafamily Violence in Cross-Cultural Perspective." In Lenore Loeb Adler (ed.), *Issues in Cross-Cultural Research in the Annals of the New York Academy of Science*, 285(1977):717–730.

――――. "A Sociological Perspective on the Prevention and Treatment of Wifebeat-

178 : : *Sheltering Battered Women*

ing." In Maria Roy (ed.), *Battered Women: A Psycho-sociological Study of Domestic Violence*. New York: Van Nostrand Reinhold, 1977.

————. "Wife Beating: How Common and Why?" *Victimology: An International Journal*, 2(3–4) (1977/1978):443–458.

————. *A Sociological Perspective on the Causes of Family Violence*. (paper presented at the Annual Conference of the American Association for the Advancement of Science, Houston, January 1979).

Straus, Murray A., and Bruce W. Brown. *Family Measurement Techniques*, 2nd ed. Minneapolis: University of Minnesota Press, 1979.

Straus, Murray A., Richard Gelles, and Suzanne K. Steinmetz. *Behind Closed Doors: Violence in the American Family*. New York: Doubleday/Anchor, 1979.

Swan, Joan. Personal communication, April 18, 1979.

U.S. Commission on Civil Rights. *Battered Women: Issues of Public Policy*. Washington, D.C.: The Commission, Publications Management Division, 1978. (This reference contains the proceedings of the Consultation on Battered Women sponsored by the Commission on January 30–31, 1978).

U.S. Department of Justice. *FBI Uniform Crime Reports*. Washington, D.C.: The Department of Justice, 1975.

————. *FBI Uniform Crime Reports*. Washington, D.C.: The Department of Justice, 1979.

Valente, Judith. "Domestic Violence Surveyed," *Washington Post*, February 27, 1979, pp. C1, C3.

Vaughn, Sharon Rice. "The Last Refuge: Shelter for Battered Women," *Victimology: An International Journal*, 4(1) (1979):113–150.

Walker, Lenore E. *The Battered Woman*. New York: Harper & Row, 1979.

Warrior, Betsy. *Working on Wife Abuse*, 6th ed. (mimeographed copies available from Ms. Warrior, 46 Pleasant St., Cambridge, Mass. 02139), 1978. First edition published in April, 1976.

Wolley, Sabra F. *Battered Women: A Summary*. Washington, D.C.: Women's Equity Action League, 1978.

Selected Newsletters

The following national newsletters will be useful to individuals and agencies interested in keeping abreast of the latest developments in the field of family violence. All of the publications mentioned are available at no charge.

Concern

Emilio C. Viano, Project Director
National Victim/Witness Resource Center
108A South Columbus Street
Alexandria, VA 22314

This monthly newsletter provides information on the status of federal and state legislation, legal developments, upcoming conferences, resource materials, research summaries, and news briefs in the victim/witness field.

NCADV Newsletter

National Coalition against Domestic Violence
1728 N Street, N.W., Suite 201
Washington, D.C. 20036

As of April 1980, NCADV was in the process of setting up a national office. The first edition of their newsletter was scheduled to appear during the summer of 1980, while this book was in press.

Response to Violence in the Family

Center for Women Policy Studies
2000 P Street, N.W., Suite 508
Washington, D.C. 20036

This monthly newsletter focuses on pending legislation, legal developments, research summaries, grant awards, publications available through the National Clearinghouse on Domestic Violence, new books and films, and upcoming conferences on violence and sexual abuse in the family.

SANE News: A National Newsletter on Battered Women

Community Health Center, Inc.
P.O. Box 1076
Middletown, CT 06457

This quarterly newsletter provides information on volunteerism, grantsmanship, legislation, and shelters and services for battered women.

APPENDIXES

APPENDICES

Directory of 89 Intervention Programs

Alaska

Juneau

Aiding Women from Abuse and Rape Emergencies (AWARE)
Room 503, Goldstein Building (99801)
(907) 586–6624
Caren Robinson, Shelter Director
24-hour hotline and shelter utilizing a network of safe homes; opened in 1977; staffed by 2 full-time and 1 part-time co-directors, 1 lawyer (volunteer), 10 volunteers, 1 CETA worker, 2 VISTA workers, and 1 secretary.

Special features. Counseling and legal advocacy, and community education; referrals are made, as needed.

Arizona

Phoenix

Rainbow Retreat, Inc.
4647 North 12th Street (85014)
(602) 263–1113
Elfrieda Russ, Administrative Assistant
24-hour hotline and shelter located in 2 buildings; opened in 1974; staffed by 6 full-time and 2 part-time counselors, 1 consulting social worker and 1 consulting psychologist, 1 vocational counselor, 4 CETA workers, 3 volun-

teers, 1 nurse intern, 1 consulting lawyer, 5 former battered women, 2 undergraduate and 2 graduate students, 5 clerical workers, 1 cook, 1 child attendant, 1 data clerk, 1 bookkeeper, and 1 administrative assistant; the program serves battered women and alcohol abusers.

Special features. Individual and group counseling, family therapy, legal advocacy, vocational services, research, individual and group out-patient program, children's program, court diversion to counseling for victim and assailant.

California

Fresno

Services for Abused Females Ent., Inc. (SAFE)
1334 East Belmont Avenue (93701)
(209) 268–6377
Randy G. Gillet, Program Director
24-hour hotline and shelter; opened in 1977; staffed by 7 CETA workers, 1 volunteer, 2 former battered women, 1 psychologist, 1 undergraduate student, 2 graduate students, and 1 secretary.

Special features. Emergency crisis counseling, long-term counseling, support groups, family therapy, and community education; SAFE serves as a clearinghouse for relevant literature. Referrals are made for legal services information, vocational services, housing information, and medical and psychological services.

Livermore

Tri-Valley Haven for Women
P.O. Box 188 (94550)
(415) 443–1955
Cathie L. C. Brown, Director (unpaid)
24-hour hotline and shelter, using network of private homes, opened in 1977; staffed by 2 full-time and 12 part-time volunteers, 3 CETA workers, 2 former battered women, 2 consultant lawyers, and 1 undergraduate student.

Long Beach

Carrie Walker Emergency House
c/o Long Beach YWCA
3636 Atlantic Avenue (90805)
(213) 432–5471
Clarice Butler, Resource Coordinator

Temporary emergency shelter provided for both abused and nonabused women; affiliated with the YWCA; opened in 1978; staffed by 1 program coordinator, 1 resource coordinator, 1 director, 1 assistant director, 8 CETA workers, and 3 counselors; specialized services are arranged through referral.

Orange

Women's Transitional Living Center, Inc.
P.O. Box 6103 (92667)
(714) 992–1931
Alice Oksman-Banner, Executive Director
24-hour hotline and shelter; opened in 1976; staffed by 1 psychologist, 3 CETA workers, and an unspecified number of counselors, former battered women (who volunteer their time), volunteers, graduate and undergraduate students, clerical staff, and lawyers available through the Community Women's Law Center.
Special features. Individual and group counseling, legal advocacy, vocational services and research; family therapy by referral to the Family Service Association.

Sacramento

Womanspace
P.O. Box 160994 (95816)
(416) 446–2811
24-hour hotline and shelter; opened in 1977; staffed by 1 counselor full time, 1 part-time counselor, 8 volunteers, 9 CETA workers, and 3 full-time and 1 part-time staff through revenue sharing. Of these staff, 11 persons are former battered women.
Special features. Individual and group counseling, family therapy, legal advocacy, peer counseling, and advocacy regarding schooling, housing, welfare, and the police.

San Jose

Brandon House-Volunteers of America
1716 East San Antonio (95116)
(408) 258–6146
Jerry G. Hawkins, Executive Director
Temporary shelter for abused women; staffed by an unspecified number of psychologists, counselors, volunteers, CETA workers, former battered

women, graduate students, nurses, clerical staff, cooks, and maintenance workers. The shelter is affiliated with the Volunteers of America, which has been in existence for 47 years.

Special features. Individual and group counseling.

San Luis Rey

Women's Resource Center
4070 Mission Avenue (92068)
(714) 757–3500
Colleen Richardson, Executive Director
24-hour hotline and shelter, using a network of private homes; opened in 1974; staffed by 1 counselor, 1 psychologist, 3 CETA workers, 1 former battered woman, and 1 secretary.

Special features. Individual and group counseling, family therapy.

San Mateo

La Casa de San Mateo
P.O. Box 652 (94401)
(415) 342–3404
Constance B. Castaneda, Coordinator
At the time this program responded to the survey (June 1978) they were *not yet operational,* but they expected to open their doors during 1978 and to provide 24-hour hotline and shelter; staffed by 2 coordinators and an unspecified number of volunteers, CETA workers, former battered women, undergraduate and graduate students, and a bookkeeper.

Special features. Group rap sessions and legal advocacy.

Santa Rosa

YWCA Women's Emergency Shelter Program
P.O. Box 3506 (95402)
(707) 546–1477
Linda Reitzell, Client Services Coordinator
24-hour hotline and shelter, opened in June 1977; staffed by 25 volunteers, 10 CETA workers, 1 counselor, 1 vocational counselor, 4 former battered women, 1 graduate student, and 1 secretary.

Special features. Individual and group counseling; vocational services.

Connecticut

Meriden-Wallingford

Battered Women's Shelter
P.O. Box 663
(203) 238–1501
Sue O'Connor, Administrative Assistant
24-hour hotline and shelter; opened in February 1978; staffed by 3 social workers, 3 counselors, 1 psychologist, 10 volunteers, 8 CETA workers, 7 former battered women, 1 undergraduate student, and 1 clerical worker.
Special features. Individual and group counseling, family therapy, legal advocacy, and vocational services.

Florida

Jacksonville

Hubbard House, Women's Rape Crisis Center
1231 Hubbard Street (32206)
(904) 354-3114
Brenda Andrews, Clerical Worker
24-hour hotline and shelter facility which can house a maximum of 22 people; opened in 1976; staffed by an unspecified number of social workers, counselors, volunteers, CETA workers, former battered women, graduate and undergraduate students, and clerical workers.
Special features. Individual and group counseling, marriage counseling (when requested), and referrals to Legal Aid and private attorneys.

Miami

Safespace: Battered Women's Shelter
P.O. Box 186 (33137)
(305) 579–2915
Sarah M. Lenett, Coordinator
24-hour hotline and shelter utilizing the top floor of an apartment building; opened in 1977; staffed by 1 administrative officer, 6 counselors, 2 social workers, 1 CETA worker, and 1 former battered woman.
Special features. Civil Assist-Escort woman with assistance of police officer, to victim's home to retrieve her personal belongings; individual and group counseling, family therapy, and legal advocacy.

St. Petersburg

Abused Women's Alternative Resource Exchange (AWARE)
P.O. Box 3154 (33731)
(813) 896-0395
Carol B. Evans, President
24-hour hotline and shelter provided at one central facility and at private homes, as needed; opened in 1977; staffed by 1 social worker, 2 counselors, 5 attorneys (part time), 2 CETA workers, 3 former battered women, 2 undergraduates and 1 graduate student, and 1 secretary. In addition, a registered nurse from the County Health Department makes regular visits; psychiatrists and psychologists are available if needed; a vocational counselor is available from the state employment office, and a physician from the nearby Family Practice Center is available at all times.

Special features. Individual and group counseling, legal advocacy, vocational services, transportation to obtain needed services, research, emergency food and food stamps, clothing and medical attention.

Tampa

The Spring, Inc.
P.O. Box 11087 (33610)
(813) 835-9481
Cathie A. Lundin, Administrative Assistant
24-hour hotline and shelter; opened in 1977; staffed by an unspecified number of volunteers, CETA workers, and former battered women.

Special features. Individual and group counseling.

West Palm Beach

Domestic Assault Shelter
c/o YWCA
901 South Olive (33401)
(305) 833-2439
Mary Kay Murray, Director/Social Worker
24-hour hotline and shelter; staffed by 4 CETA workers, 2 social workers, 1 counselor, 2 students, 1 secretary, and 1 maintenance worker. It shelters an average of 38 persons (women and their children) each month.

Special features. In-service meetings with local police, presentations on radio and television talk shows, to church groups, and women's organizations; also individual and group counseling, legal aid services, and legislative advocacy.

Georgia

Marietta

YWCA Battered Women's Crisis Center
48 Henderson Street (30064)
(404) 973–8890
Diane Kuzeff, Director
Hotline and shelter services; hotline operational Monday through Friday, 8:00 A.M. to 6:00 P.M.; affiliated with the YWCA; opened in February 1978; staffed by a director, 3 counselors, 5 volunteer lawyers, 30 volunteers, 5 CETA workers, 2 former battered women, and 1 secretary.

Special features. Individual counseling and referral for specialized services as needed.

Hawaii

Honolulu

Shelter for Abused Spouses and Children
1888 Owawa Street (96819)
(808) 841–0822
Elizabeth Nelson, Administrative Assistant
24-hour hotline and shelter; opened in 1975; staffed by 20–30 volunteers, 1 social worker, 1 former battered woman, and 1 CETA worker; 1 lawyer and 1 psychiatrist volunteer their time.

Idaho

Pocatello

Women's Advocates
c/o 454 North Garfield (83201)
(208) 232–0742; crisis line: (208) 232–9169
Jeanne Poole, Coordinator
24-hour hotline and shelter, using private homes when the shelter facility is overcrowded; opened in March 1977; staffed mostly by volunteers: 3 counselors, 5 nurses, 1 lawyer, and 10 former battered women, all of whom volunteer their time. In addition there are 45 nonprofessional volunteers, an unspecified number of graduate and undergraduate students, and 1 CETA worker.

Special features. Counseling and referral for other services as needed.

Illinois

Alton

Oasis Women's Center, Inc.
P.O. Box 1162 (62002)
(618) 466-8725
Carol Woody, Director

At the time of the center's response to the survey (July 1978), they were *not yet operational*, but the director anticipated the following full services by late summer 1978: 24-hour hotline and shelter for women in crisis, including battered women; staffed by 1 social worker, 30 volunteers, 3 CETA workers, and 2 undergraduate students.

Special features. The goal is to provide immediate access to information and referral services from the many social, health, and welfare resources in the county.

Iowa

Cedar Falls

Family Violence Intervention
524 Main Street (50613)
crisis line: (319) 277–4735;
business line: (319) 268–0141, extension 261
Judith M. Copella, Coordinator

24-hour hotline; shelter provided through network of private homes; staffed by 1 social worker, 1 counselor, 8 volunteers, 4 former battered women, and 3 students.

Special features. Counseling, public education, and public speaking; referral to other agencies when appropriate.

Kansas

Wichita

Wichita Women's Crisis Center
1158 North Waco (67213)
(316) 263–9806

24-hour hotline and shelter; opened in 1976; staffed by 20 volunteers, 3 CETA workers, 2 former battered women, and 1 clerical worker.

Special features. Individual counseling and legal advocacy.

Maryland

Silver Spring

Abused Persons Program of Montgomery County
8500 Colesville Road (20910)
crisis line: (301) 279–1331
Business line: (301) 565–5770
Cynthia L. Anderson, Supervisor

24-hour hotline and shelter; opened in January 1977; staffed by 4 CETA workers, 3 social workers, and 1 secretary.

Special features. County police work closely with the program; a mobile unit is available to pick up the victim if necessary; individual and group counseling; family therapy and legal advocacy.

Massachusetts

Acton

CODE, Inc.
P.O. Box 767
136 Main Street (01720)
(617) 263–8777
Betsy Fonta, Executive Director

Telephone crisis intervention available 24 hours a day; open in 1970; staffed by 4 counselors, 45 volunteers, 1 CETA worker, and 1 clerical worker.

Special features. Legal advocacy and referral to emergency shelter and other services as needed.

Cambridge

Transition House
c/o The Women's Center
46 Pleasant Street (02139)
(617) 354–02676
Susan Ketcham, Fund-raising Committee

24-hour hotline and shelter; opened in 1975; staffed by 40 volunteers, 6 former battered women, and 4 CETA workers.

Special features. Individual peer counseling; emphasis on self-help.

Lawrence

Women's Resource Center
Greater Lawrence YWCA
38 Lawrence Street (01840)
(617) 685–2480
Emily Defusco Perkins, Director

24-hour crisis service which provides shelter to abused women through a volunteer network of private homes; administrative offices located in the YWCA; staffed by 12 volunteers, 6 CETA workers, 2 counselors, and 1 secretary.

Special features. Family therapy and legislative advocacy.

Lowell

Alternative House
P.O. Box 2096
Highland Station (01851)
(617) 454–1436
Beverly Gelzinis, Coordinator

24-hour hotline and shelter, utilizing private homes; opened in February 1978; staff includes volunteers, CETA workers, former battered women, and a nurse.

Special features. Counseling and legal advocacy.

Natick

Women against Violence
YWCA
105 Hartford Street 01760
(617) 872–6161 or 369–6112
Jean Panke, Communications Assistant

24-hour hotline and temporary emergency shelter affiliated with the YWCA; opened in November 1977; staffed by 1 social worker, 2 lawyers, 27 volunteers, and 13 CETA workers; 80 percent of the staff is comprised of former battered women; a vocational counselor is available part time through the YWCA Women's Resource Center.

Special features. Individual counseling, support groups given by battered women for battered women; legal, welfare, and housing advocacy. At the time of the survey, outreach group counseling was being initiated in the Hispanic community.

Somerville

RESPOND
1 Summer Street (02143)
(617) 623–5900
Emily O'Brien, Outreach Worker
Telephone crisis intervention available Monday through Friday during the day; temporary shelter in a shelter facility; private homes also used as needed; opened in 1973; staffed by 1 consulting social worker and psychiatrist, 6 CETA workers, 6 volunteers, 4 former battered women, 1 nurse on call, 1 graduate student, and 1 secretary; legal assistance available through a lawyer on the board of directors.
Special features. Individual and group counseling, legal advocacy, vocational services, social services advocacy, and child care program.

Worcester

Abby's House
P.O. Box 176 West Side (01608)
(617) 756–5486
Sr. Annette Rafferty
Telephone crisis intervention available nights only, 7 days a week; temporary shelter available for a broadly based clientele including battered women; opened in June 1976; staffed by an unspecified number of social workers, volunteers, former battered women, graduate and undergraduate students. Due to staff commitments during the day, it is possible for Abby's House to be open only from 7:00 P.M. until after breakfast the next morning. Women are given shelter for 1–5 nights.
Special features. Individual counseling, food and clothing for low-income women, and referral for specialized services as needed.

Michigan

Ann Arbor

Domestic Violence Project/SAFE House
1917 Washtenaw Avenue (48104)
(313) 995–5460 or 995–5444
Rachel Shaw, Office Manager
Shelter available 24 hours a day; opened in 1977; staffed by a director, 6 volunteers, 5 CETA workers, 1 counselor, 2 graduate students, and 2 VISTA workers; most clients referred by Assault Crisis Center.

Special features. Assistance in relocating. Also located at the same address is the National Coalition against Domestic Violence, an advocate for state and federal legislation and public education on family violence. The contact person there is Kathleen M. Fojtik.

Kalamazoo

Women's Crisis Center
211 South Rose (49007)
(616) 343–9496
Carolyn A. Krill, Director

24-hour hotline and shelter affiliated with the YWCA; opened in 1976; staffed by an unspecified number of social workers, counselors, and volunteers.

Special features. Individual and group counseling, legal advocacy, vocational services, child care, and advocacy in financial aid, housing, school, etc.

Muskegon

Rape/Spouse Assault Crisis Center (of Every Woman's Place, Inc.)
29 Strong Avenue (49441)
(616) 726–4493
Sue A. Ashby, Program Coordinator

24-hour hotline and shelter; opened in 1977; staffed by 60 volunteers, 5 CETA workers, 2 counselors, 1 psychologist, 1 lawyer, 1 volunteer coordinator, 1 shelter manager, and 1 secretary.

Special features. Legal advocacy, vocational services, individual and group counseling.

Saginaw

Perfect Place
c/o 1110 Howard (48601)
(517) 754–8361
Kathy Prevost, Director

24-hour hotline and shelter for women 17 years and older with various problems; approximately 20 percent of clients are abused women; opened in 1977; staffed by 1 social worker and 7 counselors, with access to clerical staff as needed.

Special features. Individual counseling provided at the center; family therapy, legal advocacy, and vocational services available by referral.

St. Joseph

YWCA Spouse Assault Program
508 Pleasant Street (49085)
(616) 983–1561
Margaret Howard, Coordinator
24-hour hotline and shelter; opened in July 1978; staffed by 12 volunteers,
1 CETA worker, 2 counselors, 1 secretary, and 1 director.

Traverse City

Women's Resource Center
932 East Eighth Street (49684)
(616) 941–1210
Page Phillips, Counselor
Open 8:30 A.M. to 5:30 P.M. weekdays; emergency shelter provided
through network of private homes of local NOW members; opened in 1975;
staffed by 15 volunteers, 10 CETA workers, and 2 counselors.
Special features. Counseling, career library, and newsletter.

Ypsilanti

Assault Crisis Center
561 North Hewitt Road (48197)
(313) 434–9881
Jody Bisdee, Coordinator
24-hour hotline and shelter serving victims of battering and rape; temporary emergency housing available through private homes; opened in 1977;
staffed by 9 counselors, 1 social worker, 4–7 volunteers, and 1 clerical
worker.
Special features. Short-term individual counseling, legal advocacy,
and advocacy in court.

Minnesota

Austin

Victims Crisis Center
908 Northwest First Drive (55912)
(507) 437–6680
Vivian Lea Miller, Undergraduate Student Advocate
24-hour hotline and shelter in private homes, hotels, and motels; crisis

center located in a mental health center; opened in 1977; staffed by 1 counselor, 15 volunteers, and 1 undergraduate student.
Special features. Counseling and legal advocacy.

St. Cloud

St. Cloud Area Women's Center
1900 Minnesota Boulevard (56301)
(612) 252–8831
Colleen M. Anderson, Volunteer Coordinator for Battered Women's Task Force
24-hour hotline and shelter, utilizing a shelter facility and private volunteer homes; opened in August 1978; staffed by 2 counselors, 2 vocational counselors, 15 volunteers, an unspecified number of former battered women, 1 undergraduate and 1 graduate student, and 1 secretary.
Special features. Individual counseling provided at center; group counseling provided at mental health center; legal advocacy and vocational services.

St. Paul

Women's Advocates
584 Grand (55102)
(612) 227–8284
24-hour hotline and shelter; opened in april 1972; staffed by 10 volunteers, 5 CETA workers, 10 advocates, 1 lawyer part time, and an unspecified number of former battered women.
Special features. Support groups, child advocacy, and legal advocacy provided at the shelter; family therapy and vocational services available through referral.

Nevada

Las Vegas

Women's Crisis Shelter
P.O. Box 43264 (89104)
(702) 382–4428
Kate Shronmeyer, Gale Robinson, and Nancy Sutton
24-hour hotline and shelter; opened in June 1978; staffed by 1 shelter program coordinator, 1 direct service coordinator, 16 volunteers (of whom

3 are former battered women), 2 CETA workers, 6 VISTA workers, and 1 CETA-paid secretary.
   Special features. Support groups for battered women.

New Jersey

Elizabeth

Battered Women Project
YWCA of Elizabeth
1131 East Jersey Street (07201)
(201) 355-HELP
Paula T. Fenance, Project Coordinator
24-hour hotline and shelter, affiliated with the YWCA; opened in April 1978; staffed by 1 social worker, 2 CETA workers, an unspecified number of volunteers and former battered women, a teacher, and a sociologist.
   Special features. Individual and group counseling and legal advocacy by the project; vocational services provided through referral.

New Brunswick

Women's Crisis Center
56 College Avenue (08901)
(201) 932-7599
Anne Camoratto, Counselor
Hotline services provided 9:00 A.M. to 4:00 P.M. and 8:00 P.M. to midnight, 7 days a week; emergency shelter provided through a network of private homes; affiliated with Rutger's University; opened in 1974; staffed by 25 volunteers, of whom an unspecified number are counselors, former battered women, and graduate and undergraduate students.
   Special features. Individual counseling, transportation to court, and referral to specialized services, as needed.

New Mexico

Albuquerque

Women's Community Association Shelter for Victims of Domestic Violence
P.O. Box 6472 (87197)
crisis line: (505) 247-4219; administration: (505) 299-7845
   E. Armstrong, Administrative Assistant
24-hour hotline and shelter; opened in 1977; staffed by 11 counselors, 1

vocational counselor, 3 psychologists, 3 former battered women, 6 law students, 1 undergraduate student, 1 teacher, and 1 secretary.

Special features. Counseling, vocational services, legal advocacy, nutritional assistance, outreach services to abusers and battered men.

Santa Fe

Battered Women's Project
P.O. Box 1501 (87501)
(505) 988–9731
Sharon Gardner, Counselor

24-hour hotline and shelter; opened in March 1978; staffed by 1 consulting psychiatrist, 10 volunteers, 10 CETA workers (of whom 6 are counselors and 3 are social workers), 2 former battered women, 1 undergraduate student, and 1 secretary.

Special features. Individual and group counseling, family therapy, legal advocacy, research, and transportation to obtain needed services.

New York

Binghamton

YWCA Interfaith Room
YWCA of Binghamton and Broome County (13901)
(607) 772–0340
Kathy Fennell, Residence Counselor

Shelter available 24 hours a day at the YWCA; opened in 1975; staffed by 2 volunteers, 1 CETA counselor, and 2 counselors (weekends only).

Special features. Serves women in crisis, no matter what its origin.

Brooklyn

Women's Survival Space
P.O. Box 279, Bay Ridge Station (11220)
crisis line: (212) 439–7281; business line: (212) 439–4612
Ann Salmirs, Executive Director
Anne McGlinchey, Coordinator

24-hour hotline and shelter located in former maternity hospital; opened in September 1977; 36 beds; average length of stay 25 days, with some women staying for over 4 months; staffed by 10 volunteers, 4 counselors, 2 former battered women, and 2 secretaries; also, part-time recreation aide, community organizer, teachers assistant, and nutritionist.

Special features. Welfare and court advocacy provided by Brooklyn College student interns; group therapy for children residents (average age 5) led by child psychologist (volunteer).

Canton

North Country Women's Center, Inc.
P.O. Box 474 (13617)
(315) 386–4130
Rebecca Wilson, Staffer
24-hour hotline and shelter; opened in 1976; at the time of the survey, the center was located in an apartment and was looking for a house to buy or rent; staffed by 1 social worker, 1 nurse, 17 CETA workers, 5 volunteers, and 1 former battered woman.
Special features. Women who need specialized services are referred by center staff.

Cortland

Aid to Women Victims of Violence
c/o YWCA
14 Clayton Avenue (13045)
(607) 756–6363
Linda A. Hanrahan, Coordinator
24-hour hotline and shelter, affiliated with the YWCA; opened in October 1977; staffed by 35 volunteers and 1 coordinator, who is paid through CETA.
Special features. Counseling, community education, and speakers bureau.

Hauppauge

Victims Information Bureau of Suffolk, Inc. (VIBS)
501 Route 111 (11787)
(516) 360–3730
Janet A. Geller, Clinical Director
24-hour hotline and shelter; opened in 1976; staffed by 3 social workers, 4 counselors, a psychologist available on a consulting basis 10 hours a week, 2 lawyer consultants, 1 consulting psychiatrist, 10 volunteers, 8 CETA workers, 1 former battered woman doing intake work, and 3 undergraduate and 4 graduate students.

Special features. Individual and group counseling, family therapy, legal advocacy, speakers bureau, and counseling for batterers.

Port Jervis

Outreach
41 Sussex Street (12771)
(914) 856–5800
Gerald Gould, Senior Caseworker
Telephone crisis intervention available Monday through Friday during day and evening hours; opened in 1975; staffed by 2 counselors, 1 social worker, and a part-time clerical worker.
Special features. Individual counseling and referral to specialized services, as needed.

North Carolina

Winston-Salem

Battered Women's Shelter
c/o YWCA
1201 Glade Street (27101)
(919) 724–3979
Judith Kaufholz, Executive Director
24-hour hotline and shelter; affiliated with the YWCA; an answering service only (staffed by volunteers) was provided from September 1977 to April 1978; shelter opened in May 1978; staffed by 1 nurse, who is the executive director, 1 counselor, 12 volunteers, 2 full-time and 1 part-time advocate, and 1 secretary.
Special features. Individual and group counseling provided at the shelter; family therapy, legal assistance, vocational services, social services information, and housing information provided through referral.

Ohio

Athens

My Sister's Place Inc.
P.O. Box 1158 (45701)
(614) 593–3402
Sue Allen, Executive Director

24-hour temporary shelter for abused women; opened in May 1978; staffed by 50 volunteers, 5 former battered women, 15 undergraduate students, 12 graduate students, 2 CETA workers, 1 social worker, 1 counselor, 1 lawyer, 1 nurse, and 2 secretaries.

Special features. Individual counseling, group therapy, aid in finding a job and housing, and supportive aftercare; specialized counseling in areas of assertiveness training, self-defense, single parenting, and sexuality; a children's program; assistance in acquiring skills for independent living such as household management, budgeting, and consumer education.

Columbus

Phoenix House, Inc.
P.O. Box 8323 (43202)
(614) 294–3381 or 294–7876
Carol Jorgensen, Director

24-hour hotline and shelter; at the time of the survey the director indicated that the name "Phoenix House" was soon to be changed; opened in 1977; staffed by 5 social workers, 70 volunteers, 16 CETA workers, 6 former battered women, 3 graduate students, 2 clerical staff, 2 administrative staff, and 1 advocate.

Special features. Individual and group counseling, family therapy, legal advocacy, vocational services, research, public education, groups for men, and strong emphasis on working with the children, including coordination with the public schools to provide teachers for the children.

Oregon

Ashland

Jackson County Task Force on Household Violence
511 East Hersey (97520)
crisis line: (503) 779–HELP; business line: (503) 482–6213
Rosemary E. Dalton, Chairperson

24-hour hotline and shelter; opened in 1977; staffed by 1 house director, 15 volunteers, 2 counselors, 5 students, and 1 vocational counselor.

Special features. Volunteers trained as legal, social service, and welfare advocates; short-term individual and family counseling; advocacy services (which may include accompanying the woman to the hospital, police station, and through court proceedings).

Astoria

Clatsop County Women's Resource Center
P.O. Box 441 (97103)
(503) 325–5735
Sheila Lea, Coordinator
Telephone crisis intervention available on weekdays 12 noon to 5:00 P.M.; temporary shelter provided; opened in 1977; staffed by 4 CETA workers, 1 social worker, 1 counselor, and 1 lawyer.
Special features. Counseling and legal advocacy.

Corvallis

Sunflower House
128 Southwest Ninth Street (97330)
(503) 753–1241
Diana Artemis, Director of Counseling
24-hour hotline and shelter, available through a network of private homes or referral to other agencies; this is a multiservice agency opened in 1971; staffed by 2 counselors, 1 lawyer, 50 or more volunteers, 4 CETA workers, 20 undergraduate and 10 graduate students; in addition, the staff includes an unspecified number of crisis intervention workers, youth outreach workers, program coordinators, physicians, and nurses who volunteer their time.
Special features. Individual counseling, drug and alcohol counseling, family therapy, medical care, and community education on abuse; also, a man and a woman trained in crisis intervention, cardiopulmonary resusitation, and first aid available 24 hours a day.

Portland

Bradley Angle House
P.O. Box 40132 (97240)
(503) 281–2442
Michelle Carlson, Public Education Coordinator
24-hour hotline and shelter; opened in 1975; staffed by an unspecified number of counselors, vocational counselors, housemothers, children's program staff, volunteers, CETA workers, former battered women, and undergraduate students.
Special features. Individual and group counseling, legal advocacy, vocational services, and a children's program.

Raphael House
P.O. Box 10797 (97210)
(503) 223–4544
John Savage, Director
24-hour hotline and shelter; opened in December 1977; staffed by 15 CETA workers.
    Special features. Individual and group counseling, special program for batterers, vocational services, and follow-up program.

Salem

Women's Crisis Service
P.O. Box 851 (97301)
crisis line: (503) 399–7722; business line: (503) 378–1572
Sandie Hoback, Shelter Coordinator
24-hour hotline and shelter serving victims of battering and rape; shelter provided in motel rooms and through a network of private homes; hotline operational since 1973; shelter program opened in 1978; staffed by 1 paid and 2 volunteer counselors, 1 lawyer, 10 volunteers, 3 CETA workers, 3 former battered women, and 3–6 undergraduate students.
    Special features. Individual counseling, frequent outreach group counseling, and research.

Pennsylvania

Allentown

Rape Crisis Council of Lehigh Valley, Inc.
P.O. Box 1445 (18105)
(215) 437–6611
Nancy Hanahue Yarrish, Executive Director
24-hour hotline (which had functioned previously as a rape crisis center); at the time of the survey, the program was just getting started as a service for battered women; the rape crisis service had been operational since 1974; staffed by an executive director, training director, administrative assistant, and 39 volunteers.
    Special features. At the time of the survey, callers were referred to specialized services within the community.

Bloomsburg

Women's Center
Market Street Shopping Center
Box 221 (17815)
(717) 784–6631
24-hour hotline and shelter; opened in 1975; staffed by 20 volunteers, 2 CETA workers, and 1 undergraduate student.
Special features. Individual and group counseling.

Chambersburg

Women in Need (WIN)
P.O. Box 25 (17201)
(717) 264–4444
Jane Rossi, Director
24-hour hotline and shelter; opened in December 1977; staffed by 20 volunteers, 2 CETA workers, 2 former battered women, 2 undergraduate and 1 graduate student, and 1 secretary.
Special features. Counseling and community education.

Erie

Hospitality House for Women
240 East 10th Street (16503)
(814) 454–8161
Sheila Ardery, Director
24-hour hotline and shelter for 20 people; opened in 1975; staffed by 5 volunteers, 3 CETA workers, 2 former battered women, 1 undergraduate student, 1 secretary, and 1 housekeeper/cook.
Special features. Al Anon meetings held here.

Lancaster

Lancaster's Women against Abuse
110 North Lime Street (17602)
(717) 299–1249
Donna Glover, Assistant Director
24-hour hotline and shelter, located in a YWCA building for their first 2 years of operation; opened in fall 1978 in a private house with the help of Title XX federal funding and a grant from the Steiman Foundation; staffed

by 10 volunteers, 3 CETA workers, 4 counselors, 1 director, 1 assistant director, and 1 shelter manager.

Philadelphia

Women in Transition
3700 Chestnut Street (19104)
(215) 382–7017
Sarah Lynne McMahon, Co-director
Telephone crisis intervention provided Monday through Friday during the day; located in a church; incorporated in 1972; serves women with a variety of problems, including abused women; staffed by an unspecified number of social workers, counselors, volunteers, CETA workers, lawyers, graduate students, and clerical workers.

Special features. Individual and group counseling provided at the center; women are referred for specialized services, as needed.

Wallingford

Marital Abuse Project of Delaware County, Inc.
P.O. Box 294 (19086)
(215) 565–6272
Linda M. Shaw, former Director; Ginger McMahon, current Director
24-hour hotline and shelter in private homes for limited emergency housing; shelter facility being planned opened in 1975; staffed by 53 volunteers, 1 paid and 7 volunteer social workers, 21 counselors, 12 former battered women, 3 undergraduate and 5 graduate students, 1 lawyer, 12 group leaders, 2 research volunteers, and 1 paid and 2 volunteer clerical workers; in addition, 2 psychologists are on the board of directors.

Special features. Individual and group counseling, legal advocacy and accompaniment when women go to court, and research.

Rhode Island

Providence

Sojourner House, Inc.
P.O. Box 5667 Weybosset Hill Station (02903)
(401) 751–1262
Cathy Lewis, Coordinator

24-hour hotline and shelter located in a rented house; opened in 1977; staffed by 50 volunteers, 1 counselor, 3 CETA workers, and 12 students.

Special features. Group counseling, weekly outreach counseling, legal advocacy, welfare advocacy, child care programs, and research.

Women's Center of Rhode Island, Inc.
37 Congress Avenue (02907)
(401) 781–4080
Helen P. Hawkinson, Executive Director

24-hour hotline and shelter, which can accommodate up to 20 persons at a time, for women and children who have no place to stay, with priority given to women who are victims of violence; opened in 1976; staffed by 50 volunteers, 5 CETA workers, 3 former battered women, 1 director, 1 house manager, 1 dance therapist, 1 art therapist, 1 children's coordinator, and 1 secretary.

Special features. Group counseling, legal advocacy, children's services, including a nursery school for preschool children and Saturday trips with Big Brothers, art and dance therapy; a weekly parenting class for women who are residents and former residents.

Texas

Austin

Center for Battered Women
P.O. Box 5631 (78763)
(512) 472–HURT
Deborah Tucker Meismer, Director

24-hour hotline and shelter for 14 in a house owned by the city; opened in 1977; staffed by a director, volunteer coordinator, 40 volunteers, 4 CETA workers, 5 former battered women, and 1 counselor.

Special features. Counseling and legal advocacy provided at the center; referrals made for family counseling.

Vermont

Brattleboro

Women's Crisis Shelter
67 Main Street, Room 38 (05301)
(802) 254–6954
Ann Shepardson, Director

24-hour hotline and shelter; opened in 1976; staffed by 3 counselors, 20 volunteers, 1 CETA worker, 1 law student, 4 former battered women, and 2 graduate students.

Special features. Individual and group counseling, legal advocacy, couples counseling, and advocacy to all other agencies.

Virginia

Christiansburg

Women's Resource Center
203 Phlegar Street (24073)
(703) 382–6553
Judith Gatz, Counselor
24-hour hotline and shelter; opened in July 1977; staffed by 15 volunteers, 4 CETA workers, 2 counselors, 3 students, 1 secretary.

Special features. Short-term counseling, support groups, self-help workshops, library, emergency food and clothing; information and referral; a parent study group for single parents.

Roanoke

Women's Resource and Services Center
605 First Street (24016)
(703) 342–4076 or 343–6016
Geraldine C. Nolan, Manager
At the time this program responded to the survey, it provided telephone crisis intervention Monday through Friday during the day. The program reported that it was trying to establish an emergency shelter component. Their office is located at the YWCA; opened in 1975; staffed by an unspecified number of peer counselors, volunteers, and CETA workers.

Special features. Peer counseling and referral; at the time of the survey, staff were trying to organize self-help groups. In addition, special workshops are held on a variety of topics including legal rights, single parenting, and assertiveness training.

Washington

Bellevue

Women's Association of Self-Help (WASH)
11100 N.E. 2nd (98009)
(206) 454–WASH
Dottie Feldman, Director
Telephone peer counseling and support groups; began in 1975.

Bellingham

YWCA Battered Women's Program
1026 North Forest (98225)
(206) 734–4820
Kerry Anne Ridley, Counselor/Coordinator
24-hour hotline and shelter located in YWCA residence; opened in 1978; staffed by volunteers, CETA workers, former battered women, undergraduate students, and secretary.
Special features. Counseling.

Everett

Evergreen Legal Services
1712½ Hewitt (98201)
(206) 258–2681
Janet Epstein, Social Worker
Legal services agency open weekdays; service began August 1977; staffed by 3 CETA workers, 1 lawyer, 1 social worker, and 1 secretary.
Special features. Legal and legislative advocacy and crisis counseling; crisis callers needing emergency shelter are referred to Stop Abuse, Inc., also in Everett.

Stop Abuse, Inc. (formerly the Women's Survival Center)
5205 South Second (98203)
crisis line: (206) 25–ABUSE; business line (206) 258–3543
Fran Zimmer, Grantwriter/Researcher
24-hour hotline and shelter in private homes; opened in 1976; staffed by 1 director, 1 fundraiser/researcher, 1 volunteer coordinator, 25 volunteers, 7 CETA workers, 3 counselors, 1 lawyer, 1 undergraduate student, an unspecified number of former battered women who work as volunteers, and 1 secretary.
Special features. Individual and group counseling, legal advocacy, research, public education through a speakers bureau, child care and child advocacy, and provision of transportation and medical care, when needed.

Olympia

Thurston-Mason YWCA Women's Shelter Program
220 East Union (98501)
(206) 352–0593
Colleen Spencer, Support Service Counselor
24-hour hotline and shelter; office at the YWCA but shelter in a separate

facility; opened in 1978; staffed by 1 counselor, 1 vocational counselor, nurse, 12 volunteers, 3 CETA workers, 1 former battered woman, and 2 lawyers who are on call.

Special features. Individual counseling, welfare advocacy, referral for legal advocacy.

Seattle

Catherine Booth House
The Salvation Army Family Services Department
925 East Pike (98122)
(206) 322–7959
Dorothy Deering, Director
24-hour hotline and shelter affiliated with the Salvation Army; opened in 1976; staffed by 5 social workers, 1 former battered woman, 1 undergraduate student, 1 graduate student, 1 part-time child care worker, and 1 full-time housekeeper.

Special features. Individual and group counseling, legal advocacy, public assistance advocacy, assistance in finding and paying for permanent housing, furniture and food, alumnae group.

YWCA-Women's Resource Center
1118 Fifth Avenue (98126)
(206) 447–4882
Judy A. Williamson, Counselor
24-hour hotline and shelter for women in crisis, including battered women; located at the YWCA and has 7 beds; opened in 1973; staffed by 2 full-time counselors and 8 part-time counselors, 3 graduate students, and 3 substitute counselors to guarantee 24-hour coverage.

Special features. Individual and group counseling, vocational services, and small loans for food and transportation.

Spokane

YWCA Battered Women's Program
West 829 Broadway Avenue (99201)
(509) 327–1508
Patricia C. Peery, Coordinator
24-hour hotline and shelter provided by the YWCA; opened in 1976; staffed by 1 social worker, 1 counselor, 23 volunteers, and 2 full-time and 1 part-time CETA worker.

Special features. Counseling, legal advocacy, and vocational services.

Tacoma
Women's Support Shelter
405 Broadway (98402)
(206) 383–2593 Carol Richard, Shelter Coordinator
24-hour hotline and shelter facility having 37 private rooms which can house 75 people and, in addition, a network of private homes available when the shelter is full; opened 1974; staffed by 2 social workers, 5 counselors, a psychiatrist who is available for weekly consultations, 1 vocational counselor, 8–12 volunteers, 5 CETA workers, 5 former battered women, 2 graduate and 2 undergraduate students.

Special features. Individual counseling, vocational services, group counseling open to the public and advertised, and children's recreation and therapy. At the time of the survey, a group for abusive males was in the planning stage.

Yakima
Battered Women's Service Program (YWCA)
North Naches Avenue (98901)
(509) 248–7796
Rebecca VanWars, Child Development Coordinator
24-hour hotline and shelter, affiliated with the YWCA; shelter provided through shelter facility and network of private homes; opened in 1977; staffed by 2 volunteers, 2 CETA workers, 2 counselors, and 2 night resident supervisors.

Special features. Individual counseling, legal advocacy, vocational services, educational outreach—lectures and films for the community.

West Virginia

Charleston
Charleston Domestic Violence Center, Inc.
1105 Quarrier Street (25301)
(304) 343–8056 Susan B. Walter, Program Coordinator
24-hour telephone service and temporary shelter at a local church; opened in January 1978; staffed by 10 volunteers and a coordinator paid through CETA and United Way funds.

Special features. Individual and group counseling, family therapy, legal advocacy, research, and referral for other services, as needed.

Wisconsin

Eau Claire
Refuge House
P.O. Box 482 (54701)
(715) 834–9578 Greta L. Marshall, Director

24-hour hotline and shelter, opened in July 1977; staffed by 1 counselor, 11 volunteers, 10 CETA workers, 3 former battered women, and 1 secretary.

Special features. Counseling and referral for services not available at the program.

La Crosse

YWCA New Horizons Women's Center
1021½ Jackson Street (54601)
(608) 784–6419
Diane E. Gilmore, Project Coordinator

24-hour hotline and shelter, utilizing private homes; opened in 1978; staffed by 4 volunteer psychologists, 1 volunteer lawyer, 1 counselor, 25 volunteers, 3 CETA workers, and 2 undergraduate students.

Special features. Individual and group counseling, legal advocacy, and vocational services.

Milwaukee

Sojourner Truth House
P.O. Box 08110 (53208)
(414) 933–2722
Roz Read, Program Coordinator

24-hour hotline and shelter; opened in July 1978; staffed by 2 administrators, 5 house managers, 1 social worker, 12 volunteers, 6 undergraduate students, and 1 clerical worker.

Special features. Individual counseling, support groups, legal advocacy, a "legal clinic," human sexuality workshops, and house meetings.

Wasau

Abused Women's Project
Marathon Health Care Center
1100 Lakeview Drive (54401)
(715) 842–1636
Lynne Goheen, Project Developer

Extensive community education in Langlade, Lincoln, and Marathon counties; consultation to community agencies; and development of a formal reporting mechanism for spouse abuse clients at human services agencies in Wausau.

■B
List of
Community Foundations*

Foundation Names and Addresses	No. of Fnds. ( )	Year Organized
ALL COMMUNITY FOUNDATIONS	(219)	
NEW ENGLAND	(26)	
Connecticut	(11)	
The New Haven Fdn. 1 State St. New Haven, Conn. 06510		1928
The Hartford Fdn. for Public Giving 45 S. Main St. West Hartford, Conn. 06107		1925
Waterbury Fdn. c/o The Colonial Bank & Trust Co. P.O. Box 252 Waterbury, Conn. 06702		1923
The Bridgeport Area Fdn., Inc. 955 Main St. Bridgeport, Conn. 06603		1967
The Meriden Fdn. 14 W. Main St. Meriden, Conn. 06450		1932
New Britain Fdn. for Public Giving, Inc. P.O. Box 102 New Britain, Conn. 06050		1972
The Stamford Fdn. c/o Fairfield County Trust Co. 300 Main St. Stamford, Conn. 06904		1952
The Greenwich Fdn. for Community Gifts, Inc. One Lafayette Ct. Greenwich, Conn. 06830		1955

Foundation Names and Addresses	No. of Fnds. ( )	Year Organized
The Torrington Area Fdn. for Public Giving c/o Hartford Nat. Bank & Trust Co. 336 Prospect St. Torrington, Conn. 06790		1969
The Guilford Fdn., Inc. P.O. Box 326 Guilford, Conn. 06437		1975
The Greater Norwalk Community Fdn., Inc. 10 Westport Rd. Wilton, Conn. 06897		1970
Maine	(2)	
Maine Charity Fdn. c/o Maine National Bank P.O. Box 3555 Portland, Maine 04104		1921
The North Haven Fdn. North Haven, Maine 04853		1966
Massachusetts	(9)	
Committee of the Permanent Charity Fund, Inc. One Boston Pl. Rm. 3005 Boston, Mass. 02106		1915
The Cambridge Fdn. 99 Bishop Richard Allen Dr. Cambridge, Mass. 02139		1916

* Lists 219 community foundations in the United States and Canada, showing for each their name, address and year of organization.

Reprinted by permission of the Council on Foundations from their publication Status of Community Foundations in the U.S. New York, Council on Foundations, Inc., 1976.

Foundation Names and Addresses	No. of Fnds. ( )	Year Organized
Massachusetts-(Continued)		
Old Colony Charitable Fdn. c/o First Nat. Bank of Boston 100 Federal St. Boston, Mass. 02110		1955
The Cornerstone Charitable Fdn. c/o New England Merchants Nat. Bank 28 State St. Boston, Mass 02107		1953
Attleboro Fdn. c/o Attleboro Trust Co. P.O. Box 330 Attleboro, Mass. 02730		1915
Committee of the Brockton Charitable Fund, Inc. c/o First County National Bank 90 Main St. Brockton, Mass. 02403		1947
Greater Worcester Community Fdn. 237 Chandler St. Worcester, Mass. 01609		1975
Dover Fdn., Inc. P.O. Box 69 Dover, Mass. 02030		1950
Greater Fall River Fdn., Inc. 687 High St. Fall River, Mass. 02722		1967
New Hampshire (2)		
New Hampshire Charitable Trust 1 South St. Concord, N.H. 03301		1962
The Randolph Fdn. Randolph, N.H. 03571		1962
Rhode Island (1)		
The Rhode Island Fdn. 15 Westminster St. Providence, R.I. 02903		1916

Foundation Names and Addresses	No. of Fnds. ( )	Year Organized
Vermont (1)		
Vermont Charitable Fdn. RFD Box 57 Waitsfield, Vt. 05673		1973
MIDDLE ATLANTIC (31)		
New Jersey (3)		
The Plainfield Fdn. 202 Park Ave. Plainfield, N.J. 07060		1920
Trenton Community Fdn. 19 Chancery Lane Trenton, N.J. 08618		1952
South Jersey Fdn. c/o Burlington County Trust Co. 91 Main St. Moorestown, N.J. 08057		1972
New York (14)		
The New York Community Trust 415 Madison Ave. New York, N.Y. 10017		1923
The Buffalo Fdn. 812 Genesee Bldg. Buffalo, N.Y. 14202		1919
Poughkeepsie Area Fund, Inc. 35 Market St. Poughkeepsie, N.Y. 12601		1969
The Watertown Fdn., Inc. 600 Woolworth Bldg. Watertown, N.Y. 13601		1929
Central New York Community Fdn. 423 W. Onondaga St. Syracuse, N.Y. 13202		1927
Glens Falls Fdn. c/o First Nat. Bank of Glens Falls 239 Glen St. Glens Falls, N.Y. 12801		1939

214 : : *Sheltering Battered Women*

Foundation Names and Addresses	No. of Fnds. ( )	Year Organized
New York-(Continued)		
Utica Fdn., Inc. 233 Genesee St. Utica, N.Y. 13501		1952
The Tompkins County Fdn., Inc. 415 Hanshaw Rd. Ithaca, N.Y. 14850		1945
Scarsdale Fdn. 4 Richbell Rd. Scarsdale, N.Y. 10583		1923
Mohawk-Hudson Community Fdn. 877 Madison Ave. Albany, N.Y. 12208		1968
The Community Fdn. of Unadilla 98 Main St. Unadilla, N.Y. 13849		1969
Rochester Area Fdn. 315 Alexander St. Rm. 205 Rochester, N.Y. 14604		1973
The Schenectady Fdn. P.O. Box 1020 Schenectady, N.Y. 12301		1963
Corning Community Fdn., Inc. c/o Lincoln First Bank of Rochester 2 E. Market St. Corning, N.Y. 14830		1972
Pennsylvania (14)		
The Philadelphia Fdn. Two Girard Plaza Suite 1502 Philadelphia, Pa. 19102		1958
The Pittsburgh Fdn. 301 Fifth Ave. Suite 1417 Pittsburgh, Pa. 15222		1945
The Williamsport Fdn. c/o Northern Central Bank & Trust Co. 102 W. Fourth St. Williamsport, Pa. 17701		1916

Foundation Names and Addresses	No. of Fnds. ( )	Year Organized
The Erie Community Fdn. P.O. Box 1818 Erie, Pa. 16507		1935
The Scranton Area Fdn. P.O. Box 937 Scranton, Pa. 18501		1954
The Warren Fdn. P.O. Box 69 Warren, Pa. 16365		1949
The Lancaster County Fdn. 30 W. Orange St. Lancaster, Pa. 17604		1924
The Altoona Fdn. 1206 11th Ave. Altoona, Pa. 16603		1924
The Greensburg Fdn. 18 Pittsburgh St. Greensburg, Pa. 15601		1947
Central Montgomery County Fdn. 114 E. DeKalb Pike P.O. Box 534 King of Prussia, Pa. 19406		1960
The Grove City Fdn. 209 W. Pine St. Grove City, Pa. 16127		1948
Bethlehem Area Fdn. 508 Main St. Bethlehem, Pa. 18018		1967
York Fdn. c/o York Machinery & Supply Co. 20 N. Penn St. York, Pa. 17401		1961
The Ashland Trusts 816 Centre St. Ashland, Pa. 17921		1967
SOUTH ATLANTIC (26)		
Delaware (1)		
The Delaware Fdn. c/o The Bank of Delaware 300 Delaware Ave. Wilmington, Del. 19899		1920

Foundation Names and Addresses	No. of Fnds. ( )	Year Organized
District of Columbia (1)		

The Community Foundation of
Greater Washington, Inc.
1501 18th St., N.W.
Washington, D.C. 20036 1973

Foundation Names and Addresses	No. of Fnds. ( )	Year Organized
Florida (6)		

The Community Fdn. of Sarasota
c/o Southeast Banks Trust Co., N.A.
P.O. Box 267
Sarasota, Fla. 33578 1958

Winter Park Community Trust Fund
c/o Barnett Bank of Winter Park
P.O. Box 1000
Winter Park, Fla 32790 1951

Palm Beach County Community Fdn.
411 S. County Rd.
Palm Beach, Fla. 33480 1971

Dade Fdn.
955 S.W. 2nd Ave.
Miami, Fla. 33101 1967

Pinellas County Community Fdn.
1253 Park St.
Clearwater, Fla. 33516 1969

Southwest Florida Community Fdn.
c/o The First National Bank
in Fort Myers
P.O. Box 130
Fort Myers, Fla. 33902 1976

Foundation Names and Addresses	No. of Fnds. ( )	Year Organized
Georgia (3)		

Metropolitan Fdn. of Atlanta, Inc.
1330 Healey Bldg.
P.O. Box 1357
Atlanta, Georgia 30301 1951

Savannah Fdn., Inc.
428 Bull St.
P.O. Box 9119
Savannah, Ga. 31402 1953

Metropolitan Augusta Fdn.
P.O. Box 36
Augusta, Ga. 30903 1964

Foundation Names and Addresses	No. of Fnds. ( )	Year Organized
Maryland (1)		

The Community Fdn. of the
Greater Baltimore Area, Inc.
Suite 915
One Charles Center
Baltimore, Md. 21201 1973

Foundation Names and Addresses	No. of Fnds. ( )	Year Organized
North Carolina (6)		

The Winston-Salem Fdn.
2230 Wachovia Bldg.
Winston-Salem, N.C. 27101 1919

Greater Charlotte Fdn., Inc.
301 Brevard St.
Charlotte, N.C. 28202 1958

Elizabeth City Fdn.
c/o Hugh K. Marr
P.O. Box 14
Elizabeth City, N.C. 27909 1959

Salisbury Community Fdn., Inc.
c/o Security Bank & Trust Co.
P.O. Box 1327
Salisbury, N.C. 28144 1944

Rocky Mount Fdn.
150 Howard St.
Rocky Mount, N.C. 27801 1954

The Polk County Community Fdn., Inc.
165 Wilderness Road
Tryon, N.C. 28782 1975

Foundation Names and Addresses	No. of Fnds. ( )	Year Organized
South Carolina (3)		

The Spartanburg County Fdn.
545 Montgomery Bldg.
Spartanburg, S.C. 29301 1943

The Greenville County Fdn.
P.O. Box 2145
Greenville, S.C. 29602 1956

Anderson Community Fdn., Inc.
P.O. Box 183
Anderson, S.C. 29622 1970

Foundation Names and Addresses	No. of Fnds. ( )	Year Organized
Virginia	(3)	
Norfolk Fdn. 406 Royster Bldg. Norfolk, Va. 23510		1950
The Portsmouth Community Trust 2115 High St. P.O. Box 668 Portsmouth, Va. 23705		1965
The Greater Richmond Community Fdn. 809-B Mutual Bldg. 9th and Main Sts. Richmond, Va. 23219		1968
West Virginia	(2)	
The Greater Kanawha Valley Fdn. P.O. Box 3041 Charleston, W. Va. 25331		1960
Parkersburg Community Fdn. 16 Citizens Bank Bldg. P.O. Box 1762 Parkersburg, W. Va. 26101		1963
EAST NORTH CENTRAL	(73)	
Illinois	(9)	
The Chicago Community Trust 208 S. LaSalle St. Chicago, Ill. 60604		1915
The Aurora Fdn. 32 Water St. Aurora, Ill. 60507		1948
The Moline Fdn. c/o Moline National Bank 506-15th St. Moline, Ill. 61265		1953
Rockford Community Trust c/o First Nat. Bank & Trust Co. 401 E. State St. Rockford, Ill. 61101		1953
Community Fdn. of Champaign County P.O. Box 826 Champaign, Ill. 61820		1972

Foundation Names and Addresses	No. of Fnds. ( )	Year Organized
Illinois-(Continued)		
Oak Park-River Forest Community Fdn. c/o Oak Park-River Forest Community Chest 1042 Pleasant St. Oak Park, Ill. 60302		1959
The Rock Island Community Fdn. 213-20th St. Rock Island, Ill. 61201		1967
Sterling-Rock Falls Community Trust c/o The Central National Bank of Sterling 302 First Ave. Sterling, Ill. 61081		1968
The Arcola Fdn. 127 South Oak Box 524 Arcola, Ill. 61910		1975
Indiana	(5)	
The Indianapolis Fdn. 615 N. Alabama St. Indianapolis, Ind. 46204		1916
The Fort Wayne Fdn. 215 W. Washington Blvd. Fort Wayne, Ind. 46802		1956
The Portland Fdn. 1329 S. Meridian St. P.O. Box 1094 Portland, Ind. 47371		1952
The Brookville Fdn. 511 Main St. Brookville, Ind. 47012		1956
Kosciusko County Fdn. 1610 E. Center St. Warsaw, Ind. 46580		1968

Foundation Names and Addresses	No. of Fnds. ( )	Year Organized
Michigan	(22)	
Kalamazoo Fdn. 3321 SB Bldg. 151 S. Rose St. Kalamazoo, Mich. 49006		1925
Grand Rapids Fdn. 300-C Waters Bldg. Grand Rapids, Mich. 49502		1922
The Fremont Area Fdn. P.O. Box 9 Fremont, Mich. 49412		1951
Muskegon County Community Fdn. Lumberman's Bank Bldg. Webster at First Muskegon, Mich. 49443		1961
Vicksburg Fdn. 108 E. Michigan Kalamazoo, Mich. 49006		1936
The Jackson Fdn. 505 Wildwood Ave. Jackson, Mich. 49201		1948
The Flint Public Trust 1010 Genessee Bank Bldg. Flint, Mich. 48502		1950
The Greater Lansing Fdn. c/o American Bank & Trust Co. P.O. Box 300 Lansing, Mich. 48902		1947
The Ann Arbor Area Fdn. 2301 Platt Rd. Ann Arbor, Mich. 48104		1963
Detroit Community Trust c/o Detroit Bank & Trust Co. 211 W. Fort St. Detroit, Mich. 48226		1915
Berrien Community Fdn., Inc. P.O. Box 68 Benton Harbor, Mich. 49022		1952
Midland Community Fdn. P.O. Box 289 Midland, Mich. 48640		1973

Foundation Names and Addresses	No. of Fnds. ( )	Year Organized
Oakland County Community Trust c/o Detroit Bank & Trust Co. 211 W. Fort St. Detroit, Mich. 48226		1965
Allegan Fdn. P.O. Box 15 Allegan, Mich. 49010		1970
Port Huron District Fdn. P.O. Box 285 Port Huron, Mich. 48060		1944
Alpena Area Community Fdn. 150-C N. State St. Alpena, Mich. 49707		1974
Leelanau Township Fdn., Inc. Northport, Mich. 49670		1945
Grand Haven Area Community Fdn., Inc. 202 Security Bank Bldg. Grand Haven, Mich. 49417		1971
Greater Battle Creek Fdn. 512 Michigan National Bank Bldg. Battle Creek, Mich. 49014		1926
The Colon Fdn. 108 W. State St. Colon, Mich. 49040		1963
Traverse Area Fdn. 407 National Bank and Trust Bldg. Traverse City, Mich. 49684		1972
The Adrain Fdn. 2711 E. Maumee St. Adrian, Mich. 49221		(c)
Ohio	(28)	
The Cleveland Fdn. 700 National City Bank Bldg. Cleveland, Ohio 44114		1914
The Columbus Fdn. 17 S. High St. Suite 707 Columbus, Ohio 43215		1943

Foundation Names and Addresses	No. of Fnds. ( )	Year Organized
Ohio-(Continued)		
The Greater Cincinnati Fdn. 812 Gas & Electric Bldg. 139 E. Fourth St. Cincinnati, Ohio 45202		1963
The Stark County Fdn. 618 Second St., N.W. Canton, Ohio 44703		1963
The Ashtabula Fdn., Inc. P.O. Drawer A Ashtabula, Ohio 44004		1922
Youngstown Fdn. P.O. Box 450 Youngstown, Ohio 44501		1918
Richland County Fdn. of Mansfield 38 S. Park St. Mansfield, Ohio 44902		1945
The Van Wert County Fdn. 101½ E. Main St. Van Wert, Ohio 45891		1926
The Troy Fdn. c/o First National Bank & Trust Co. 910 W. Main St. Troy, Ohio 45373		1924
Akron Community Trusts 1 Cascade Plaza Akron, Ohio 44308		1955
Hamilton Community Fdn., Inc. 323 N. Third St. Hamilton, Ohio 45011		1951
The Toledo Community Fdn. One Stranahan Sq. Rm. 141 Toledo, Ohio 43604		1924
The Dayton Fdn. 110 E. Second St. Dayton, Ohio 45402		1921
The Mount Vernon Community Trust 111 S. Mulberry St. Mt. Vernon, Ohio 43050		1944

Foundation Names and Addresses	No. of Fnds. ( )	Year Organized
The Lorain Fdn. c/o Lorain National Bank 457 Broadway Lorain, Ohio 44052		1947
Licking County Fdn. for Public Giving 36 N. Second St. Newark, Ohio 43055		1956
The Scioto County Area Fdn. 48 National Bank Bldg. Portsmouth, Ohio 45662		1974
(Canton Welfare Federation) Community Memorial Trust 618 Second St., N.W. Canton, Ohio 44703		1960
The Sidney Community Fdn. c/o Garmhausen, Kerrigan & Elsass Ohio Bldg. Sidney, Ohio 45365		1952
The Springfield Fdn. 35 S. Spring St. Springfield, Ohio 45502		1948
Salem Community Fdn., Inc. P.O. Box 483 Salem, Ohio 44460		1966
Lake County Fdn. 50 Liberty St. Ext. Painesville, Ohio 44077		1932
Bryan Area Fdn. P.O. Box 651 Bryan, Ohio 43506		1969
Mercer County Civic Fdn. P.O. Box 145 Celina, Ohio 45822		1960
Galion Community Fdn. 312 E. Payne Ave. Galion, Ohio 44833		1957
The Tipp City Fdn. c/o First National Bank & Trust Co. 910 W. Main St. Troy, Ohio 45373		1943

List of Community Foundations : : 219

Foundation Names and Addresses	No. of Fnds. ( )	Year Organized
Ohio–(Continued)		
The Fayette County Charitable Fdn. 604 S. Fayette St. Washington Court House, Ohio 43106. .		1953
The Marietta Community Fdn. c/o The Peoples' Banking & Trust Co. P.O. Box 666 Marietta, Ohio 45750		1974
Wisconsin	**(9)**	
Milwaukee Fdn. 161 West Wisconsin Ave. Suite 5146 Milwaukee, Wis. 53203		1915
Oshkosh Fdn. c/o First Wisconsin National Bank 111 N. Main St. Oshkosh, Wis. 54901		1928
LaCrosse Fdn. c/o LaCrosse Trust Co. 311 Main St. LaCrosse, Wis. 54601		1930
Madison Community Trust Fund c/o First National Bank of Madison 1 S. Pinckney St. Madison, Wis. 53701		1942
Cambridge Fdn. Main St. Cambridge, Wis. 53523		1948
Kenosha Fdn. c/o First National Bank of Kenosha P.O. Box 280 Kenosha, Wis. 53141		1926
The Ashland Fdn. 100 Second St., West Ashland, Wis. 54806		1930
The Fort Atkinson Community Fdn. c/o Godfrey & Kahn 780 N. Water St. Milwaukee, Wis. 53202		1973
Racine County Area Fdn., Inc. P.O. Box 444 Racine, Wis. 53401		1976

Foundation Names and Addresses	No. of Fnds. ( )	Year Organized
WEST NORTH CENTRAL	**(14)**	
Iowa	**(4)**	
Waverly Community Fdn. c/o State Bank of Waverly Waverly, Iowa 50677		1962
Community Welfare Fdn. of Cedar Rapids P.O. Box 2107 500 Merchants Nat. Bank Bldg. Cedar Rapids, Iowa 52406		1949
Davenport Area Fdn. 409 Putnam Bldg. Davenport, Iowa 52801		1967
Waterloo Civic Fdn. 1003 W. Fourth St. Waterloo, Iowa 50702		1956
Kansas	**(1)**	
The McPherson Community Fdn. 901 Main St. McPherson, Kans. 67460		1964
Minnesota	**(4)**	
The Minneapolis Fdn. 400 Foshay Tower Minneapolis, Minn. 55402		1915
The St. Paul Fdn. 355 Washington St. St. Paul, Minn. 55110		1939
The Rochester Fdn. 247 First National Bank Bldg. 201 S. First Ave. Rochester, Minn. 55901		1944
Duluth Community Trust c/o Northern City Nat. Bank 306 W. Superior St. Duluth, Minn. 55801		1943

Foundation Names and Addresses	No. of Fnds. ( )	Year Organized
Missouri	**(1)**	
St. Louis Community Trust 7733 Forsyth Blvd. Suite 1854 St. Louis, Mo. 63105		1915
Nebraska	**(2)**	
The Lincoln Fnd., Inc. 215 Centennial Mall South Lincoln, Neb. 68508		1955
Merrick Fdn., Inc. 1615-17th Ave. Central City, Neb. 68826		1960
North Dakota	**(2)**	
Fargo-Moorhead Area Fdn. c/o Merchants National Bank & Trust Co. 505 2nd Ave., N. P.O. Box 1980 Fargo, N.D. 58102		1960
The North Dakota Community Fdn. P.O. Box 885 Casselton, N.D. 58012		1976
EAST SOUTH CENTRAL	**(7)**	
Alabama	**(2)**	
The Greater Birmingham Fdn. P.O. Box 9096 Birmingham, Ala. 35213		1959
The Mobile Community Fdn. First National Bank Bldg. Rm. 1514 Mobile, Ala. 36602		1976
Kentucky	**(2)**	
Blue Grass Fdn., Inc. 2020 Nicholasville Rd. Lexington, Ky. 40503		1968
The Owensboro-Daviess County Community Fdn. 1619 Frederica St. Owensboro, Ky. 42301		1973

Foundation Names and Addresses	No. of Fnds. ( )	Year Organized
Tennessee	**(3)**	
Community Fdn. of Greater Chattanooga, Inc. 1033 Volunteer Bldg. Chatanooga, Tenn. 37402		1963
The Memphis-Plough Community Fdn. First National Bank Bldg. Suite 1521 Memphis, Tenn. 38103		1969
Community Improvement Fdn. of East Tennessee 1212 Pierce Pky. Suite 101-A Knoxville, Tenn. 37921		1939
WEST CENTRAL	**(13)**	
Arkansas	**(1)**	
Arkansas Community Fdn., Inc. P.O. Box 3071 Little Rock, Ark. 72203		1976
Louisiana	**(2)**	
Shreveport-Bossier Fdn. P.O. Box 1106 Shreveport, La. 71156		1961
Baton Rouge Area Fdn., Inc. 1753 Convention St. Baton Rouge, La. 70802		1964
Oklahoma	**(2)**	
Oklahoma City Community Fdn., Inc. 1300 N. Broadway Oklahoma City, Okla. 73103		1969
The Tulsa Fdn. c/o First National Bank & Trust Co. of Tulsa P.O. Box 1 Tulsa, Okla. 74102		1919

Foundation Names and Addresses	No. of Fnds. ( )	Year Organized
Texas	(8)	
Dallas Community Chest Trust Fund 4605 Live Oak St. Dallas, Tex. 75204		1953
Navarro Community Fdn. 531 First National Bank Bldg. P.O. Box 1035 Corsicana, Tex. 75110		1938
Dallas Fdn. 3300 Republic Bank Tower Dallas, Tex. 75209		1929
San Antonio Area Fdn. 201 N. Saint Mary's St. San Antonio, Tex. 78205		1964
Waco Perpetual Growth Fdn. 1801 Austin Ave. Waco, Tex. 76701		1958
Amarillo Area Fdn., Inc. 1001 Fisk Bldg. Amarillo, Tex. 79101		1957
Waxahachie Fdn., Inc. 200 Overhill Dr. Waxahachie, Tex. 75165		1968
El Paso Community Fdn. c/o 1808 State National Plaza El Paso, Tex. 79901		1975
MOUNTAIN	(2)	
Colorado	(2)	
The Denver Foundation 70 W. Sixth Ave. Suite 310 Denver, Colo. 80204		1925
Colorado Springs Community Trust Fund 1622 N. Corona St. Colorado Springs, Colo. 80907		1928

Foundation Names and Addresses	No. of Fnds. ( )	Year Organized
PACIFIC	(20)	
California	(12)	
The San Francisco Fdn. 425 California St. San Francisco, Ca. 94104		1948
California Community Fdn. P.O. Box 54303 Terminal Annex Los Angeles, Ca. 90054		1915
The Santa Barbara Fdn. 11 E. Carrillo St. Santa Barbara, Ca. 93101		1928
Pasadena Fdn. 16 N. Marengo Ave. Suite 219 Pasadena, Ca. 91101		1953
The East Bay Community Fdn. P.O. Box 688 Oakland, Ca. 94604		1928
The Humboldt Area Fdn. P.O. Box 632 Eureka, Ca. 95501		1972
The Corcoran Community Fdn. P.O. Box 457 Corcoran, Ca. 93212		1965
The San Mateo Fdn. 1204 Burlingame Ave. Room 10 Burlingame, Ca. 94010		1964
Community Trust of Santa Clara County 393 E. Hamilton Ave. Suite B Campbell, Ca. 95008		1955
Fresno Regional Fdn. 1171 Fulton Mall Room 1221 Fresno, Ca. 93721		1966
Glendale Community Fdn. 420 N. Brand Blvd. Suite 614 Glendale, Ca. 91203		1956

Foundation Names and Addresses	No. of Fnds. ( )	Year Organized
California–(Continued)		
San Diego Community Fdn. P.O. Box 2671 San Diego, Ca. 92112		1975
Hawaii	(1)	
The Hawaiian Fdn. c/o Hawaiian Trust Co., Ltd. P.O. Box 3170 Honolulu, Hawaii 96802		1916
Oregon	(4)	
The Oregon Community Fdn. 319 Yeon Bldg. Portland, Ore. 97204		1973
The Benton County Fdn. P.O. Box 911 Corvallis, Ore. 97330		1953
The Pendleton Fdn. Trust P.O. Box 218 Pendleton, Ore. 97801		1936
Salem Fdn. c/o Pioneer Trust Co. 109 Commercial St., N.E. Salem, Ore. 97301		1942
Washington	(3)	
The Seattle Fdn. 520 Joshua Green Bldg. Seattle, Wash. 98101		1946
Greater Spokane Community Fdn. 1006 Old National Bank Bldg. Spokane, Wash. 99201		1974
Stanwood-Camano Area Fdn. 642 Broadway P.O. Box 458 Stanwood, Wash. 98292		1961
UNITED STATES	(212)	

Foundation Names and Addresses	No. of Fnds. ( )	Year Organized
CANADA	(7)	
Vancouver Fdn. Suite 2211 1177 W. Hastings St. Vancouver, B.C. V6E 2K3		1943
The Winnipeg Fdn. 800 Mercantile Bank Bldg. 305 Broadway Winnipeg, Man. R3C 0R9		1921
Calgary & District Fdn. 1210-205 Fifth Ave., S.W. P.O. Box 9114 Calgary, Alta. T2P 2W4		1955
The Hamilton Fdn. 20 Gloucester Rd. Hamilton, Ont.		1954
The Victoria Fdn. 877 Island Rd. Victoria, B.C. V85 2V1		1936
The Regina Community Fdn. 202 - 1102 Angus St. Regina, Sask. S4T IY5		1969
Community Fdn. of Ottawa & District United Appeal of Ottawa-Carleton 85 Plymouth St. Ottawa, Ont. K1S 3E2		1968

Index

Abused Persons Program of Montgomery County, MD, 29, 35, 91, 191
Abused Women's Alternative Resource Exchange (AWARE), St. Petersburg, FL, 15, 171, 188
Abusive males, 28, 29, 112, 131–132, 136, 158–159, 162, 163–166
Administration of shelters. *See* entry under Shelters
Advisory boards, 38–41, 61
Advocacy, 28, 29, 56, 86, 146, 149
Aid to Battered Women, Cedar Falls, Iowa, 27, 148–154, 190
Aid to Women Victims of Violence, Cortland, NY, 26, 199
Aiding Women from Abuse and Rape (AWARE), Juneau, Alaska, 33, 53, 183
Alcoholism, 11, 16, 18, 20, 78, 80, 87, 104, 124, 183–184, 202, 204
American Friends Service Committee, 6, 140, 171
Antler, Stephen, 103–105, 173

Batterers. *See* Abusive males
Board of directors, 36–38, 101

Bradley Angle House, Portland, OR, 202
Brandon House, San Jose, CA, 16, 185–186
Brooklyn Legal Services Corporation B, 98, 111, 174
Busiest day for callers, 22–23

Catherine Booth House, Seattle, 29, 35, 209
Center for Women Policy Studies, 12, 165–166, 174
CETA (Comprehensive Employment and Training Act), 10, 36, 41, 45–46, 53, 100, 101, 156
Charleston Domestic Violence Center, WV, 92, 210
Children of battered women, 3, 4, 11, 16, 18, 29, 43–44, 57, 59, 61, 112, 118, 121, 137, 158–159, 170
Chiswick Women's Aid, London, England, 165, 170, 174
Church, the role of, 133–140
Cleveland Foundation, The, 48–49, 51–52
Client's needs. *See* entry under Social work

223

United States Commission on Civil
Rights, 156–157, 164, 178
United States Department of Labor,
45–46
United Way, 102

Victims Crisis Center, Austin, MN,
30, 195
Victims Information Bureau of Suf-
folk, Inc., (VIBS), Hauppauge,
NY, 29, 163, 164–165, 199
VISTA Volunteers (Volunteers in Ser-
vice to America), 42, 43
Vocational rehabilitation, 4, 7–8, 28,
100, 103, 147, 166–168
Volunteer homes. *See* Shelters

Walker, Lenore, 170, 178
Warrior, Betsy, 8, 156
Welfare. *See* Public assistance and
Social work
Wichita Women's Crisis Center, KA,
30, 190
Winston-Salem Battered Women's
Shelter, NC, 16, 34, 51, 146–
148, 200
Women against Abuse, Lancaster,
PA, 13, 171, 204–205
Women in Transition, Philadelphia,
31, 205

Women's Advocates, Pocatello, ID,
30, 91, 189
Women's Advocates, St. Paul, MN,
29, 196
Women's Association of Self-Help
(WASH), Bellevue, WA, 28–29,
35
Women's Center, The, Providence,
RI, 29, 34, 206
Women's Crisis Service, Salem, OR,
14, 25–26, 34, 203
Women's Crisis Shelter, Brattleboro,
VT, 33, 93, 206–207
Women's Crisis Shelter, Las Vegas,
NV, 33, 196–197
Women's Resource Center, Law-
rence, MA, 92, 192
Women's Resource Center, Traverse
City, MI, 31, 92, 195
Women's Support Shelter, Tacoma,
WA, 35, 209–210
Women's Transitional Living Center,
Orange, CA, 34, 185

YWCA, 15, 26, 29, 35, 41, 45, 54–83,
99, 102, 113, 122, 138, 156, 184–
185, 186, 192, 195, 197–200,
207–211.
YWCA Battered Women's Crisis Center, Marietta, GA, 33, 189
YWCA Battered Women's Program,
Bellingham, WA, 29, 207–208